Praise for Matthew F

RUNNING TO T

"Athletes in any sport stand to learn from Larsen's methods, and Futterman turns in a fluent yarn reminiscent of Plimpton and McPhee."   —*Kirkus Reviews*

"Fast-paced. . . . An inspirational road map for runners. . . . *New York Times* sports editor Futterman enthusiastically documents the life of renowned American running coach Bob Larsen.
                                                                                    —*Publishers Weekly*

"*Running to the Edge* is at its heart a vivid, fascinating, and affection-ate portrait of a man who changed the sport of running in America and of the sport that changed him. . . . I can't think of a runner who wouldn't enjoy this book."   —Ed Caesar, author of
                                        Two Hours: The Quest to Run the Impossible Marathon

"A captivating narrative. Futterman gives us an informative history of American distance running while telling a fascinating story about a group of unconventional San Diegan boys who unexpectedly com-peted for a national cross country championship in 1976 against the well-established major running clubs. Futterman profiles a young coach, Bob Larsen, who was developing training methods that would later turn UCLA into a national running powerhouse and help lead Meb Keflezighi and Deena Kastor to become Olympic marathon medal winners."
                                        —Bill Pierce, coauthor of *Run Less, Run Faster*

"At the core, running is about pushing one's self to the limit. Mat-thew Futterman's *Running to the Edge* is a fascinating account of Bob Larsen's journey to uncover the secrets of optimal run training, initially for himself and then for his runners. The story is riveting. If you love running, this book will knock your shoes off—highly recommended!"   —Jordan D. Metzl, MD, author of
                                                        Dr. Jordan Metzl's Running Strong

"Matt Futterman's definitive examination of this primal human sport—distance running—richly serves a subject he knows intimately and rewards the reader with a captivating ride. This is a classic American underdog tale, populated by appealing oddballs, in search of answers to an age-old mystery: Why do we run?

—Mark Frost, author of
The Match and creator of *Twin Peaks*

"Many running fans know about marathon star Meb Keflezighi and perhaps even about his longtime coach, Bob Larsen. But few have heard about Larsen's life and coaching before Meb. That's the story told for the first time in *Running to the Edge*, a tale about the ragtag, improbably named 'Jamul Toads' running club and how Larsen's training methods turned the toads into national-class gazelles. . . . Readers will feel themselves drawn into the Bob Larsen–Jamul Toads ethic, and they'll cheer out loud for the little-known underdogs. I know I did."

—Amby Burfoot, 1968 Boston Marathon champion,
former editor in chief of *Runner's World*, and author of
Runner's World Complete Book of Running

"Packed with valuable knowledge elegantly conveyed, *Running to the Edge* is an inspiring and eye-opening look into the evolution of the distance running tradition. Matthew Futterman beautifully translates his passion and curiosity for running into a book that speaks to runners of all abilities."

—Alexi Pappas, distance runner and star of *Tracktown*

Matthew Futterman

RUNNING TO THE EDGE

Matthew Futterman is deputy sports editor of *The New York Times*. He has previously worked for *The Wall Street Journal*, *The Philadelphia Inquirer*, and the *Newark Star-Ledger*, where he was a part of the team that won the Pulitzer Prize for Breaking News in 2005. He lives in New York with his wife and children. In his spare time he runs marathons.

www.mattfutterman.com

RUNNING
TO THE EDGE

Also by Matthew Futterman

Players: How Sports Became a Business

RUNNING
TO THE EDGE

A Band of Misfits and the Guru Who
Unlocked the Secrets of Speed

Matthew Futterman

ANCHOR BOOKS
A Division of Penguin Random House LLC
New York

FIRST ANCHOR BOOKS EDITION, APRIL 2020

Copyright © 2019 by Matthew Futterman

All rights reserved. Published in the United States by Anchor Books,
a division of Penguin Random House LLC, New York, and distributed
in Canada by Penguin Random House Canada Limited, Toronto.
Originally published in hardcover in the United States by Doubleday,
a division of Penguin Random House LLC, New York, in 2019.

Anchor Books and colophon are registered
trademarks of Penguin Random House LLC.

Photograph on page viii courtesy of Robert Lusitania.
Photograph on page 277 courtesy of Marathonfoto.

The Library of Congress has cataloged the Doubleday edition as follows:
Name: Futterman, Matthew, author.
Title: Running to the edge : a band of misfits and the guru who
unlocked the secrets of speed / Matthew Futterman.
Description: First edition. | New York : Doubleday, 2019.
Identifiers: LCCN 2018049020
Subjects: LCSH: Running—Training. | Running speed.
Classification: LCC GV1061.5 .F88 2019 | DDC 796.42071—dc23
LC record available at https://lccn.loc.gov/2018049020

Anchor Books Trade Paperback ISBN: 978-0-525-56257-3
eBook ISBN: 978-0-385-54375-0

Author photograph © Blaga Ditrow
Book design by Michael Collica

www.anchorbooks.com

Printed in the United States of America

For my girls

Author's Note

I wrote this book because I have long been fascinated by something I do not possess, which is speed. Every runner I have ever known—including an eighty-five-year-old woman in northern California who ran seven-hour marathons, and Eliud Kipchoge, the otherworldly Kenyan who runs them in just under two—shares a desperate desire to run faster.

I started searching for a story that might explore what drives so many of us, from the very fast to the very slow, to begin, or end, or break up our days by heading out to the streets or the trails to run some miles. Sometimes we don't even know how far we will go when we start. And isn't that the beauty of it?

Then I saw a picture of a running team from the mid-1970s. They had scraggly hair and hopeful eyes, ridiculous (or amazing) uniforms with a toad logo, and the kind of lean physiques that only thousands of hours of roadwork can produce. I knew their coach, Bob Larsen, from his work with the marathon champion Meb Keflezighi, but I had no idea this was where it all began.

Those guys called themselves the Jamul (pronounced "HA-mool") Toads. They looked a little nuts, which is how most people felt about nearly every runner who logged heavy mileage back then. I had a hunch they embodied the obsessive and rebellious spirit at the roots of this strange endeavor and that those runners and their coach could help me understand why we run. As I unearthed their story, I realized it went so far beyond what I expected.

I like to think the spirit of those Toads, so visible on that photograph, is timeless. It lives on today at every level of this beautiful pursuit.

Matthew Futterman
November 2018

"It is the brain, not the heart or lungs, that is the critical organ."

—Roger Bannister *Miler. Neurologist.*

Contents

RUNNING
TO THE EDGE

Prologue

Athens, Greece, August 29, 2004

Bob Larsen has lost his mind.

That's been the word around the campfire in running circles for a little while now. For three years he's been dragging runners up to Mammoth Lakes in California's southern Sierras, preaching the benefits of running and sleeping so far above sea level. There, and only there, they will find what they need to avoid getting laughed at by all those Africans—the Kenyans and Ethiopians and everyone else at the top of the game, runners who barely consider Americans to be participants in the same sport anymore. Judging from the results of the past couple of decades, they really have no reason to.

And yet, Bob Larsen believes as strongly as he believes anything that after these Olympic Games they will. That's why everyone who knows anything about running is certain that Bob Larsen has cracked. Sure, he spent the 1970s figuring out how to run so far, so fast, before anyone else had cracked the code. Then he produced all those national champions and Olympians at UCLA in the 1980s and 1990s. But this idea that runners from his part of the world can figure out how to keep up with the folks born and raised to be champions in East Africa's highlands, well, that just seems a little loony.

Bob Larsen does not think so . . . though maybe it is, and maybe Larsen is a little loony himself. Case in point: He spent several days hunting for the coldest freezer in the Olympic Village, comparing set points and feeling inside them, searching for the one that will keep the ice vests he wants his marathoners to wear (until right before the starter's pistol fires) as cold as possible. He finds the coldest one in the kitchen near the village dining hall. He finds this pushy New York woman who works there. She promises she can barrel her way through any obstacle. She gets the vests into the freezer the night before the race, and gets them to him the next day.

Bob could sense the eye rolls and the sideways glances from the other coaches when he told them of his quest for the perfect freezer. That was just fine with Larsen. This is how it was back in the 1970s, when he took that first group of hippie runners no one took seriously and he elevated them to national prominence. When no one sees you coming, you have them right where you want them.

For a moment one week earlier, on the middle Sunday of the Olympic Games, the running world stopped and had to reconsider Larsen's sanity. On that day, American Deena Kastor came from way, way back in the women's marathon and sneaked onto the podium with the bronze medal, the first U.S. distance medal since 1984. Deena who? Kastor had been one of the runners Larsen and his partner in crime, Joe Vigil, started shuttling up to Mammoth Lakes a few years back, high in the Sierras. And here in Greece, she wore the ice vest to the start line, then raced the plan Larsen and her coaches had designed for this crazy, blazing hot Olympic marathon.

The course followed the trail that gave the race its name—the road from Marathon to Athens, the one Pheidippides ran to announce the Greek victory over the Persians. Pheidippides collapsed and died after delivering the message. To avoid that fate in the heat of the Athens summer, Kastor's coaches told her to let everyone else fight for the lead early, and especially during that largely uphill stretch between miles 2 and 20. They bet the heat and the stress of the course would produce widespread panic among even the elite of the field. Panic produces mistakes. Let the others make those mistakes, and then pounce. They did, and then she did.

Still, that was the women's race, the Larsen skeptics whispered. The women's field lacked the depth and firepower of the men's competition. Kastor had done well, but the African men had proven themselves an entirely different life form. Unapproachable.

Larsen can feel those doubts, the subliminal snickering, as he rides to the start line with his prized protégé, the twenty-eight-year-old Meb Keflezighi. Exiting the bus, Meb gets the ice vest pulled on tight. For ten years he has done nearly everything Larsen has told him to do, and he isn't about to stop now. Larsen let him come to Athens for the Opening Ceremony. Then he put Meb on the first plane back to a hotel in Crete, where they had set up a base camp for training in the weeks ahead of the Games.

More fun in the Athletes Village, Meb said.

More sleep on Crete, said Bob. And that was that.

Weeks before this marathon, which is scheduled for 6 p.m. on the final day of the Games, Meb drove the course with Larsen.

"What do you think you can run out here?" Bob asked him.

"In this heat, 2:11 or 2:12," Meb said.

"I agree," Bob told him. "And if you do that you are going to get a medal."

On paper, Meb should have no shot at the podium. There are 101 runners in the field. He has the 39th fastest personal best for the marathon in the competition. His best is 2:10:03. Kenyan Paul Tergat, the world record holder and favorite, has run a 2:04:55. That's more than a full mile ahead of Meb's best pace.

No one knows about the work though, the work that Bob and Meb have put in, running to the edge of exhaustion, the work that is at the very foundation of every lesson Bob has delivered to every runner he has guided the past forty years as he quietly tries to solve the secrets of distance running. It's a place he knows is filled with the truths that can only be found when we go to the place we fear more than any other—and stay there. Because when you go there, day after day, what happens in the race is not about how pristine your practice track is, or whether there is a certain logo on the side of your shoe or on the singlet across your chest. It might be a winged foot, or a swoosh, or even a toad. The race, and winning the race, will be about being the best version of yourself on the day you are supposed to, and what happens when you pursue that edge without fear. Nothing else.

In the warm-up area before the race, Bob and Meb don't speak of any of this. They barely talk at all. "Just another little race," Bob tells Meb with a wink. There is no need for any last-minute reminders. Meb knows everything he needs to know. He knows to keep an eye on the Italian Stefano Baldini, who has a proven record of running strong in the heat. It's in the low 80s as race time approaches. There is nothing more to say.

As Meb goes to the start, finally discarding the vest, Larsen loads into a van for coaches that will take him to the 10-mile mark. He will wait there for his one live glance at Meb during a race they have worked for a decade to reach.

As he stands at the side of the course a little less than an hour later, Larsen begins to see the lead pack approaching. They are cruising over that historic route at faster than five minutes per mile, a time that seems inhuman to most for even one mile, much less 26. Then, he spots Meb, just behind them, trudging along. Meb may not be the most beautiful runner, but he is right where Larsen wants him to be, tucked just behind the lead pack, right where no one can see him coming.

"Perfect!" Larsen says to his charge.

Meb flashes a thumbs-up and a smile. Larsen does the same. Then Meb is gone.

It really is perfect, Larsen thinks, the kind of perfect that exists out there at the very edge of sanity, which is actually a place that is not very insane at all. This is where Larsen has always landed during this never-ending quest . . . the elusive perfect he has spent a lifetime searching for. Always, the closer he gets to it, the further it stretches out of reach. Or does it? As Larsen watches Meb and the lead pack disappear down the road, he wonders if he's finally found it.

ONE

Bobcat

Bob Larsen can't remember a time when he didn't run.

During the first dozen years of his life, a life on the farm in the lake country of Minnesota, he runs because he has to. Here, much of Bob's life involves figuring out the fastest way to get from point A—his home in the woods—to point B. Sometimes he saddles his horse, but more often than not, he arrives at the same answer—running. He runs to school. He runs to his friends' houses. He runs because his family's log cabin and farm are a two-mile trek on a narrow lane to the closest road. That road is a dirt road. So is the 15-mile route to Detroit Lakes, the closest town. Down that road is the rest of the world—school, and friends, the closest stores, none of which are very close at all.

The nearest friends are three miles away. His one-room school, with one teacher for all eight grades, heated with a wood stove, is two and a half miles from the cabin. A general store is even farther. When Bob is nine, his mother teaches school a few miles into the hinterlands. She brings Bob and his sister, LaDonna, with her in the family coupe. On the way, they pick up a few Native American kids from the White Earth Reservation who only rarely attended school in the past. They are older and bigger than Bob and LaDonna but in the same grade. Everyone wedges into the coupe and bounces along the dirt road to the schoolhouse.

At recess, the children run through the woods playing cowboys and Indians, climbing trees and hiding in the branches, covering long distances by moving as quickly as they can, then trekking back when the school bell rings. Bob almost always chooses to be an Indian. The Native American kids usually play the cowboys. They chase each other all around the land near the school. No one can catch Bob.

The next year Bob and LaDonna return to their regular school. In the afternoons, they often hustle home on a shortcut through the woods along the shores of the lake and streams on the edge of the neighboring game refuge. There are deer and foxes and turtles. If they get hungry they stop to pick wild berries and chokecherries.

Their farm is roughly 600 acres, with decent farming conditions, though not as good as the pricier land farther to the south. The soil is rich, and there are wide, level expanses. Half the land remains wooded, but there is still plenty of space to grow alfalfa, corn, and wheat every summer, and occasionally potatoes and other crops. Bob's mother has a large vegetable garden. In the fall, she cans the vegetables so her family can eat them through the long winter. They raise cattle—milk cows and calves, bulls and steers. They also have pigs, sheep, chickens, and a few turkeys kicking around. One gets slaughtered for Thanksgiving, another a few weeks later for Christmas. They have horses to ride and horses to plow. Bob owns a horse. He pays $90 of his own money for it, money he earned selling baby pigs at the county fair. With the exception of the milk cows, the number of animals they raise depends on the expected price of the meat at the market in Detroit Lakes, where they rent space in a freezer, store some of their meat for sale and some for personal use. On the farm all they have is an icebox. They cut the ice for the icebox out of the lake using hand saws during the winter. The plow horses pull the ice cakes onto the shore and up to the barn. They cover the ice with sawdust, which keeps it for the summer.

When Bob was young he helped milk the cows by hand twice a day. Eventually, his family gets a milking machine. They drink this milk, raw. It is rich and thick. So is the butter they churn from it, and the ice cream his grandfather makes with the hand crank during the summer.

Their cabin sits about thirty meters from Buffalo Lake, which is almost entirely surrounded by woods, creating an intense sense of a family alone in the wilderness. There is also a pond in the middle of the property. Run to the other side of the farm and the shoreline of another lake appears. Minnesota.

Bob runs to get from the cabin to the barn, to round up the cows for milking twice a day. He runs to get to the fields, and sometimes to go into the woods to explore and to find wild berries. Every day he shovels manure, and during the winter, snow. Muscles take root in his upper back. Before he was eight years old, he learned to drive the team of horses pulling a wagon or a sled. None of this is easy, but it is the only life he knows—all farm kids do this sort of physical work daily, the kind that pushes them to the edge of exhaustion. And there is a payoff. They get strong from it. The strength makes them confident, and when they are challenged they believe they will have an advantage over kids who don't grow up on farms.

For Bob Larsen, this sense of physical superiority drawn from hard work will never go away. He will learn how to use it for himself and to pass it down to runners he turns into champions. He will feel it when he runs with the bulls in Pamplona. He understands bulls, he understands work, he understands self-reliance, and he understands how to move quickly using only the power of his legs.

He doesn't yet know how important these ideas will be to a truth that he will spend a lifetime searching for, or that he will come as close as anyone to finding it. He doesn't know that he will understand the secrets to the East African domination of long distance running before even the Kenyans and Ethiopians do. He doesn't know that he will write the blueprints of training for an activity that will become a worldwide movement, and he will impart this knowledge to two generations of star long distance runners, that they will include collegiate and national champions and Olympic medalists, that one of them will pull off perhaps the most inspirational triumph in distance running history, and that he will do all this in relative obscurity during the next half century.

For now, Bob Larsen is still on a remote farm in the middle of Minnesota, happy as can be, until suddenly it all ends. Life on the farm comes to an abrupt completion on a spring afternoon in 1951 with a freak accident. Bob's father falls out of the haymow on the second floor of the barn. It's one of those hazards that make farm life among the most dangerous existences on the planet.

His father's injuries aren't fatal, but his back is wrecked, not catastrophically, but the farming days are over. There is simply no way to haul bales of hay or milk cows or drive the plow horses or drag the slop out to the pigs.

In the summer Bob's parents will head south and west. They will need money for the journey. Bob will collect the few hundred dollars he has earned through the sale of pigs birthed by the sow his father had given to him. He will give it to his parents. They promise to pay him back. Then they leave. Bob and his sister stay behind in Minnesota with their grandmother until his parents figure out where they are going to end up. They pause in Las Vegas to consider making a life in the desert. It is 104 degrees in the shade. They push on to San Diego, where a new life, warmer than Minnesota, cooler than Las Vegas, begins.

San Diego, Fall 1954

There are moments when the boy from northern Minnesota does not like high school, when he misses the family farm and the one-room schoolhouse, the simplicity of life far, far away from the big city. He misses the horses and the cows, even the smelly chickens and all the work the farm required. There are times when he feels alone. These people out here on the coast of southern California he has gotten to know the past few years are a little different, which could make any teenager slightly uncomfortable.

Then there is gym class. Gym class has always been the time when he runs. In junior high school, these were dashes, 50 yards, 100, maybe 300 at most. The teacher lined the boys up in the schoolyard. A track was chalked off on the concrete. Bob Larsen took his spot at the front and felt no discomfort at all. He knew the boys around him would give him a chase, maybe finish within a few yards or even closer some days when he wasn't feeling his best, but almost always he would hit the finish line first. He likes to hit the finish line first. When he runs he is at home, even through middle school, when no one ever feels at home.

Now he is in tenth-grade gym class, his first at this dizzyingly large institution with 3,000 students called Hoover High School. A teacher named Raleigh Holt is lining the boys up for another one of these runs. He tells the boys that since they are in high school, they must run longer than they did before. This test, and it is a test, because Raleigh Holt needs it to be for reasons that will soon become clear to Bob, stretches 660 yards. They will need to be fast, but this 660-yard run is also about being strong, Mr. Holt says. Larsen stands at the front, as usual. His strawberry-blond hair is cut in a 1950s buzz. His eyes are bright and wide, focused, like they always are when he is about to run. The expression on his face is blank. Inside, where no one can see, he can feel the grin begin to emerge, because he knows what is going to happen next.

When he first arrived in San Diego, Bob joined a fitness program at the local YMCA. It was not far from his house, northeast of downtown in a neighborhood called North Park. After the farm, nothing felt far away. They did sprints and shuttle runs up and down and across the gym floor, the rubber on the bottom of their shoes squeaking with every twist and turn. They did sit-ups and push-ups and pull-ups and chin-ups. It was tiring for some, but Bob didn't really get tired. He does not tire the way the other kids do.

And now he knows he isn't going to get tired on this 660-yard run his gym teacher, Mr. Holt, is describing like a trek to the Mexican border. Bob hears the boys around him moaning. He thinks about the farm, of all those runs through the woods and across the property. They were so much longer than 660 yards. Weren't they?

Yes, they were. Bob knows how this will go. He knows what it's like to work to the edge of exhaustion. He knows that work is the reason there will be so much daylight between him and the other kids after they leave the starting line. They will get tired. He will not.

For a moment, when Mr. Holt is done speaking, the gym teacher stands silently in front of Bob. When the whistle blows Bob will sprint to the lead, the air coursing through that strawberry blond buzz. He will never look back. He won't have to, because he knows who surrounds him—a bunch of kids from the city, and he knows they don't have a prayer of keeping up with him. By the end, roughly 100 seconds later, his nearest classmate is 30 yards behind.

When gym class is over, Mr. Holt strolls over to Bob. He knows the boy isn't from here. He also knows he is going to turn Bob into one of the stars of the Hoover High School track team and one of the top runners in San Diego. He is fast. He just needs a little work.

Before very long, for the first time, Bob begins to *train*. Like the racing in gym class, the training comes fairly easily. In this unenlightened era, unless you are a sprinter, there is little variation. Like everyone else who is remotely connected to running, Mr. Holt knows about the regimens the great Czech runner Emil Zátopek put himself through on the way to winning the 5,000- and 10,000-meter races and the marathon at the Helsinki Olympics in 1952. In training, Zátopek rarely runs any distance longer than a half mile at a time. Occasionally he might go as far as a kilometer, or 1,200 meters. Rarely though. But he does these repetitions over and over. A morning session and an afternoon one. He will do ten 880s, with a brief rest between each one, or twenty 440s, at a pace far faster than what he will race at in those long distance competitions. His competitors are in awe of these. They listen to Zátopek speak of running twenty 440s in succession, each one faster than 65 seconds. Their legs begin to burn. It's not possible, they think. They are right. For them it is not.

Holt has adapted these workouts for his Hoover High School students—in other words, he has made them significantly easier. Monday through Wednesday the routine is almost always the same. The boys (it is all boys, because there is no girls team) run three 1,320s—three laps around the dirt track—with a solid 5 or 10 minutes of rest between each one. The next day they run eight 440s. Between each quarter mile, they walk a full lap of the track, which takes about five minutes. On Thursdays they "jog," though they call it easy or light running. Fridays they race at track meets. They are expressly told not to run on weekends. Best to rest up for the next week. Same goes for summer. No running then. Summers are for recovery. So is winter.

Thanks to a collection of very fast boys at the high school, it seems to work. Bob becomes an essential part of a team that almost never loses, even though nearly every star runner on the team, including Bob, spends weeks on the injured list. It will force him to understand that in running health is just as essential as speed. He learns early on that all the talent in the world is worthless if you can't get to the starting line. Only later will he understand that the injuries he and his teammates are experiencing are likely the result of an imbalanced training regimen, of every runner on the team doing the same thing day after day, an endless stream of intervals around and around the hard dirt track in black leather running spikes. It's a valuable nugget that he will store away until he begins in earnest that quest for running truth.

Bob and the Hoover boys try not to think about the pain. They focus on their numbers. They are all breaking 4:30 in the mile. The best of them can get down around 4:20 on a good day. By the time they are done, everyone knows they are among the best runners in southern California. As a senior, Bob is the top miler in the city, a star recruit for San Diego State University, where he gets to consider the most important concept that any runner confronts—what comes next.

What comes next is an up-and-down year of adjusting to life as a college runner and battling injuries. At the first practice, Larsen and his teammates are sent out on a three-mile warm-up run on the grass at Aztec Stadium. On other days, they do a warm-up run on the roads around the university. This is interesting and different, farther than Bob has ever run in one stretch. The grass feels good under his feet, especially since he is training in the thin leather racing flats that provide little cushion. Then it is back to the interval training on the track that he is too familiar with. All those quarter-, half-, and three-quarter-mile near-sprints around a rock-hard dirt oval. Three weeks into the season, his shins are shot. He shuts down for two weeks, then comes back, then another shut-down. It goes like this all year, even into the spring, when the injuries grow especially frustrating because for the first time Bob is starting to feel genuinely fast.

San Diego, Summer 1958

Bob Larsen knows how to run only one way—as hard as he can, to the edge of exhaustion. This is how he approaches each training session, each interval of 200, or 400, or 800 meters. He sets a simple goal—expend so much effort that when he takes his final step he has nothing left to give. Then, the only thing his body can do is collapse.

There is a simple explanation for why he does this. He worships Roger Bannister, the Englishman who first broke the four-minute mile. He has studied the photograph of Bannister collapsing after the finish on that gray day at the Iffley Road Track in Oxford on the 6th of May, 1954. When the race ended, and Bannister had broken four minutes for the mile by six tenths of a second, he fell limp, unable to stand without the help of those around him. So Bob runs and then collapses just as the Oxford medical student did that day.

His teammates think it might be a recipe for future injury, maybe even death. They also find it to be a bit of a hoot. They watch their teammate falling to the track at the end of each interval, leaving everything he has out there like the English guy who ran in a way that not long ago most thought was unthinkable, and they shake their heads. Bob simply believes this is how you have to run to be as great as Bannister. Seek the threshold and then cross it. Later, as his quest for running truth evolves, he will realize he wasn't far off. But right now it's just the beginning of his journey, one he doesn't yet know he's on, to understand what it really takes to run very far, very fast.

Only in the last few months, as a member of the track team at San Diego State, where Bob is a freshman, has he begun to consider himself fast. The Aztecs are a spartan operation. The head trainer, the man responsible for the health of the athletes, is the same man who hands out the jocks and shorts before practices and collects them for the laundry after. There are no ice baths or hot tubs. The team showers are outside. Bob loves it, and like Bannister, he loves to run the mile. He can stay with the leaders in nearly any race and finish in the 4:20s. He can also run the 200 in 25 seconds. He has wheels, though the occasional stress fracture makes him feel like he has a few broken spokes.

At the end of the spring season, his coach told him and the other men on the team to remember they are not in high school anymore. They need to get some running in during the summer. They need to come to the track, put in the time, do the work, run those intervals. Keep the rest short between each one, and push as hard as you can, will yourself around those turns even when your lungs are screaming.

Bob isn't sure how that's going to work with his schedule. He now lives in El Cajon, not all that close to the university, and he has a job at the local Shell station that he is fairly certain is going to sap all his energy. Two days into summer, he knows he is right. There is little rest for the gas station attendant of the late 1950s. This is the era of the gas station worker as automobile valet. At the Shell station, Bob does a whole lot more than simply pump gas. He washes and waxes cars, changes the oil, checks tire pressure, and, if need be, changes the tires, too. He is on his feet ten hours every day. When he arrives home, he collapses on the couch in his parents' living room. The last thing in the world he wants to do is run.

After two days he realizes the only way he is going to get his miles in is to avoid the couch at all costs when he walks in the door. He decides to go directly to his room. He changes into shorts and a running singlet, slips on his shoes, and heads out the door for a run.

A few months before, a podiatrist had molded a crude early version of an orthotic to slip into his thin leather running shoes. He told Bob it might soften his landing and help with the stress fractures in his shins. The hard plastic wedge is as thick as an old Coke bottle. As he runs on the roads in his neighborhood, alone in the summer twilight, he can feel the orthotics cushioning his arches.

He often heads over to El Cajon High School, about three miles away, at a pace that would allow him to have a conversation with a buddy if there was anyone else around to do these distance runs with. At El Cajon High, he finds a few other boys doing summer workouts, sometimes on the track, sometimes barefoot on the grass fields next to the school. Then Bob heads back onto the road to run home. Sometimes, when he gets close, he realizes his legs and his body are just beginning to feel good, so he keeps going, adding on one and then two and then three or four more miles as the evening cools and darkness descends.

The miles click by. Sometimes, mile six is easier than mile five. He will test his pace for a few miles one day, clicking off 3 miles in 16 minutes or so in the middle of the run, then easing back toward the finish. He finds the roads liberating, so different from the round-and-round of the track. Sometimes the route makes up itself. He just follows it, sometimes quickly and sometimes less quickly, however fast and wherever his legs tell him to go.

The miles become addictive, the part of the day that Larsen thinks about all afternoon at the Shell station. San Diego is a big city compared with the farm in northern Minnesota where Bob spent the first dozen years of his life. But it is still something of a small Navy town. Larsen runs through streets of low-rise buildings and past block after block of modest California ranch homes. Everywhere he sees sailors in their whites, officers in their dress uniforms, heading over to a friend's house for dinner. Downtown, enlisted sailors wander the city's streets, in port for a few days and searching for some female company and something to do.

He is always bone tired when his shift at the gas station ends, but after a few weeks he knows as well as he knows anything that if he just avoids his couch and gets out on the roads, within minutes his energy will rise. Some days he only flirts with pushing the gas pedal to the floor. Miraculously, he feels no pain in his shins. The running is pure joy, just as it once was back on the farm in Minnesota.

Some days he pushes hard, even to the edge in spurts, that moment of liminality, when the ritual is giving way to a kind of transcendent exhaustion and he has no idea what will come next. Pain? Nirvana? Some combination of the two—the most painful kind of pleasure or the most pleasurable form of pain? He wonders if a joyful, physical pain can serve as a pathway for a deeper, wider realm of understanding. It's like that moment when the point of a thumbtack is first piercing the fleshy part of a fingertip, and it feels strangely good. How long can it last?

In August, he signs up for a race in Balboa Park that is called the Balboa Park 8 Miler. The event attracts the top runners from the region, college competitors and a few recent graduates, who still train, dreaming of maybe making an upcoming Olympic team before getting on with the rest of their lives. It is 1958—there are no recreational runners, people who will eventually be called "joggers." They simply do not exist yet. All summer long, as he racks up those miles in dusk on the crowded roads of central San Diego County or on a trail across one of the dusty canyons, Bob Larsen never sees another soul running the way he does.

On the start line of the Balboa 8 Miler, he sees the best runners in the region and that's all. This is the fourth edition of the race, which was started in 1955 by an SDSU alum named Bill Gookin. Gookin had set school records at SDSU and had a shot at national success in the middle and long distance races. He and his teammates weren't ready to give up competitive running, so they formed the San Diego Track Club and began to organize "all-comer" meets and this eight-mile distance race over the hybrid terrain of rolling Balboa Park and the surrounding streets and boulevards. Most of the closest races were in Los Angeles, a day's drive round-trip back then. Bill

Gookin and his small crew are the only serious adult runners for miles around. Gookin is there on the start line with Bob Larsen. So are roughly 50 to 100 other men. There are no women, who do not compete in races longer than 400 meters.

At the sound of the gun, Larsen takes off to the front. He knows this is where he belongs. He has thought this for some time now.

As he runs the first miles of the Balboa 8, he has a summer of bliss in his legs, all those dusky ventures, mile after mile of pushing to find the moment when his legs or his lungs will give way. They never do.

He has never raced this far, but five miles in he is still up front. He is floating over the grass and concrete, clicking off miles at a 5:30 pace and feeling he could run to San Francisco like this if he wanted to. One by one, the runners in the lead pack fall off until it is no longer a pack anymore, just Bob Larsen sailing across the course, 100 and then 200 yards ahead of the rest of the field. Down the stretch he is waving to his buddies watching beside the course. The endorphin-fueled euphoria is coursing through his body. There is no way he can know this, but he is having the greatest long distance running day of his life. He crosses the finish line in 44 minutes flat. He is nineteen years old. He cannot imagine and does not know a purer form of happiness.

In fact, there is plenty he doesn't know. Most importantly he has no idea why he is having this magical day. He doesn't know that within those long runs in the evenings, the hard ones and the less hard ones, and even those exhausting days at the gas station, lies the secret to his success this day in Balboa Park. He doesn't know that this is the secret he will chase as he evolves from Bob Larsen, surprise winner of the 1958 Balboa 8, into "Bobcat" and "CBL" (short for Coach Bob Larsen)—a man who teaches others that they can find strength that they never thought they had if they can fear-lessly search for it, again and again. He has no idea or plan for any of it as he accepts the congratulations. All he knows is that he is the Balboa 8 Mile champion, that he has just pulled off an epic run and he should probably celebrate, though not too much, because this race is over, and his mind goes very quickly to what comes next.

Why We Run

So, a question: Why do we run?

Bob Larsen has sensed from his first days in the sport that the answers are equal parts science and existential philosophy. He knows that running can be many things—a form of medicine, a means of escape, a mission, a destiny—all at once.

First some science. The human body bends in the direction of decay. Without regular and increasingly challenging activity, the systems of the body slowly, or in some cases quickly, descend into inefficiency and malfunction. After people reach roughly their mid-twenties, bones lose their density, and muscles lose their mass. Mitochondria, the tiny structures within each cell responsible for converting nutrients into energy—hence their reputation for being the body's power plants—get worse at doing their job with each passing year. Muscle cells shrink, and fat cells grow. This happens to people who are wiry and fit, and those who are round and out of shape.

A body that is in training and then stops training experiences all this in microcosm, a quick descent from in-shape to out-of-shape that mirrors the aging process in a way that is adjusted for time and age and the level of fitness that was reached before the break in training began. The fittest athletes experience the decay more acutely than anyone because they have more ground to lose. Good runners who can complete 5 kilometers in 20 minutes may lose only 10 seconds, or less than 1 percent, after a week of inactivity, but after a month that 5K time may grow by more than a minute as the body's ability to circulate and use oxygen efficiently drops by roughly 12–15 percent. After two months, efficiency has dropped by more than 25 percent. Endurance is among the first traits of fitness to go, even among the most fit. Scientists compare this phenomenon to the changes that a pot of hot water and a boiling one will experience when they are removed from heat. After five minutes, the pot of water that was boiling will still be hotter than the other one, but it will have lost a higher percentage of its heat than the pot that was merely hot.

The challenge for humans—or the subset of people who care about such things, including those who can run very fast for a very long time—is how to keep the body on a slow boil. The idea is to train the body so that the heart is very good at pumping blood. The 60,000-odd miles of blood vessels need to be especially good at getting blood to the corners of the body where oxygen is needed most, especially to the muscles that work the hardest during a physical exercise. Fortunately, vigorous training increases the number of capillaries, which are the tiniest blood vessels responsible for feeding oxygen to muscles. It also increases the size and the quantity of mitochondria, those power plants charged with transforming nutrients into energy and supplying that energy to our billions of cells.

Here is what happens when our bodies run: We breathe harder, and we force our hearts to pump more quickly. This forces our blood vessels to dilate, so more blood filled with oxygen can get to the muscles that need it. When the muscles use up their initial store of complex sugars, also known as glucose, which they use to produce energy, the muscles throw off hydrogen ions and carbon dioxide. That causes capillaries to dilate, allowing for even more blood flow and oxygen to the muscles.

A body that has trained also produces a vastly different group of metabolites, those small molecules essential to the chemical reactions that must occur in all living organisms that want to survive. Those reactions include converting food to energy and into the various proteins and other organic substances essential for cells to thrive, and also for the elimination of waste.

The well-trained body has far more glycerol, which breaks down fatty tissue, than the untrained one, and far less allantoin, which can bring on a condition known as oxidative stress that causes cell damage. In this way, every run becomes a battle against decay and death—a battle none of us will win but which many cannot resist fighting.

The evolutionary biologists tell us we are bred to be distance runners, that we owe our very existence to it. Think of early humans, they say. They live in the Serengeti. They are hungry. Their brains, compared with the size of the rest of their bodies, are so much larger than nearly every other animal's brain. Keeping that brain alive requires well-nourished, oxygenated blood. At any given moment, the brain uses 20 percent of the blood that's in the body. The brain uses all that blood to fuel the electrical impulses that neurons use to communicate with each other and keep the body's cells in working order. Keeping that blood healthy requires thousands of calories every day.

Plant food is fine, but it can be hard to get enough of it on the African plain. Animal meat is better. There is a problem though—nearly all the animals are faster than the humans. That makes them hard to capture and kill. Early humans don't have guns and bullets to shoot them. They have rocks and spears. Advantage animal.

Humans, though, have a secret weapon: sweat glands. They have the ability to cool themselves through perspiration. They also have muscles and lungs that adapt to activity. The more activity, the bigger the capacity of the lungs and muscles. In a 100-meter race, or even a 1,000-meter race, the humans don't have a chance against the animals. However, give a human a few months to practice and stretch that distance to 3,000 or 5,000 or 10,000 meters, and things start to get interesting. The animals can't cool themselves. Think of dogs and horses that pant feverishly in the heat, especially after exertion.

The early humans are also blessed with an intricate series of muscles in the back of the neck that allow the head to stay upright and balanced when the rest of the body is moving at full speed. The Achilles tendon helps, too. The roughly eight-inch elastic strand that attaches the calf muscle to the heel is a near perfectly designed energy storage unit for an animal that wants to run on two feet. It is one of nature's most delicately designed springs, storing and then releasing energy every time the foot hits the ground and pushes off. Other primates, such as chimpanzees and gorillas, have their own unique advantages, but they would kill for the human Achilles tendon.

Sweat glands, muscles in the head and neck, an Achilles tendon in each foot—these are priceless tools. So when it comes to long distance running, advantage human. Blessed with these gifts from nature, humans learn how to run constructively in groups, how to take turns giving chase and tracking their prey. They learn how to run their prey into submission.

The evolutionary biologists preach the gospel of the "Running Man," who lives on in the spirit of the Tarahumara Indians in Mexico, those ultra-marathon champions celebrated for their barefooted dominance in trail races across the Rocky Mountains.* And yet, while the scientists can explain with fascinating precision why humans can run, and how we perfected this skill thousands of years ago chasing zebra and ibex on the African plain, we haven't had to run our prey to death for thousands of years. We really don't have to run anymore at all. So why do we?

Because it makes us thin? Yes, for some. Because it allows us to win races? For the luckiest of us, those blessed with speed, this, too, may be true. Because it makes us feel good? Who doesn't crave the rush of endorphins that courses through our bodies after even a mediocre run, to say nothing of those magical days when we stop even though it feels like we could just go and go and go.

All this is true, but maybe another answer has to do with battles. Now comes the philosophy.

We relish those fights against time and decay and death, even if we know they are ultimately unwinnable. With each step, each stressed breath, every elevation in the heart rate that restarts the process of improved oxygen circulation and capillary production and metabolite efficiency, each extra second we save on a clock that measures how we are, or are not, letting time slip away, we can better fool ourselves into thinking that aging and expiration are optional. Or that they have been delayed for another day.

There are other battles we run from, too. Consider Frank Shorter for a moment. After all, he is the supposed father of the American running boom. In an earlier era of Olympic telecasts, Shorter won the gold medal in the 1972 Olympic marathon in Munich in front of a captivated U.S. television audience drawn to the Games that year in record numbers. That was the year Palestinian terrorists took

---

* Daniel Lieberman, a Harvard evolutionary biologist, lays all this out extensively in Chris McDougall's *Born to Run,* and did so for me during interviews about "Running Man" I have conducted with him.

hostage and killed eleven Israeli athletes. Shorter watched it from his balcony in the Olympic Village, a mere forty yards across a grassy yard from the terror. Then, a few days later, he became the first American to win the race since 1908, inspiring 1970s America, so worn down by war and the sense of everything coming apart, to begin to lace up its shoes and run.

Shorter first became a star runner at the Northfield Mount Herman prep school in Massachusetts and then a college champion at Yale. He has long been rather matter-of-fact about why he ran. In his memoir, Shorter compared running to reading a book.

> *After a while, you're not really conscious of reading. It's just images through your head. It's the same with running a marathon. People always ask me why I do it. Well, I am good at it, and we do the things we excel at. But also, I just like being out there. I like it better than anything else I've ever done. I like being able to think about it as I go along. I get so seriously involved with the race, with what my body is doing, I don't have time to notice things around me.*

Or even what might have been inside him, which, as he would only realize later, was sort of the point.

In his sixties, Shorter accepted he could no longer bury memories of his troubled childhood in Middletown, New York, where he was raised by an abusive, alcoholic father. Publicly, Shorter's father was revered as the dedicated town doctor. In private, he was a monster. He abused Shorter and his eight brothers and sisters. He raped his daughters and beat a young son who suffered from Down syndrome. As the second-oldest brother, Shorter tried to protect his siblings as best he could. As soon as his father entered the home, life became a chess game of motion. How could Frank move to intercept his father, distract him from unleashing his cruelty on the rest of the family. To be still was to surrender, and Frank didn't like to surrender. Running became an extension of the movement and activity. Shorter ran to school, and to his friends' homes, one in particular, a few miles away, that became, secretly for him, an oasis from his father. If he was running he was safe, moving beyond the reach of the abuse.

Shorter is now seventy-two years old. He still runs.

So, we run to avoid death, to play at that game of transcending our finite reality, for a moment, so as to imagine we are more than this single life in the most endorphin-juiced way.

And we run away from trauma with the miles of body in motion. And here is one more possibility—maybe running is a way of re-imagining the life-death duality. This is a part of what I do on some of my most special days as a runner, even though I toil far off the elite pace in marathon after marathon. The run can be a meditation-in-motion, a cleansing of all the sensory realities we encounter. The run is white noise, a way to simply experience time as a body, a piston, that exists away from the mind and only in the body as a live reactive presence. Running is escapism, but it is also the opposite. It can be the ultimate expression of being awake and alive only as a body that occupies space and time. A painter doesn't merely create a painting. When he is painting and creating at his best, he is a part of that work of art. This is how it can work for the runner and the run.

Now, another question—how do we run best?

Greek coaches poked their charges with forked sticks and told them to practice holding their breath. Roman athletes practiced abstinence, slept a lot, and had slaves lash their backs with rho-dodendron branches. A nineteenth-century miler (and boxer) named Captain Barclay filled his day with uphill, half-mile sprints, moderate six-mile walks, and lying in bed naked for a half hour at high noon. Training at intervals of a half mile to 1.5 miles with rest in between becomes an approach at the dawn of the twentieth century. In the 1920s, the Finnish legend Paavo Nurmi gets Olympic glory after indulging in long training runs at a steady pace.* Emil Zátopek becomes the greatest runner ever doing as many as seventy 400-meter intervals at 65–70 seconds in a single training session.

For a twenty-year-old Bob Larsen, champion of the 1958 Balboa Park 8 Miler, running (and the attempt to figure how best to prepare to run) becomes the ultimate puzzle. Within weeks of that triumphant day, he is back in school, back in training, doing his coach's interval workouts around the track at Aztec Stadium. His lungs have

---

* For a terrific and deeper explanation of these methods and others, see Neal Bascomb's *The Perfect Mile*, from which these practices are taken.

never felt so big, but his shins are starting to ache again. He runs for three weeks, then he has to take two weeks off. Then he returns for another three weeks of intervals, racing his teammates through a series of quarter- and half-mile repeats over and over, as though they are at the national championships each day. Every week, seemingly, another one of them goes down with another leg injury. Only Bill Gallagher, one of Larsen's teammates from Hoover High School, manages to stay healthy. Bill is majoring in engineering. His class schedule and his lab work only allow him to train two or three times a week with the rest of the track team, and he isn't breaking down. But he isn't getting much faster either.

Even more frustrating, Larsen and his teammates know how close they are to being exceptional. They aren't blowing away the competition, but they can do the math. At practice, before and between and after those intervals, they sit on the infield grass and tally up and multiply and divide the times they have run and compare them to the national records that their contemporaries have set—records that stand at 8:46 for two miles, 14:16 for the 5,000.

Larsen has just won an eight-mile race in 44 minutes, 5:30 miles, and it wasn't very hard. He can get to 4:20 in the mile. He and his teammates can breeze quarters in 65 seconds or so. This is not so different than the workouts Roger Bannister did in the run-up to breaking the four-minute mile—10 quarter miles beginning at a 66-second pace, a couple of minutes rest between each one, and slowly trying to knock a few seconds off the quarters and cut down on the intervals of rest as the race approached.

"Those records," Larsen tells his teammates every afternoon, "they're soft. We can break them."

There is one problem. They can't stay healthy. If they aren't healthy they can't train, and if they can't train they can't improve. This is not only a problem for Larsen and the rest of the Aztecs at San Diego State, but for seemingly every top American runner. All of them, at one crucial moment or another, get saddled by injury. Shin splints, stress fractures, tweaked knees, sore ankles, pulled quads and hamstrings and calves. The Europeans are clearly putting up better times than the Americans, but maybe they aren't any faster, Larsen thinks. Maybe they are just healthier. Maybe they have solved the injury puzzle, so they are able to train more.

One morning in the fall of 1959 Larsen puts a foot on the floor as he climbs out of bed. His leg, weakened from the stress fractures, now buckles. Larsen collapses to the floor, pain coursing through his shins. He takes a few days off from training. The pain subsides. Then he tries to run again. He begins to think he just might have the engine of a Cadillac, but he has been stricken with the body of a Rambler.

His mind churns. More than ever now he is looking for the big answers he senses are out there . . . a truth that will connect training and injury and ability in some kind of transcendent way.

At meets he quizzes opponents who win races, asking them what their workouts are. They give answers like "10 by 600" or "8 by 800." He asks them why? They shrug and say they do what their coach tells them to. There is no trial and error. No one thinks about running technique much either, other than some chatter about long strides vs. short ones.

Then he gets a break. In San Diego's kinesiology department he discovers a new PhD recipient named Frederick William Kasch. A native of Chicago, who played baseball at the University of Illinois, Kasch arrived in San Diego in 1948. He teaches a range of courses in exercise physiology and applied anatomy, and he develops the then-revolutionary idea that regular exercise can make the heart stronger and prevent heart attacks. It can also help someone with a bad heart make that most essential of all muscles stronger. He develops a fitness program for adults to prove his theories, measuring their capacity when they first show up and then tracking their progress as the weeks go on. This at a time when the consensus within the scientific community is that to exercise vigorously after the age of thirty-five is to flirt with a catastrophic cardiac event.

There are others who are researching the path Larsen is following. He discovers the writings of Woldemar Gerschler, a German coach and researcher who, along with Zátopek, forms the bedrock of European interval training. Gerschler, the director of the Freiburg Institute for Physical Education, built the connection between fitness and pulse rates. To many it sounds like a silly concept, but people pay attention to him because before World War II he trained the great German half-miler Rudolph Harbig. Harbig cut two seconds off the world record in the 800 meters in 1939, lowering it to a then unheard-of 1:46.6. Gerschler establishes a series of hypotheses based on the concept that the heart is just another muscle that can be trained. The more and harder you run (or swim or ride a bike), the slower your heart will beat when it is not under stress. And even though your heart is beating more slowly, it will still pump the same amount of blood. As you exercise more, the heart can pump at a slower rate, thus working less hard, even as you increase your stress level.

There is also Percy Cerutty, the eccentric Australian coach known for his intense, primitive, captive training camps in Portsea, Australia. Cerutty, an authoritarian coach with a shock of white hair and a build so wiry his ribs and sternum are visible through his skin, discovered running in midlife after a nervous breakdown at forty-three. He spent hours walking, and then running in the Australian countryside to regain his health. He stuck to a diet of mainly vegetables and whole grains. By the 1950s he was holding training camps that adhered to a rigid regimen of weight training and gymnastics exercises, sprinting up crazy steep sand dunes that were often no more than 30 yards high for as long as an hour, and sessions of interval training and runs as long as 20 miles, with runners varying the pace.

Finally, there is Arthur Lydiard, the Kiwi running guru who is becoming one of the early advocates of running for health. He runs with a group that will become known as the Auckland Jogging Club. It includes runners at all levels and is believed to be the first running club of its kind. Lydiard pushes a system built around volume. He wants his runners pounding out 100-plus-mile weeks. He does not care if the pace is merely healthy. "Train, don't strain" is the Lydiard mantra. The distance builds a foundation of endurance, Lydiard insists, and once the foundation is there, it can be expanded through speed work. Bill Bowerman, the Oregon track coach who will later help found a little shoe company named Nike, visits Lydiard in 1962. Upon his return, his Oregon runners take up "jogging."

Larsen doesn't know what to believe. He knows how he feels, that the more he ventures out onto the roads to log miles, some of them very fast miles, the stronger he is in competition. The power comes from inside his chest and his lungs. He knows that science is beginning to establish a connection between running and the strength of the cardiovascular system. It is young and raw science, fringe really, but he believes it because it's what he is experiencing. Slowly, he begins to convince his teammates to follow him through miles off the track, sometimes on the roads, sometimes a three-mile loop on the hard-packed sand of a nearby canyon. They play around with pacing, taking turns leading the way. They force each other to become less comfortable than they otherwise would be on their own. They are a good team, among the best in the country, if a click or two below world-class.

When Larsen graduates in 1961, he decides not to go anywhere. He takes a job coaching the distance runners on the SDSU track team. He also begins doing his graduate work in kinesiology and physical education, whatever can keep him hanging around Kasch's lab. He teaches swimming and wrestling. He has puffy cheeks, and the same strawberry blond buzz cut that he arrived at school with four years before. He could probably still pass for a freshman rather than a graduate student.

At his team's first workout, he gathers the group at the track, then tells them they aren't running on the track, at least not to start. They head out to the roads and the canyons, and they begin to push. They fool around with "fartlek"—the art of speeding up for short bursts throughout a run of 3 or 5 or 8 miles. When they do train at the stadium, it's not about head-to-head competition through a series of 400s and 800s and 1,320s. That will beat them up long before the big races.

Instead, he lets the boys run free. Running isn't about being brought onto a track to be beat up each day. It's about moments of enlightenment that can be found only when you seek out that edge, that threshold, and stay there. Backing off the interval training, his boys come back fresh each afternoon. They don't get hurt and they win more often than they lose.

He's circling something approaching a piece of the truth, but it needs fine-tuning. So when the year is over Larsen takes a job at a local high school in eastern San Diego County, a place where he can experiment and make mistakes for the next four years without concern, where no one will expect him to win.

Given where he wants to go and what he wants to do, which is understand and reimagine how humans run so he can begin to develop the fastest runners in the world, Larsen's decision is akin to someone wanting to eventually manage the Yankees believing that the inevitable path to the Bronx begins at a tiny school where most people don't even know how to play baseball. Some are skeptical. Everyone is. Good, Bob thinks. Just how I like it. It's easiest—and sweetest—to win when no one sees you coming.

He will spend six months in the military and six months traveling in Europe, and then the journey begins.

Monte Vista High School, San Diego, Fall 1963

The track and field program at Monte Vista High School, to the extent that there is one, is awful. In front of the school there is a scraggly dirt track that is barely level. It backs up to dusty hillsides scattered with arroyos. Twenty miles to the west, near the ocean, San Diego earns its well-earned reputation as one of the most temperate places in America, some 300-plus days a year of dry mid-70s sun, with cool breezes rolling in from the Pacific. But here, inland, that sun bakes the earth hard and dry and the mercury regularly heads toward 90 and above during the running seasons of fall and spring. It's hardly the most inviting place to spend a fall or spring afternoon. Dragonflies buzz through the afternoon air. The hills are scattered with the occasional pine or palm tree. Small collections of ranch houses will eventually cover the landscape in every direction except south. That way, there are mountains and then there is Mexico.

The other reason this place isn't known for track and field is there are only 1,200 students. They learn in a series of low-slung brick buildings. Some schools in the region have 3,000. That means a far smaller pool of talent. With the program on the losing end of most meets for years, the best athletes flock to the traditional stick-and-ball sports. Monte Vista track gets the leftovers. Given that, Larsen can only hope to challenge the big schools in a normal track meet, where teams score points based on how they place in races as short as 50 yards and as long as two miles.

Cross country is different though. All a team needs for cross country is five decent runners. A team's top five finishers account for its point total, which is equal to the number you get when you add up what place they finish in a race. Like golf, the lowest score wins. A sweep happens when a team finishes with the first five spots in a race and a total score of fifteen. One plus two plus three plus four plus five.

This math is Bob Larsen's friend. Success in cross country is also more about toughness than speed. Runners compete on trails and hills instead of tracks. Times don't matter. It is all about out-running the guy in front of you, and the one in front of him, and the one in front of him until there is no one left to out-run. Do that, ignore the pain, or ignore it more than the guy in the other-colored singlet, and be fortunate enough to have teammates to do the same, and you win.

Bob Larsen will never forget this math. It brings him comfort. Limit his pool of talent all you want. He will find his five scorers and teach them how to run.

On the first day of practice in the fall of 1963, Larsen assembles the sign-ups and tells them to follow him. At first they don't really understand what is going on. The track and field coach is supposed to be the guy who wears a windbreaker in the middle of the track. He blows a whistle and barks instructions. Bob Larsen is not that guy. He is twenty-three years old and fast and fit. He is pretty sure he is beginning to know how to make other people that way, though anyone who knows anything about teenage athletes and high school track would be right to think Bob Larsen was a little delusional for having any designs on optimism with this gangly group. They had done nothing that might suggest they had anything resembling speed or potential, or much in the way of desire. They will learn, Bob thinks.

Together they start to run. He leads them far away from that dirt track at Monte Vista. It doesn't matter that basically every high school kid trains almost exclusively on tracks at this time. They go north on the roads through Casa de Oro and Mt. Helix and Mt. Miguel and south and east into the back canyons of the wildlife refuge, through a riverbed and across dirt trails that few had ever thought to run before. The high school is built near the top of a hill. No matter which way they go, they quickly descend, which means on the way back they will have to go up. They find the steepest hills, dirt ones and paved ones, and they sprint up them. "Keep up with the coach," he tells them as he pushes the pace without warning.

He forces them to go hard for longer than they expect to, and to rest for less time than they ever have. He rarely relents, even on the hottest days. In truth, he is lucky he never loses a kid back there in the canyons, but they do keep up. They do more than that. He loves to run hard and now so do they, and now they have someone to follow. They learn that they can survive when they are pushed, that they can endure discomfort and sometimes pain, that they are tougher than they ever realized they might be, that they can run until they find their edge, and then push beyond it. After a few weeks, a boy named Bruce Hamilton, who transferred into the school that fall, becomes the front-runner, pushing the pace in training the way Larsen has shown him to.

By the end of the fall season, they are the best small-school team in the region. But they are learning something else. Larsen is teaching these young men (boys, really) how to love running. He is teaching them to live at the threshold, to experience the primal joy of doing what the body is meant to do . . . run miles and travel distances. As much as he is teaching them about the toleration of pain, he is also opening up a pathway to a truth that can connect the body and the mind, one fast step at a time.

Acapulco, Christmas, 1963

As Christmas 1963 approaches, Larsen yearns for a tropical vacation, or at least one that he can afford on a salary of about $5,000 a year. He convinces a few buddies to drive down to Acapulco with him to swim in warm waters and have cocktails by the sea. But as the holiday draws nearer, one by one Larsen's friends decide they have other family obligations that are going to keep them stateside. So Bob Larsen does what Bob Larsen does—he goes it alone. He drives his VW bug through the night down the Pacific coast until he reaches Acapulco. There he finds a quiet spot near the beach and parks his car. He sets up camp and calls this place home for the next week.

Each morning he rises and heads onto the beach. All he can see is sand for miles north and south. It is the perfect place to run.

The sand feels so good under his feet he doesn't bother with shoes. He starts slowly, silently pushing himself across the beach, his toes sometimes grazing the incoming water. As he begins to move faster, he notices his feet and his legs are doing something they have never done before. Running barefoot, he isn't running as much as he is bounding. It feels fast. All morning, each morning he does it up and down the beach, through intervals and fartleks, and hard long runs, the front of his foot hits the ground and then pops back up. His legs are lighter, like they were meant to move this way.

Larsen realizes he is on to something, one step closer to truth and meaning. He thinks about how he has always run, how seemingly everyone he knows runs. This is all he has to go on because he has barely read a word on running mechanics—not because he hasn't wanted to, but because barely any literature on the subject exists. All the runners he knows load off their heels. They land on the heel and follow through the step like this: heel-mid-foot-push-off-the-toe, as though it's just a walking motion only faster.

There, on a deserted beach, he believes he has come upon a better way—the mid-foot strike. If running is all about the push off the toe, why waste all that time on the heel? On the beach, where being fast is all about not sinking into the sand, running becomes the act of popping the knee, of springing the foot as quickly as possible, up and through off the toe and then back down again, right under the center of gravity, a tap on the ground instead of muscling through each stride. Every step gets pre-loaded on the way down and then boom, off again, like a roadrunner, churning and churning away. Pop-pop-pop-pop-pop. Eventually, people will call this "heel recovery."

He thinks of his boys at Monte Vista. If he can change the power of their hearts and lungs, he can change the way they run, too. The pieces of the puzzle start to appear. He knows they are a long way from coming together, but he begins to see how it all might one day take shape.

San Diego, New Year's Eve, 1963

Bob Larsen pulls back into San Diego just before New Year's. He knows his boys at Monte Vista and everyone he will ever coach will all reap the benefits of this Mexican sojourn. At the moment, however, none of that is even a dream. There is a more pressing matter at hand. It's New Year's Eve. Bob has been in Mexico, running. All his friends have dates for tonight. He does not.

Fortunately for Bob, his fraternity brother, Mike Neil, offers to come to the rescue. Mike is in law school. He knows a girl, a senior at San Diego State. Blond, light eyes, sweet, fun, good company, and strangely available at the last minute. His buddy, who's been up to God knows what in Mexico these past weeks, needs a date for New Year's Eve. Mike offers to set them up. Susan is her name. Why not, Bob figures. It's not like he has a lot of other possibilities.

They go to a party. There are some drinks, plenty of easy conversation, some laughs. She is, indeed, everything Mike told Bob she was. Yes, she says after that first date, she'd love to see him again.

Bob has sworn off marriage until his thirtieth birthday. He wants to get some money in the bank, get started on a career. He knows soon after marriage there will likely be children, and he'd like not to be figuring out someone else's life while he is still figuring out his. Does he know then that a little more than five years later, on December 21, 1969 (just shy of his thirty-first birthday), they will become Bob and Sue Larsen? Of course he does not, but he sure does like how that first date went.

Monte Vista High School, Grossmont College, San Diego, 1964–70

Mexican epiphanies aside, Larsen's runners at Monte Vista look like a collection of misfit toys. A kid named Don Olsen is maybe five and a half feet tall with long gangly arms. Danny Ungrich could blaze through two laps around the track but often dies after that. Rodney Stevens and David Matheny insist on running barefoot, regardless of the surface, and they often get distracted by the wildlife along the trails behind the school. They stop running to explore.

There is a pond at the bottom of the canyon. Larsen warns everyone on the team to watch out for rattlesnakes. If he sees one near the trail as he leads the pack through workouts, he yells "snake" so the boys trailing him know to beware. During one training session, Larsen doesn't realize Matheny and Stevens have not heeded the "snake" warning and decide to have a look. As Larsen ascends the hills back toward the high school, the boys pick up a rock and kill the snake. When they return, one of them has a dead rattlesnake draped around his neck.

Most days though, they run with the intensity and drive that Larsen relishes. He tells them to run to the threshold, to that edge where you are running at a pace that is as hard as you can go without having to slow down. It's the precipice between aerobic, where the lungs learn to breathe almost normally throughout the activity, and anaerobic, where they do not and the power does not depend on the efficiency of the cardiovascular system. Maintain that, for as long as you can.

They listen, and they push themselves to the edge. He begins to take the heart rates of his own boys through their workouts. He sees that when they push the tempo to the edge on those runs to the threshold, their hearts approach 140–160 beats per minute, before quickly recovering. They can learn to keep it there, he tells them.

In the off-season, Larsen decides his boys might benefit from running in some local road races. There are only a few to choose from but the races will keep them running. He wants them to run as part of a team. He is sure that runners train and race faster when they are part of a group than they do when they run alone. The big cities have their "Athletic Clubs," these hoity-toity organizations like the New York Athletic Club that are as much about high society as they are about athletics. Larsen looks at his surroundings, the dusty mountains around eastern San Diego County, and thinks, this must be the most unlikely place in the world for someone to form an "athletic club." Which is exactly why he wants to put one here.

On his drives through those hills, he once arrived at a one-stoplight neighborhood called Jamul (pronounced "Ha-MOOL"), a place with little more than a grocery store, a church, and a gas station. "Jamul" means "bad water" in a Mexican-Indian language. The mountains there are covered with scraggly shrubs and boulders the size of Volkswagens. Perfect, he thinks. He has the name for his team—the "Jamul Athletic Club." His boys love it. So does he. He cuts a few J's out of fabric. His girlfriend, Sue, sews them onto used singlets. They have their uniforms. Now they are a proper club, a team that runs all year round.

The next year they move up to compete with the large schools, and the year after that no one can touch Monte Vista in distance running and cross country. Larsen is building something. What it is he doesn't quite know, but his team is the distance power of San Diego.

After spending four years at the little high school out in the sticks, Larsen's phone begins to ring. On the other end of the calls are college coaches. What is he feeding those boys? One call comes from the University of California at Irvine. Another from Pomona, one of the prestigious Claremont schools some forty miles inland from the Los Angeles coast. A coach from Cal Poly calls, too. All want the same thing. They want Larsen to help coach their kids.

He lands at Grossmont Community College, a school that sits atop a hill in El Cajon, ten miles east of San Diego's Pacific shore. There are glorious, 360-degree views of the valley below, the mountains to the north and south, the ocean to the west. The dirt track is at the top of the hill.

On the surface, it's a curious choice. Why not go with a more academically known—or bigger—school. Oddly though, junior colleges in late 1960s California are a hotbed of running talent. These schools don't have powerhouse football teams, but in many cases their sports teams, especially the track teams, are very, very good, often far better than the state's four-year schools. The four-year college education explosion, the idea that it is essential for success, has yet to occur in the U.S. So every year there are any number of very fast graduating high school seniors who opt for the two-year, local college route.

A couple hours north, László Tábori, a Hungarian former world record holder in the 1,500 meters, is guiding one of the country's best track teams at Los Angeles Valley College. Tábori is a protégé of Mihály Iglói, another Hungarian, who, like Tábori, is in the first ring of running royalty. If a junior college is good enough for Tábori, it's plenty good for Bob Larsen. And once again, there is that underdog advantage that Larsen is drawn to. No one would ever predict that Grossmont Community College will ever become a running superpower. Larsen is going to be coming almost from nowhere again, which is the place he really likes to come from.

Plus, the Grossmont post comes with a job teaching physical education and a $20,000 a year salary, significant money at the time. Regulations will limit his recruiting to a small region of San Diego, but he isn't worried. He's in the middle of a puzzle and he's pretty sure he's going to solve it.

Now Larsen needs a plan.

There are two prevailing schools of thought in distance training. There are the disciples of Lydiard, the Kiwi, who don't think much about pace and instead focus on volume—a minimum of 100 miles each week. "Train don't strain." Avoid injury by not going too hard. In the other school are runners and coaches obsessed with intervals—Zátopek and his scores of 400s, and Iglói and his twice-daily interval sessions. Avoid injury by not adding on unnecessary mileage, they say. Both have little science backing them up. Larsen thinks he can create a third way, by marrying the two. Then he will back it up with numbers and trophies to make it last.

The miles Larsen envisions are on the roads and trails, off the track. The question Larsen really wants to answer, the one he thinks he might discover in this next level of competition, is this—how long can you stay away from the intervals, stay off the dangers of the track, and still compete successfully? Larsen is sure of one thing, that eventually the track becomes the enemy.

It's a strange thing about a track. There is something about those eight lanes and that quarter-mile oval, the scattering of curiosity-seekers who always seem to pause as they wander by. From the first moment a spike hits the dirt (or the cinders, or eventually the rubber) a runner on a track wants to be great in that moment. He wants to win every lap, every interval, wants the stopwatch always to read a split second less than it did the lap before. The best runners crave competition, no matter who it is—a rival or a teammate—to be one step farther ahead or one step closer to the front than he was the previous day. But do that on a track day after day, month after month, and the breakdown will come. The oval shifts the mind's frame of reference in some mysterious way, and the psychological toll is simply too taxing.

Larsen has learned that roads and trails are different. Out there, the mind expands beyond 400- and 800-meter intervals, referred to by runners as "splits." A runner can explore and conquer the barriers and limits that everyone who has never done this sort of thing assumes exist. At some point, on nearly every run, the runner begins to believe that, yes, you can keep doing this, at this pace, maybe forever. Larsen's goal is to rewire his runners' brains to experience competition in a different way, to enjoy the push of body and speed as they have never done before, and to want to search for each new limit again and again.

So this is what Bob Larsen tells that first collection of Grossmont runners as he gathers them in the summer before school begins. He says he knows what their old teammates and high school competitors who have ventured elsewhere are likely doing right now. He knows they are going to be hearing about it. It's what runners do, after all—they talk about running, the way golfers talk about irons and drivers and the latest technological innovation, or the hip turn that might give them an extra 10 yards off the tee. Pitchers in baseball trade secrets about how they grip a ball, where each fingertip touches each seam, and the angle at which the arm powers through the slot. Runners talk workouts. Interval patterns. Weekly mileage.

Larsen tells his boys they are never going to match what the other guys are doing on the track. Those other teams are going to do so many more quarter and half and mile repeats than we will ever think about doing, he says. He tells them not to worry. He is going to make sure the boys of Grossmont run themselves into the shape of their lives, not by next week, or for the first race of the season, but for when it counts, at the end of the season, when the championships are won.

The summer, he says, will be all about building the base, putting in the miles on roads, and on trails, and at the beach, up hills and down, 60, 70, 80, 100 miles a week, whatever their legs can take. Each runner will find his limit. His body will tell him where it is.

Then, after several weeks, when the fitness is there, they will begin in the middle of those runs on the roads and through the canyons to chase the edge, to find that spot where one click more is too fast to maintain, and one click less feels just slightly too comfortable. They will hold it there, for five miles, and then six and seven, as long as they can. For some of them, that pace will be sub-five-minute miles. For others, it will be slower. They will try to hang with the pack as long as they can. This is not about high mileage or low mileage, it's not about 65-second quarters, or 2:10 halfs, or 4:30 or 5:20 miles. It's about the search for the edge. They won't search for it every day, but several times each week. Then, when the big meets approach toward the end of the season, they will back off the search and increase their time on the track, to find that short burst of speed they will need to bring the finish line close.

The boys trust Larsen, trust the man they call "CBL" and what he tells them. The trust equation is unspoken but perfectly conveyed. They trust him when he starts out on the runs with them, and he orders them to stay behind him for the first 15 minutes, and then 20, and 25, so they get into the warm groove. They know eventually he will let them go. Then he will take a shortcut to the latter stages of the loop and wait. There, Larsen will give them those few words they need to hear to get to the end. He limits these to simple phrases that remind them to stay relaxed but not let up.

Out there on the roads and trails, away from the track, the boys stick together but always end up in something that looks like a race, pushing each other to get the pace up a few clicks faster, to get back to that hilltop track, high above their heavenly city where each run begins. He checks their heart rates when they get there and between intervals, and this is what the numbers say: the longer they stretch out the threshold runs, the longer they can run intensely without pushing their heart rates to that maximum pumping level of roughly 180 beats per minute, which means their bodies are becoming more efficient. This is what he knows to be the definition of fitness. He knows the numbers can only mean one thing, that their bodies can do more while using less energy. If they can keep getting better at that, they will have more gas in the tank to push the pace as a race moves into its last miles.

As a team, they can't win the big meets at first, can't challenge for a state championship. They don't have the depth yet. But Larsen can see the progress, especially among his better runners. They show up at the big invitationals in Long Beach and at Mt. San Antonio

College and score with the best runners from the biggest schools in California.

Bob Larsen knows why this is happening. He believes his search for the edge is making them as fast as they can possibly be, faster than they ever imagined. He believes in their hearts, that his way is getting them all closer to the truth—that marriage between having the strongest engine and the healthiest legs that gives the elite runners the belief that they can run fast forever. Now he just needs to find some more of them. If he can find the right runners, he believes he can win anything.

And so the hunt begins.

East Hampton, New York, September 2015

This race I run, the Hamptons Marathon, starts this year in the woods in an area called The Springs, several miles away from some of the most expensive beachfront property on the eastern seaboard. The race winds for eight miles by farms, summer home developments, a tennis club, a fruit and vegetable stand, along roads with substantial names—Accabonac, Old Stone Highway, Abraham's Landing. Then it jags sharply south and east, through the preserved acres of Napeague State Park. There, Long Island, some twenty-five miles wide at its widest, can be measured in yards. The briny air of Napeague Bay to the north, the pounding surf of the Atlantic to the south, both visible with a swivel of my head.

Here, approaching the 10-mile mark of the race, the wind begins to pick up for the first time on this late September morning. It's coming off the ocean, from the southeast. Through the first nine miles, the stands of trees beside the road provide the occasional protection. There is no rhyme or reason to when they are there and when there is a clearing. When there are trees, the air is mostly still. When they disappear, it whips across Cranberry Hole Road like someone giving you a little shove to the hips.

The landscape is dead flat out here, which is the point. I like the flats. I can run fast in the flats for hours, barely getting tired. Today I need to go faster than I have ever gone before if I am going to run fast enough to qualify for the Boston Marathon, the only major U.S. marathon that requires a qualifying time. I am now forty-six years old, and I have been at this marathoning game, and trying to qualify for Boston, for nearly a quarter century.

The downside is the flats also allow me to see what's ahead. The sun is still on its way up, dead in my face and almost blinding if I don't squint, but I can see. I'm not wearing sunglasses. Stupid mistake. A squinting face is a tight face. Tight face, tight body. Shaded, relaxed face makes for a loose, relaxed body. That's one of many reasons marathoners pray for cloud cover. I have a nylon baseball cap on to keep the sun off the top of my head, but the sun isn't high enough for the cap to do the job yet. So there is blinding sun. It's manageable, but uncomfortable.

The September air is crisp. I started the race with an old pair of socks on my hands to keep my fingers warm. They're tucked into my shorts now, navy blue short running shorts, with zip pockets to hold the gel packs I eat every seven miles. The last one, the one that is supposed to get me through the final five miles, inevitably turns my stomach. I might skip it.

I'm also wearing a white running shirt with a Butch Cassidy cartoon on it. It's the shirt of the charity team I run with named Hole in the Wall Gang. The charity supports a camp by the same name for kids with cancer, HIV, and other miseries. The Hole in the Wall was the hangout of the outlaw Butch Cassidy and his gang, the place where they felt safe. The camp is where these hard-luck kids are supposed to feel safe, where they can play ball, and fish and swim and climb treehouses without a parent four steps behind worrying about what catastrophe might await. I often run marathons in Hole in the Wall shirts or bandannas or sweatbands. When I am hurting or dreading the next miles, I look at the Butch Cassidy cartoon and I think of those kids. Sometimes it helps. Sometimes I'm helpless.

I should probably think of them now, because what I am thinking about is what I am seeing off in the distance, maybe a half mile ahead. There, Cranberry Hole hits Lazy Point Road and the course takes a hard right, due south into the Napeague meadow—dead into a 20-mile-an-hour wind off the ocean. This is what I have been worried about the past twenty-four hours.

No, the past ten months.

I am not an elite runner. Never have been. I try to train the way they do, though, the way Bob Larsen taught them to, only slower, of course. I only recently realized I run this way because of him. I chase seconds, trying to cheat time.

There is a simple reason why I am running here today. The reason is the wind. Not this wind, but the wind of November 2, 2014—the day of the New York Marathon, almost a year earlier. I was injury free and in the best marathon shape of my life that day. I was ready to climb the mountain that every workaday marathoner wants to climb. I was ready to run fast enough in New York to qualify for Boston, the holy grail for long distance runners. Every other marathon in the world has a very simple formula for building a field of runners. Sign up, pay an entry fee, show up on the starting line. Run when the gun sounds.

Boston, uniquely, is for the elite, or rather, the elite in each age group.*
The younger you are, the faster you have to run to qualify for the field of the
country's oldest and grandest marathon. On that day in New York I had just
turned 45, which put me in the 45–49-year-old age group. This gave me an
extra 10 minutes to play with. Now I could run a 3:25 and make it to Boston,
rather than the 3:15 I had to run when I was 44. A month before the race, I
did a 24-mile training run in just over three hours. In other words, I almost
could have walked the last two miles that day and likely still finished under
the wire. I was going to get a time that was going to put me into the top
10 percent of marathoners in my age group in the most populous country
in the world where running is a big, competitive deal. I was on the edge of
elite (for my age group). Athletically, I have never been elite. But finally, on
November 2 in New York, this was going to happen.

Then came the forecast—20–25-mile-per-hour winds from the north.
The first 19 miles of New York head due north. Steeling myself in my living
room the night before the race, I got a text from Meb Keflezighi, who
won the race in 2009. Through my job as a sports journalist, I had gotten
to know Meb from writing about him. He and I understand my version of
a marathon is nothing like his, but sending words of encouragement to a
fellow runner the night before what figures to be an ugly race is the sort
of thing he does.

"Pain is in the forecast for all of us tomorrow," Meb wrote. "Good luck."

This is what running does. It draws together me and Meb, two people
who could not be more disparate in talent and potential. Yet we race on
the same course, cross the same start and finish, train with the same
framework of training designed by the same coach, only at far different
speeds. There will be pain for Meb and a different, though not entirely
separate, pain for me. There always is.

On that day, we ran with the feeling of someone's hand on our chests
pushing us in the other direction for 19 miles. Impossible. There went five
months of training, gone with the wind.

It was just like the wind that was about to whack me in the eleventh mile
of this mostly flat Hamptons race. On all the topographical maps and elevation charts and marathon guides, this course looks like the perfect place to

---

* Yes, you can get a number for Boston through a charity that requires minimum
fundraising of $7,500, which is wonderful. It's just not the way countless runners,
both the serious and dilettante, dream of making it to the starting line in Hopkinton.

finally get under 3:25, to finally get an ounce of revenge on the twenty-two boys who made my high school's varsity soccer team in 1985 when I did not, and all those college tennis players who, unlike me, knew how not to choke away second set leads. Unfortunately for me, topographical maps do not show the wind.

I've put New York behind me, but as I turn into Napeague Meadow, my eyes squint. I'm trying desperately to qualify for Boston again, to get to the finish under 3:25. Out there is the ocean. Here, upon me, is a wall of wind as hard as anything I have felt in nearly a year.

There are plenty of strategies for running into the wind in the middle of a race.

Go harder, get through it fast, and don't let it knock you off your pace. That way, when the course turns or the wind shifts, it feels like you are running downhill.

Or, ease up, don't waste precious energy fighting, know that everything is temporary.

Or, believe there is a narrow corridor, a passageway through that wall of air. Find it, and run free.

I try all three of these within a half-mile span as I head south through the meadow in mile 11. I keep my eyes up. I try to think not of the wind but of the horizon on the ocean that I can just barely make out. The scenic beauty is all that you have during a tiny marathon like this with just a few hundred participants and even fewer spectators. Mile after mile passes with no one cheering you on, no roars of support or DJs or marching bands or any of the other pomp that big-city races offer. It's just you, often running hundreds of yards away from the closest competitor, and the trees and the sky and whatever else fills the landscape. You take it in. You remind yourself how lucky you are to be able to be doing this, and you take another step, and then another.

Right now though I feel far more snakebit than lucky. My race plan— 1:38 for the first half, 1:42 for the second, has a five-minute cushion. I can have a few subpar miles along the way and still get under 3:25 and get to Boston.* Those slow miles aren't supposed to happen until the final

* The age-based qualifying standards for the Boston Marathon can be deceiving. There are more people who meet the standards than there are spots in the race. So the Boston Athletic Association has set up a fastest-to-slowest system for registration. The result is that to get a spot in the race, you usually have to run between

10 kilometers of the race, when I generally begin to slow down, no matter how hard I train or how good I feel through the first 20 miles. A gust kicks up. Did I just take a step backwards?

Then I notice a runner coming toward me. He's moving at a pretty good clip, but nothing crazy. It's my first hint that there is an end to this. Then there is another one coming at me. That can only mean one thing. There is a turnaround somewhere up there. But how far? I swore I studied the course map closely last night. Wait, now it looks not all that far at all. Just up at the 11-mile mark. We're dead into the wind for a mile, and then it's at my back for a mile. An even trade. Maybe in marathons and in life, if we are lucky, eventually everything evens out.

one and four minutes faster than the qualifying time for your age. With more people pursuing running seriously each year, the time needed to actually get a spot in the race keeps dropping.

The First Horse: Ed Mendoza

The best part of the day for most kids in the South Park neighborhood of downtown San Diego is the worst part for Ed Mendoza. It's the moment in the afternoon when word spreads through the streets that sports are happening. Could be baseball, could be basketball, could be football. Sometimes they are heading over to Balboa Park, sometimes it's just at one of the local schoolyards down the street.

Theirs is a comfortable working-class neighborhood, packed with factory workers, plenty of Mexican descent like Ed's family. It's not fancy, sort of no-frills, with rows of low, stucco houses crammed next to each other. As long as they keep clear of the roughest part of town, Logan Heights, which is about a mile south, they are just fine on the streets alone. Wherever they end up, bodies are needed and everyone in possession of an able one is expected to show, girl or boy.

Ed usually goes, but grudgingly. Ed is twelve years old. He's not much of a sports guy. The big problem is he's smaller than darn near everyone. Always has been. It's taking him forever to get to five feet, and it's pretty clear from the size of his parents and uncles and cousins that the growing is going to stall out pretty soon after that. He's little more than a twig, and he's not one of these quick little spark plugs either, a kid who can dart around the basepaths or spring free on a passing route. His legs just don't turn over very quickly. As for the rest of his body, his arms and hands don't seem to coordinate like the other kids. Every time a baseball or a football flies at him is an adventure. His hands shoot out to meet it. Other boys seem to let it settle effortlessly into their control. There is no part of any sport that has ever happened effortlessly for Ed. Hitting a baseball is nearly hopeless. On the basketball court, at his size, just getting the ball up to the rim is a challenge, and plenty of those shots end up getting smacked right down into his face.

The worst part though is when the teams are picked. All the kids in the neighborhood stand in a clump. Two claim captain-hood, then set out to divide the group one by one. Ed hates this part more than anything, not because he is always the last one picked. He won't be, though sometimes it's close. He hates it because his kid sister, Evelyn, usually tags along with him. She's four years younger, but she's the kid who has yet to find a sport she can't do. She's the one who can smack a baseball and catch any orb flying toward her like it's a crystal egg. Her arm is a gun. Every time the captains for the day in South Park begin to choose teams, Evelyn Mendoza is going to get picked before Ed does. Getting picked after your little sister who is four years younger than you are is really about as miserable as it gets.

Things aren't much better at Rolondo Elementary School, where Ed dreads the annual Presidential Physical Fitness Test, a series of runs, jumps, throws, and exercises that get measured and, depending on your performance, reward you with either a patch for a silver or a gold award, or, for the best performers, a faux-fancy certificate with LBJ's signature on it. Ed does all right on the push-up and sit-up test, but he's slow as molasses in the 50-yard sprint. He has no strength or power. Pull-ups are a struggle. As for the shot put, that heavy little ball, plenty of girls can put a shot farther than he can.

The idea that Ed will one day become one of the great natural runners to emerge from California, and Bob Larsen's first Olympian, isn't even a kernel of a thought at the moment. It's not even worth the dream. Ed wouldn't know how to create that dream at this point.

The experiences are enough to turn Ed off to sports for a couple years—what he thinks is a lifetime. That is fine with his parents and aunts and uncles and cousins. They spend most weekends barbecuing and drinking anyway. Everyone smokes cigarettes as they recount the family legends that have landed the Mendozas in San Diego, in the booming middle of the twentieth century, in the richest, most powerful country that has ever existed. They talk of how his grandfather, Aurelio, spent his formative years riding a donkey from Michoacán, on Mexico's central coast, to the fields of southern California. There he picked fruits and vegetables and somehow made enough money to buy a zoot suit and a convertible. Citrus, watermelon, lettuce, there was always some crop in season.

Ed's father, Eugene, became one of the few from the Mendoza clan to graduate from high school. Then he lied to the military, claiming he was already eighteen, so he could ship off to Europe to fight in World War II. That's the story he hears over and over.

Before Ed starts eighth grade, his parents tell him and his sisters, Evelyn and Lorraine, they are moving to the suburbs, La Mesa, fifteen miles east of downtown. More space, a bigger yard. Room for a backyard pool in a land of seemingly endless possibility.

Ed rolls with the move just fine, and the next year, in the fall of 1967, he enters Helix High School. There's a big redheaded kid there a year older than Ed. He's nearly seven feet tall and his name is Bill Walton. Everyone says he's the best basketball player in the country, the next Lew Alcindor, the star center for UCLA, who will later change his name to Kareem Abdul-Jabar. Ed only has the vaguest idea who Lew Alcindor is but he gets the message that because of Bill Walton, basketball is about the biggest thing going at Helix High School. Ed is a few inches over five feet. So much for that.

Early in the year though, in gym class, his teacher lines the boys up on the track and tells them they are going to be tested on how fast they can run 600 yards. Ed tells the teacher that sounds really far, he's not sure he can make it. Ed feels himself slowing down in the final 10 yards of a 50. The gym teacher laughs, tells him it's one and a half times around the track. Anyone can do that he says, just don't kill yourself at the beginning and keep breathing.

Ed does what the teacher says, starts out steady and lets the air pass gently in and out of his lungs. Halfway around the track he actually feels pretty good, so he pushes. One by one, the other kids begin to come back to him. Then with a couple hundred yards to go, there is just one lead pack with a few kids struggling to get to the finish. Ed motors by them and is barely breathing hard when he crosses the finish line. Funny, he thinks, I was more tired after those 50-yard sprints in the Presidential test back at Rolondo Elementary. Then it's on to the rest of his day.

When the school bell rings, he gets called into the gym teacher's office. Turns out this gym teacher, Mike Muirhead is his name, is also the school's track and field coach. There's another kid there, too. A senior who's got stringy blond hair down to the middle of his back. Muirhead tells the boys he has brought them in because they tied for the fastest times in the school in the 600-yard run. Ed doesn't quite get that. There's a couple thousand kids at Helix. He figures this school must have the slowest collection of boys in southern California. The coach says they are actually pretty fast. He wants them to join the track team.

The boy with the long hair looks up at Muirhead and says, "I like to smoke, Coach."

Muirhead tells him he probably won't fit in with the team, that track probably isn't for him. With that, the senior with the long hair heads on his way.

Ed stays. Muirhead asks him what he thinks. Ed tells him there are two problems. "I'm slow," he says, "and I hate running."

This is when Muirhead realizes Ed doesn't really have a clue about how track and field works. He doesn't know that boys race at different distances, that there are 100-yard races and two-mile races, that the entire fall season is dedicated to something called "cross country," where the boys run over hills and trails for 1.5 miles as freshmen and then longer as they grow older. He tells Ed he'll never have to worry about sprints, or about losing, that with his natural talent, he might even be able to get a varsity letter as a freshman, the same letter that Bill Walton has on his jacket for being the best high school basketball player in the country.

"You're not slow, Ed," Muirhead tells him. "You're fast."

Ed has never heard anything like this before. He's not sure he believes Muirhead. It all sounds kind of crazy but the guy does seem to know what he is talking about.

The next day after school Ed heads to his first cross country practice. He does a series of laps around the track with the rest of the boys. There are short periods of rest between each lap. It's not easy to keep up at first, but the more laps they do, the easier it becomes. On the third day Muirhead tells the freshmen they need to run a one-mile time trial. If they can break six minutes, they will run in the next day's race. Ed runs hard but it's his first time running this far. He has no idea how to pace himself, or when to kick. He finishes in 6:04 and isn't all that tired. Only one freshman finishes ahead of him, in 6:01. Ed hears Muirhead tell the other freshman he will run the race the next day. He tells Ed he won't. Muirhead says the other kid has broken six minutes in the past. Ed tells his coach he is as sure as he has ever been about anything that he will beat that other boy. The other kid has been out here since the beginning of the season training for at least three weeks. Ed's been training for three days. Muirhead thinks for a second. The kid is right. From the looks of it, he's a special case, a little fireball, with these deep dark eyes that get this laser beam focus when a competition begins. He also has a natural motor like nothing Muirhead has ever seen. The engine takes a little time to rev, but once it turns on it doesn't seem to stop.

Muirhead tells Ed, fine, he can run the race the next day, just don't tell anyone he bent his six-minute rule. One other thing, Muirhead says, you might want to get some decent shoes.

That night Ed and his mother head to the closest shoe store, where they realize they don't know what they are looking for. Running shoes don't really exist in 1967. Some brand called Asics sells something called Tigers. New Balance has something called a Trackster, but those are mainly just available in specialty stores, not in the neighborhood shoe store where Ed and his mother are. Ed spots something made by Keds. To him, it looks like a fast shoe. Soft sole, nice fit around the top part of his foot. He'll take them.

The next afternoon, Ed heads out to the track for his first race. A few minutes before the start, he approaches Muirhead with a question. "How do I do this?" he asks.

Muirhead tells him it's pretty simple. One lap around the track, then the one-mile trail around the outside of the school, and then back to the track for one more lap. And since it's your first race, Muirhead says, how about you start at the back and then see how many people you can pass. Simple enough?

It is.

Ed hangs back on that first lap around the track but as they head out onto the trail around the school, he starts running the other boys down. He goes by them with little effort. It seems like they are suddenly standing still and he is not. He's cruising. The other guys sound like they are being tortured, huffing and wheezing through the course. As they head around the bend and re-enter the track there is just one boy left in front of him. Ed tries to push up but the kid keeps getting away from him. He tries again to reel him in.

He inches closer, and then he notices the varsity runners begin to wander out to the edge of the track to see how this all is going to end up. Then he starts to hear them.

"Go kid, come on Helix," they are saying. He realizes they are actually cheering for him. They yell "Helix" because they don't know his name. In fact they have no idea who he is, but he's wearing their uniform. The code says you cheer for the guy wearing your uniform. Ed wants to give them what they want, that last burst that will send him past the only competition left. He searches for one last gear but just doesn't quite have it. He runs out of track and the race is over. A few of the varsity boys stroll over and pat him on the shoulder, tell him he ran a good race. Then he sees Muirhead.

"Do you have any idea how good you are?" he asks.

Ed gives him a shrug of the shoulders. Muirhead tells him he is going to run this race every week for the rest of the season. Then the coach says something else. "I'm pretty sure you are not going to come in second again," he says.

Muirhead turns out to be right. Ed runs the table the rest of his freshman season. He's plenty fast. This little twig of a body he has, this contraption that seemed like it was never any good for anything athletic, it turns out there is something it can do very well. It can run farther, faster than most of the other bodies the other kids Ed's age have, even the ones far bigger than his, and even many of the ones that are older. Ed doesn't really know why, but he doesn't much care. For the first time in his life, he feels like there is a physical purpose to his existence, a use for the skin and the bones that nature has given him. He is here to run.

By the end of the season, Ed is at least the third-best kid on the team. Everyone knows before long he's going to be the best. Muirhead bumps him up to varsity for the final race, and he nearly wins that. It's a two-mile race and it turns out he's better at two miles than he is at the freshman distance of a mile and a half. The farther you go, the better you are going to be, Muirhead tells him. He finishes in third place, a little disappointing since he's used to winning, but he doesn't mind because he's on the varsity now and is pretty sure he's going to get one of those letters everyone in the school covets.

Only he doesn't. He gets a freshman certificate, and he's pissed. Muirhead tells him he's got to be in the top seven for 75 percent of the races to get the letter and he wasn't. Ed tells him if you look at his times, look at how he did in all those practice runs, he actually was in the top seven, but the coach kept him in the freshman races.

Again, the kid is right. He was better than just about everyone on the team, but this time Muirhead isn't giving in. Come back next year, or even in the spring, and you'll get your letter. Ed says this isn't fair. Here he had finally found a sport he was halfway decent at, and the coach is giving him a hard time about giving him a letter he's pretty sure he deserves. He's fifteen years old and doesn't really have the capacity to understand how to play the long game, or much interest in putting up with adults and their stringent rules. As far as he's concerned, he's done with running.

Maybe there are other sports he can try. Like wrestling, where you only battle against kids your own size. Only, as it turns out, Ed is a terrible wrestler, forever in chokeholds and cradles and getting thrown to the mat. It hurts. A lot. He quits after a few weeks.

Muirhead gets wind of this. Coaches in the same school talk to each other—especially when a kid who might be the most gifted runner the school has ever seen spends the first two weeks of the winter season rolling around a wrestling mat.

He catches up to Ed in the hallway the next day. "Ed," he says, "you really ought to think about coming back to running. I know you wanted that letter, I know you are upset, but I guarantee if you run for the team in the spring you are going to get that letter and a lot more."

Ed asks him how he knows. "What if I'm not good enough?" he says.

"Ed," Muirhead says, "you are definitely good enough."

And so it begins—Ed Mendoza's life as a runner. Like nearly everyone else in that era, Muirhead is an interval person through and through. He believes in the sanctity of the 400- and 800-meter repeat as though it is the word of the Lord. Every Monday is 400-meter repeat day. The schedule, like his rules, rarely shifts. His boys head for the hard dirt track of Helix High School after school for sixteen 400-meter intervals. At the beginning of the season, the pace is 75 seconds per lap with 90 seconds of rest between each one. By the end they are running 65-second laps with 50 seconds of rest. The fastest boys can sometimes inch down toward 62 when they are really pushing. Tuesdays the workout is thirty-two 200s to work on speed. Wednesday is for dual meets against other schools, Thursdays it's eight 800s. Friday is rest day. Saturdays are for larger invitational meets.

One night Ed reads in a magazine about Jim Ryun, the Kansas boy who became the first high schooler to break the four-minute mile. Ryun does twenty 400s each day. Ed tells Muirhead he wants to try it. When he finishes, his legs feel as though they are going to buckle. Muirhead asks him how it went. Ed tells him he is glad he did it because now he knows he never wants to do it again.

He is getting faster though, much faster. By the end of the season Ed cracks 10 minutes for the two-mile race. He's the best kid on the team already as a freshman. He gets that letter, and as school comes to an end, Muirhead tells him to make sure he gets out and runs four times a week in the summer. The rules prohibit Muirhead from supervising any practices, but he wants his boys to stay in shape, so they will be ready to go when cross country season rolls around in the fall.

Ed isn't sure exactly what this all means. Run over the summer? Where? With whom? It is 1968. He's not sure he's ever seen someone running on the streets. Is he supposed to come to the school track and do laps on his own when no one is there? That sounds pretty miserable to him. What will he say to his parents, his cousins? To them, summers are party time. Long lazy nights sitting outside, smoking cigarettes and passing bottles and listening to music. No one he knows has ever just upped and gone running in the morning or the middle of the afternoon or the evening.

That summer Ed has a job washing cars down near the beach. He vacuums the cars before they get run through the machines, and he wipes them dry after they emerge. He collects the nickel or dime or quarter from the driver, tosses it in the tip jar and it's on to the next car. Over and over, for eight hours. There are worse jobs. He knows that. But this one is utterly exhausting. His body feels like he has been tumbled through a dryer by the end of each day. He's glad he spent the spring training with the track team. He feels like that training has gotten him in shape for this job, but he sure doesn't have any energy to run when his days end. And weekends, well, running somehow just doesn't happen. He'll figure it out once the season comes. He knows he's as fast as anyone in the school at this point anyway. What does he have to train for?

The season begins with something called "hell weeks"—two weeks of preseason practices, two practices a day. Muirhead doesn't screw around. At the first practice, he says, let's see who did some running over the summer. He runs the boys through sixteen 400s on that hard dirt track at Helix High. Ed's legs nearly fall off by the end, but he forces himself to make it through, then comes back for more in the afternoon.

By the time school starts, whenever Ed starts running on the track, he feels like there are thumbtacks sticking into the inside edges of his shin bones, up and down the crevice where the muscle connects to the bones. As the weeks pass, the pain mounts, the thumbtacks begin to feel like small nails. By October, it feels like someone is twisting a screw into his tibias with each step. This little body of his, the body he had begun to think had been blessed with this one special skill, the ability to run far fast, is letting him down.

He begins to think maybe he had been right all along. Just as he wasn't put on this earth to play sports with sticks and balls, perhaps he wasn't meant to run either. For those precious moments last fall when he was breaking tapes at the finish line, or beating everyone else in the two-mile time trials in practice last spring, the running had given him a kind of stature and confidence he had never felt before. He was no longer the little twig getting picked after his sister down at the park or mauled on the wrestling mat. He was as big as anyone at the school—well, maybe not that big redhead Bill Walton, but everyone else. Now this is going away.

He tells Muirhead about the pain, and Muirhead tells him he has to go to a doctor. The doctor examines him and takes some X-rays and tells him he has a series of hairline fractures in his tibias. The only way they will heal is with rest. His cross country season is over. Take it easy, Muirhead tells him. There's another track season in the spring.

The winter is long. The only running Ed does is in his mind. He imagines his legs turning over effortlessly, sending him around the track as fast as he knows he can go when he can run without pain. Bored in classes, his grades slip—though he never was much of a student. He watches the clock tick through each day. He gets one C after another. Good enough, he figures. Then finally, spring comes and he is cleared to run again, time to get back to the track and Muirhead's weeks of 400s and 800s and 200s. At the first race of the season, he runs alone, finishes the two-mile distance in 9:51. It's as fast as he has ever run and he hasn't trained for months. Maybe this body isn't cursed after all, he thinks. But then, a few weeks into the season, the thumbtacks return. A few days later, so do the nails. Before they turn to screws, he tells Muirhead he needs to back off, rest a bit, even if it means losing some fitness. Muirhead agrees.

This is how it goes for the rest of Ed Mendoza's high school running career. His running life becomes a frustrating experiment about how fast a gifted runner can go on so little training. He wretches and dry heaves after one race, barely runs for the next two weeks, then drops his two-mile time to 9:36, and then 9:25.

In Muirhead's eyes, Ed is officially becoming a freak. He's barely training and yet the seconds are falling away. Muirhead is hardly a student of the physiology of the sport. He has no earthly idea what is going on, only that Ed seems to have this freakish motor that needs just the slightest hint of what he wants it to do. Then it downshifts and powers up, and then it just goes.

Ed comes in second at the section finals, earning himself a place at the state championships. Again after little training, he opens with a 4:30 mile and his final time drops to a blistering 9:09, making Ed the best two-miler in the San Diego region. He is only halfway done with high school.

"You are going to be the best runner our school has ever had," Muirhead says. Then comes the message he has delivered time and again. "The farther you go, the better you will be."

Farther? Did he really say farther again? Ed wonders. He tells Muirhead about his mile split. He was at 4:30 and on cruise control. I'm going to be a miler, he tells Muirhead.

A miler, Muirhead asks? Why a miler?

"I'm going to be like Jim Ryun," Ed tells him.

Over the summer, Muirhead gets up to speed on how to handle runners with a proclivity for shin splints and stress fractures. He doesn't have much experience with guys like this. Muirhead tells Ed he is consulting with the smartest running coaches he knows, including the coach at Grossmont Junior College, Bob Larsen. Larsen agrees with Muirhead that he's got to put Ed on grass and keep him there, because God has played a cruel joke on Ed, giving him nearly everything a distance runner could dream of having except bones that splinter under the kind of stress that any decent runner should be able to handle.

In the fall, Ed and the cross country team spend all season training on grass at San Diego State University. Ed stays healthy, goes undefeated, and finishes third in the regional championships.

The third-place finish comes with a useful lesson. Ed was leading with 200 yards to go but got caught at the end and finishes third. Now Ed is beginning to learn who he is as a runner; it's not so far off from the runner he thought he was when he was getting pasted in 50-yard dashes in elementary school. On the spectrum of freakishly fast distance runners, he is, in fact, slow. To win, he's going to need a healthy lead before the breakaway in the final sprint. He isn't going to beat people at the end of races. He is going to be a front-runner, the guy who gets a lead, pushes the pace, dares you to keep up, then finds a way to hang on because you realize too late how he made you spend your last reserves when you didn't even realize it.

But when the spring season rolls around, Ed has to train alone, since the rest of the team needs time on the track. Training becomes drudgery. He begins to skimp on the workouts. The hesitance, the doubt, the memories of being that boy who wasn't much for sports, creep back slowly.

One day, Muirhead hands him the workout before he heads off to the grass—twelve 400s at 64 seconds each, with one minute of rest in between. Ed does seven and gets bored. On another day, the minute rest becomes two. On yet another he feels his lungs cinching and his quads turning to rubber in the final stretches of the quarter miles. Instead of fighting, he fades.

None of this is his fault, though he doesn't realize it. He will before too long, when he learns that to train alone is to set oneself up—not specifically for failure, but for a failure to get everything out of a run that you can. When your teammates make you push on, challenge you not to fade, they convince you to ignore the cinching in the lungs and the rubberizing of your quads so you can stay with the group. Suffering becomes a brotherhood, and when women start competing at these distances, it will be a sisterhood, a family that is always with you.

Without the necessary work, his strength wanes. Three races into the cross country season, the nails in his shins return. It lingers for months. The doctor for the San Diego Chargers tells him to ride a bicycle and swim to maintain his fitness, and when he is pain-free to go back to the grass. He grinds his way back to the state championship for the two-mile. The main competition is a kid from the other side of the county named Dale Fleet, who was nothing a year ago. He puts up an eye-popping 8:53. Ed finishes eight seconds back. It's enough to allow him to see once again the person he wants to be. But how can he get there?

When he gets home, he pulls out all those letters he has from all those colleges across the country offering him a spot on their track teams. He's thinking about Oregon. Steve Prefontaine, the golden boy, is there. Or UCLA, he likes that track. Or Kansas, alma mater of his hero, Jim Ryun, even if Muirhead is right and he never will be a miler.

At school, he brings up the letters with Muirhead. The coach shakes his head. Ed, he says, what kind of grades do you have? Ed is a C student, passable, but not much more than that. Do you like schoolwork, Muirhead asks? He knows the answer. Not much, Ed says. Then Muirhead tells Ed about the plan he worked out for his star runner months ago. He explains why the coach from the nearby junior college has been showing up at so many of the Helix races lately. Of course Larsen has been watching, dreaming of putting together a group that can help him figure out what happens when a team runs as a collective on that edge, and what that might say about this most primal of activities.

Muirhead lays it on the line. Ed, you wouldn't last a semester at a four-year school. You are going to Grossmont, and you are going to get your grades up and learn how to be a student, and you are going to run for Bob Larsen.

Ed has one question. Who is Bob Larsen?

—

It takes just one race for Larsen to decide Ed Mendoza is the most talented runner he has ever seen. He thinks he's probably the most talented young runner around, probably the best one ever to come out of San Diego. Ed is small for sure, but he has the build of a thoroughbred. His lower body is packed with the power muscles where it counts, in the gluteus maximus. Yet his legs become toothpicks below the knees, so light and easy to turn over. And that motor. Perfect, Larsen thinks. For crying out loud, the kid was practically the state champion and he has basically been injured for the better part of three years. He's very nearly beaten everyone from the Oregon border to Mexico and he's barely trained. Larsen knows he will need to keep him healthy. And Larsen is pretty sure he, more than anyone, knows how to do that. The truth is becoming clearer to him, and Larsen thinks he knows how to push Ed to the edge without pushing him over it.

A few nights after Muirhead talks to Ed, Larsen arrives in Ed's living room. He explains what is happening at Grossmont, how he is gathering the best runners in San Diego's East County on his team. Larsen knows Ed is thinking about that sensation of nails driving into the bones of his lower legs when he wants something too much. Larsen tells him not to worry about injuries. On the edge of the Grossmont track, Larsen is going to build a soft trail for Ed. He's going to cover it with sawdust. That's where Ed will do his work, right alongside the rest of the boys on the team. His runners always stick together, always run in a group, whether they are running for Grossmont or the Jamul Athletic Club that Bob has going in the off-season. They are together every weekend, when they gather in Bob's front yard, head out, and push each other to the edge, then race back to Bob's front porch, where his wife, Sue, is waiting with a pitcher of lemonade.

It's going to take a little time, he says. Becoming the runner you want to be, the person you want to be, can take years, but this is what it means to run for him, Bob says, to be a part of the team. Sometimes you might find yourself out there on the roads by yourself, but you will never run alone again.

Ed likes the sound of that. And Larsen has his first true horse.

Larchmont and Mamaroneck, New York,
November 1979, September 1985

I remember the rain. And I remember the pancakes.

The running boom has officially arrived in my seaside town of Larchmont, New York. The town has organized its own five-mile race. If the big city twenty-one miles to the southwest, visible from the park along Long Island Sound, can hold a five-borough marathon, one-square-mile Larchmont can figure out a way to cram a five-miler zigzagging through its streets. I am ten years old, the youngest of three brothers. My oldest brother, David, who is fourteen, mentions at dinner one night his intention to run the race. This is roughly ten days before race day. By the end of dinner, David's two little brothers, Danny, who is twelve, and I, have taken up the challenge. We are running, too. We train some, running a mile or three through the neighborhood in late afternoons a couple of times. We declare ourselves fit.

The day before the race, my plans change. My soccer team wins a playoff game. We advance to the next round. Our game is scheduled for the following morning. It overlaps with the start of the race. I can't do both. I'm going to play soccer. The team comes first.

Then comes the rain, maybe about forty-five minutes before the start of my soccer game. We are down at the fields warming up in a downpour. By the opening whistle, the skies are dumping on us. By the end of the first quarter it's a torrent.* The field floods. The game is called. I head home, five blocks away.

By the time I arrive back at 17 Cherry Avenue, the rain has eased. David and Danny are loading into the car to head to the race. I ask if I can come. Sure, my dad says. But we have to go now. I run into the house and put on a dry pair of shorts and a T-shirt. I change out of my cleats and into the

---

* Yes, in 1979 we are still too clueless about the beautiful game to know there are no "quarters" in soccer, only halfs.

classic royal blue Nikes with a yellow stripe that are required footwear in 1979. Then I am out.

In the car, on the way to the race, I find out what I missed while I was attempting to play soccer. Pancakes. My mother decided that her boys need a nice big breakfast before they run five miles.

At the start line, I edge up to the front with the fast guys, even if I don't belong there, because that's just sort of the kid I am at that age. The rain has slowed to a steady drizzle. It's not warm, but not cold. I have no plan other than to get from the start to the finish as quickly as I can. When the gun sounds I go.

I have no idea where my brothers are until the race is nearly over. Around the four-mile mark, my brother Danny passes me. He's friendly about it, tapping me on the arm to say hello as he runs a few steps ahead, then heads to the end. I crank away for another few minutes, nearly keeping up. I cross the finish line in 40:15 a few seconds behind Danny. It's not a great time, but not a bad one either, especially for a first race, especially for ten years old. But I have felt something—or rather, I have NOT felt something, which is overwhelming fatigue. I felt something much closer to the opposite. I did not actually get tired. I had many more miles in me. Of course I have no idea what this is. Only later will I understand it as a kind of beckoning to experience a state of fullness that I will seek again and again.

We wait several minutes, until finally, David, the eldest, makes his way to the chute. He's had a bad trip. Danny isn't feeling great either, both of them are on the verge of puking. I'm fresh as a daisy. Now we know. Pancakes, just before a race. Not a good idea. Dodged a bullet with that one. I make a note to remember it. I have also slaughtered my oldest brother. I will remember that, too. Good thing; six years later, I will need the memory.

It's almost evening, the end of the second soccer practice of the day, on the last day of the second week of preseason for my high school soccer team. All summer I've trained alone on a field across the street from my house, juggling, making up moves, shooting with my right foot and my left against the fence until they are nearly equal. I'm working so hard because I need to. I spent sophomore year substituting on the junior varsity. Now I have to try out for varsity, so I can play fearlessly on the varsity the way my older brother did, because I love to play and because I desperately need to keep struggling to match those older siblings.

The final scrimmage is winding down. I've had a good two weeks. Not perfect, but good enough to make it, I think. I may not get much playing time as a junior, but this is a senior-heavy team. Keeping me on it will build depth for the next year when they are gone. Plus I'm scrappy. I don't get tired, or at least I don't show it. Not even on that night the first week when coach calls us back for a third training session and says to leave the balls at home and just wear a comfortable pair of running shoes. We run for the better part of an hour. Sprints and Indian Runs, where the last guy in the line has to overtake the first guy as the line circles the field over and over. And then we do an all-out three-miler. By the end most of the team is walking. I'm not.

But now I'm trying to get through this scrimmage without doing anything stupid. I'm the right defender. Our superstar, the kid who is deciding between college offers, is in the central defense, and when he gets the ball about 40 yards from our goal and starts dribbling fast toward me, I know I am supposed to make space for him. I'm going to make this run the coach had us working on in training the other morning. I'm going to run at him and pass him just off his back shoulder. He can leave me the ball to take it to the other side of the field, or keep carrying it to the right sideline, into the open space I have left for him. I'm going to look smart and coachable here. I think this move will help me clinch a spot on the team and launch my varsity career. Really, that career has about two and a half seconds left.

I don't notice that as I sprint at our superstar, a defender has moved up to challenge him. I don't see the defender lunge at the ball at the last second, just as I am about to pass that back shoulder. I don't see the superstar take a half step back, putting his shoulder right in line with the spot where my cheekbone meets my nose. I feel it though, the crushing impact of shoulder meeting face. I crumple to the ground in a bloody mess.

I'm not sure who helps me to the sideline, or who fetches the ice pack for me, one of those white plastic things that freeze up when you punch and shake it. I do know that within a few minutes, with blood still dribbling down my face and nose and my cheekbone still feeling like someone slammed a hammer into my face, the coach is sitting next to me and starting to talk. He tells me that while I am much improved, I'm just not physically strong enough. The move I thought would prove that I possessed a high soccer IQ has proven that I'm too weak to play with the big boys. Maybe spend another year on junior varsity, he suggests. Maybe you will grow a little more, get stronger, maybe you will be ready next year. I take the ice pack away from my face and glance over at the coach, to make sure that this isn't some kind of hallucination, that he really has chosen to cut a kid while his blood is still making an ugly mess of an ice pack. Indeed he has.

When the school year begins the next day, I walk into the track coach's office.

I think I want to run cross country, I tell him. See you at 3:15, he says.

The rest of my life begins then, though I'm not all that good at it. I spend that first season struggling to get under 20 minutes for 3.1 miles, the distance we race. I can't run a six-minute mile. I can stick with my closest friend on the team, our best runner, when he slows up for the seven- and eight-mile runs in practice, but when race time comes he's running 15:45 and I'm a half mile back hoping not to finish last.

But there's a thing I begin to know, when I am scampering through the woods on the Leatherstocking Trail, making my way across one village border and then another, covering distances that most people only travel in cars. As the miles pile up and I bump up against the occasional wall, drifting toward frustration or defeat, I end up finding the crack in the wall and pushing through, becoming a part of this activity in a way I have never been a part of something before. My runs to the edge are about suffering, and about emerging from a shadow, as the foot finds the next turnover and then the next, pushing off a rock, hopping over a tree root, and on and on. To flirt with the edge is about pain, but also the pure exaltation that comes with flying through the woods. I know that my brothers have never done this before.

Another Piece for CBL: Tom Lux

Larry Lux is pissed.

He's got this little brother, Tom, eight years younger. Good kid at heart. Always has been. Scrawny little guy. Scraggly mop of dirty blond hair. But seventh grade Tom can be kind of a wiseass these days. He thinks he's a big shot. He's spending his afternoons with a new group of friends, a bunch of mini-greaseballs, smoking cigarettes, planning all kinds of minor dereliction. It's nothing dangerous yet. Just punk stuff, stuff that pisses off an older brother like Larry Lux.

Larry's not worried his little brother is going to end up in San Quentin. Not yet anyway. He'd just rather not see Tom piss away his teenage years with a bunch of kids who don't look like they want to make much of their lives.

Larry is pretty sure the bright-eyed kid brother he knew before Tom became the kid he is right now is still in there somewhere. That kid had this innocent exuberance for life. He'd come home from school bragging about how he'd beaten everyone in gym in some race. The kid was fast, always had been; even when he was little he had this natural way of making his body move, everything flowing together, circling around in sync. Winning races down at the park or at school used to happen so often that Larry and the rest of the family just took it for granted. That's who his little brother was and it lit him up. The fast kid.

But just the day before Tom came home to the family's simple, clapboard ranch house in Spring Valley, out on the edge of the arid hills of the East County. Your basic middle-class neighborhood in nearly idyllic 1960s San Diego. Tom was griping about the 660-yard race the gym teacher put them through. He finished with the last clump of boys. Said he didn't give a crap about it, that it was for losers and dorks anyway. Larry is pretty sure this is pure bullshit, but it annoys the hell out of him to have to listen to it.

It's a Saturday afternoon, and Tom is hanging around the house, not up to much. Larry figures it's just a matter of time before Tom and his crew head off to nothing good. Larry is athletic and he's done a reasonably long cycling ride that morning, and he doesn't have much to do himself. He finds Tom on the edge of the front porch, tossing pebbles, maybe in the direction of some squirrel that's now run off, maybe at nothing at all.

"Hey," Larry says to Tom, "you didn't like coming in last place in that race the other day, did you?"

Tom turns to his brother, and in that moment the kid headed for low-scale delinquency disappears. The boy who doesn't do much but grunt at anyone over the age of sixteen looks up at his brother and shakes his head.

I can fix it, Larry tells him. Then he tells Tom to get in his car. They are going to play basketball. In the way that little brothers are wont to do, he unquestioningly follows his brother to the car.

They drive several miles away, to a park near San Diego State University. Larry kills the engine. "We're here," he says to Tom.

Tom is a little curious. They've never come here to play basketball before. On the way they passed several other basketball courts between Spring Valley and this court in College Heights. Whatever, if this is the court where his big brother wants to play basketball, this is where they will play. He sees Larry begin to open his driver's side door, so Tom opens his and gets out of the car. He begins to walk toward the courts, his eyes staring at the ground. He has no idea Larry isn't behind him. When Tom is far enough away, Larry yells through the open car window to his little brother. Holding out a stopwatch, he tells Tom there is only one way to get home, and only one way to become a good runner. He starts the car and starts the watch. Tom doesn't understand exactly what's happening until Larry pulls out of the parking lot. Then he gets it. "Bastard," he thinks.

Then Tom begins to run.

When he gets home a little less than an hour later, Larry is sitting on the front steps with the stopwatch. He hits the button and stops it. He shows it to his little brother. "Pretty good," he says.

Larry tells Tom he is a natural. He just needs to train. "I'm going to turn you into a runner," he says.

Larry has reached the little kid inside Tom, the kid he was before junior high school and cigarettes and trying to act cool and impress people by doing things that aren't especially impressive at all. It's just what Tom needs to get shaken off the idiot path—that and, eventually, Bob Larsen.

Larry has said Tom Lux is going to be a runner, and because Larry is the big brother, he gets special dispensation from Tom, so that's what Tom is going to do.

There is a steep incline out their back gate. The path rises sharply for a few hundred yards. It's called Dune Buggy Hill. They start running it together several afternoons a week. It's pretty brutal. It makes your knees feel like they are going to buckle and your chest feel like someone is stepping on it. But every time Larry says it's time to run Dune Buggy Hill again, Tom listens.

He listens as Larry talks about high school and college championships, the Olympic Games, the four-minute mile. He tells Tom he can achieve whatever he wants if he works at it. They run all spring and summer, often on the hill. Sometimes they leave their shoes on the front porch and run barefoot on the dusty trails through the low hills of the valley. Larry and Tom never talk about who to hang out with at school, or that smoking cigarettes and whatever comes after that won't do your brain much good over the long haul. They don't have to. They run.

Tom doesn't finish in the back of the pack in gym class for the rest of seventh grade. When eighth grade begins there is another classwide race. Three laps around the 220-yard chalk-line track in the schoolyard. Tom Lux laps the field and wins. The coach at the local high school, Monte Vista—a guy named Bob Larsen—is watching. He does this every year to see what talent might be on the way to the high school, which boys he might be able to keep off the football field or the baseball diamond. Larsen heads right for the boy who beat everyone else by an eighth of a mile in a race only slightly longer than a third of a mile. He tells him to keep running and to try out for the track team when he gets to high school. Tom Lux listens to him. He always will. A half century later he will say there are two people who saved his life—his brother, Larry, and Bob Larsen.

Unfortunately for Tom Lux, by the time he shows up at Monte Vista the next fall, Bob Larsen is gone, off to Grossmont College for the next chapter of his life. But the boys who trained under Bob before he left for Grossmont still follow those same regimens. They hammer those four- and five-mile tempo runs, where they search for that precipice of unsustainable fatigue and stay just short of it from start to finish nearly every afternoon. Lux follows along until he becomes one of the kids leading those tempo runs. By the time he's done at Monte Vista he's one of the best runners in the region. His mile time drops to 4:28. He can click off two miles in 9:30. There are a few better guys out there. But when Ed Mendoza is too hurt to run, when Dave Harper and Dale Fleet, these two horses from Clairemont High School in the western suburbs of San Diego County, are racing somewhere else or having an off day, Lux can win.

By the end of his senior year he's talking to Bob Larsen again, this time in Tom's living room. Larsen has had his eye on Tom Lux for a while, thinking he may help him turn Grossmont into something real. Tom would let him inch closer to having five runners who can win any race on any day. Better yet, Tom can be another of his lab rats, and let Bob, who is three years into his Grossmont coaching venture, take the next step of his quest. His distance teams were undefeated locally through 1969 and 1970. The results are sweet, but Bob Larsen is still searching for that larger truth, and he feels that winning on a bigger stage will come along with it.

Bob Larsen's runners win because he has taught them to run differently than nearly everyone else. He isn't sure what the exact ingredients of the methods are, but there are elements he knows are essential. Long hard runs that are more about quality than volume. Intervals as the races approach to find speed, preferably on a soft track. Barefoot jaunts. It's coming together. The flashes of success and constant progress make him feel more right than wrong.

And yet the naysayers are still out there, still wondering why Bob Larsen is working his tail off trying to turn this little college team called the Griffins into something they were never supposed to be, and probably never will be. Why does he care so much? Doesn't he have anything better to do? Does he really think this is going to lead to anything? He can't recruit from outside his little district. Does he actually think anyone in running's first tier will ever trust anything that some junior college coach has to say?

To his runners, Larsen's secret sauce reveals itself subtly, especially to younger runners. He comes across as a simple, happy man with plain tastes and an even tone. During training or races he stands in the infield with a stopwatch, making sure his runners know their pace. But he doesn't bark those numbers the way other coaches do, or try to rouse more speed with hollers from the grass. It might just be a suggestive three or four or five words—"maybe pick it up here" or "relax those shoulders," "use those arms." He isn't Vince Lombardi, and he isn't a mad scientist or a masochist. He is himself.

His methods, still evolving but almost revolutionary for their time, don't require huge leaps of faith. Rather, his runners must have faith in themselves, in their ability to run faster when they are most tired. Also, running is a sport that celebrates solitude. It is the essence of individual pursuit, but his runners will almost never train alone. Like a peloton in a cycling race, the group is always stronger than the individual. The lone runner, training by himself, can slack off and slow with little consequence. But the group pushes together. Whoever is having an off day inevitably reaches deeper to keep up. If he can't, he steels himself not to let it happen again, to lead the group next day. His betterment, everyone's betterment, becomes the purpose. We run on our own, but always together.

Another cornerstone—when you think you are running hard, run harder. Try to keep running harder for longer than you think you can, bringing your body and your mind closer to the edge, that moment when the ritual becomes the revelation. This is the origin of what eventually everyone will refer to as the tempo run. The tempo run doesn't have to be very long, but it shouldn't be short. Also, it must be fast, not faster than you might go in a race, though perhaps farther.

The tempo run cuts against two pieces of conventional wisdom, to the extent that in this pre-boom era of running such a thing even exists. The conventional wisdom holds that if your race distance is 10,000 meters, or 6.2 miles, then you need to train at a longer distance than that. But you will likely run a little slower than your race pace for 8 or 10 miles or even longer. Larsen wants his troops to do that sometimes, too. That's why they gather at his house on Saturday and Sunday mornings for the start of those 18- and 20-mile runs that sometimes loop back around to the Larsen home and the pitchers of lemonade that Sue Larsen always has waiting. Sometimes they punish themselves running as hard as they can up the five miles of switchbacks on Mt. San Miguel. At the top they pause for a moment to gaze out to the Mexican countryside. He lets them love the run and the running. Then they sprint back down.

Sometimes Sue drives the Larsen van out to the beach with the lemonade. She meets the team there, watches them finish those long runs with hard sprints across the sand from the jetty to the pier. Then, when they can hardly stand, she drives them back to the east county.

But Larsen also wants his boys to hammer four- and five- and eight-mile runs at a pace they might hold for the race. ("At tempo.") How fast? Enough so that it hurts, because eventually it starts to hurt less, which means it's time to go even faster.

The tempo run also doesn't have to exist on its own. It can exist as miles five through eight of a 10-mile run, or miles 13–19 of a 20-miler. The group works this out. It is an extension of Zátopek's absurd regimen of 20 or 30 or 70 quarter-mile bursts, the so-called intervals. The shorter distances harden his heart and lungs for the longer ones. This makes some sense to Larsen. The intervals have their place in the life of any runner. So why not press the cardiovascular system for as long as it can be pressed? Press it too hard, at a pace that the interval obsessives are always shooting for, and you can't go far enough to get a good workout. But press it just hard enough to reach that moment when you believe you can run fast forever, when you have reached the perfect edge, that is the essence of the tempo run. That is how you transform the internal engine, adding the extra cylinders with new capacity, making it possible for the runner to transform an everyday training session into something that can truly be epic, running to the very edge of what feels possible.

Larsen may not yet fully understand the biology of why this works. That will come later, when the sports scientists start to study the physiology of training. He will learn that what his regimen is doing is training the body to deal more efficiently with the stress of lactic acid. When his runners begin to run for him, their systems are like the kid driving a car for the first time, squeezing the steering wheel with both hands, shoulders tense, eyes darting all around, struggling to deal with the stress. With practice though, that kid can drive a car while listening to the radio and eating a sandwich.

When a body trains hard, it has to break down carbohydrates and glycogen to use them for energy. The process produces lactic acid, which then becomes lactate, though that process creates more hydrogen than a body not used to dealing with the stress can easily manage. Too much hydrogen makes the body too acidic. The human body prefers to have a nice balance between acid and base. The tempo runs train the body to get better at using the lactate as a source of energy, of converting the lactic acid to a new form of glucose.

Think of the assembly line worker trying to manufacture a machine using parts on a conveyor belt. Speed up the belt, and the worker will struggle to keep up. But over time the worker improves to maximum efficiency. This doesn't happen with quick bursts of speed (think intervals). It only happens if the conveyor belt steadily gets faster and then maintains its speed for longer and longer periods, or, in distance running terms, if the body can efficiently produce and use glycogen for a longer and longer time.

Larsen has ways of lifting his foot off the gas pedal, too. His boys always want to go longer. The age of volume is dawning. They hear stories of marathon champions, some not much older than they are, logging 160-, 180-mile weeks. There is a certain machismo in big numbers, a certain security. This is the way the mind of a gifted young distance runner works—if 10 miles is a great workout, then 20 miles must be doubly great. Then the almost inevitable breakdown occurs, even in the bodies that crave the otherworldly high from the 15th or 17th 5:30 mile the way a heroin addict craves that next rush. Run a little less, Larsen tells them, just make sure you are going hard, making every mile count. Then, when you are ready, boost the volume. At a certain point, and this is the magical point he searches for with each runner, intensity and volume are in equilibrium. Run as intensely as you can for as long as you can, each week and month during the season and then no more, because more is not necessarily better.

Unlike the competition, his runners do things others don't. They are on the beach nearly every week, cruising barefoot across the sand to build up the muscles in their feet and ease the pounding in the bones and joints. In this way they learn to run the way God wants a human to run, how to land on the middle of the foot, and lead with the knee, and keep their feet under their bodies, rather than stretching for every yard on every step, and reduce the contact time between the foot and the ground.

Larsen's ideas aren't fully formed, but they are starting to come together. Liberate the run from the track, and even from the paved road. Make the hard runs even longer. Seek the edge, except in those moments when your body honestly tells you not to.

As the Grossmont Griffins push each other to the limit each day, running in a small pack on the hot streets around campus, or across the open, rolling arid valley, dodging the chaparral with a hop here, a sidestep there, they play a running version of follow the leader, taking turns setting the pace for the pack. The only rule is everyone has to keep up with the leader. No one knows when or for how long the leader will push the pace. It might be for 100 yards or it might be for a mile. Just keep up, for as long as you have to, or for as long as you can. That's how the game works.

All Larsen needs now is some pure talent. And that is about to come.

After Tom Lux commits to Grossmont in the spring of 1971, Larsen returns to the Lux home one evening carrying a notebook. Now it's time for you to become a real runner, he tells Tom. He hands the notebook to him and tells Tom to start running every day and to write down the speed and distance of each run when he finishes. He tells Lux he is going to get a call from one of his teammates, a guy named Neil Branson who has run for Larsen this past year. Run with Branson this summer, Larsen says. He knows what to do.

Larsen had never seen Branson until he walked into his office the previous summer to introduce himself and tell the coach he wanted to run for him. Branson was twenty-three years old, just starting college after a long stint in the Coast Guard. Larsen gave him a once-over and figured he was a good twenty-five pounds overweight, maybe more. He was pretty sure this wasn't going to work. But he decided to give Branson a notebook and tell him to run every day for two weeks. Log your runs, he said. Then come back.

Larsen assumed he would never see Branson again. When Branson returned two weeks later, several pounds lighter but still a long way from a decent fighting weight, Larsen told him to do it again, for another two weeks. Branson did that, too. Finally Larsen let him on the team. By the end of the season, Branson was in Grossmont's top five, helping the Griffins to three straight blowouts against San Bernardino, Chaffey, and Riverside City to finish the season undefeated. Now Branson had a summer job—getting Tom Lux in shape to compete at the college level.

Lux and Branson spend the summer running up and down the dusty hills of eastern San Diego County. Occasionally Ed comes, too. Tom and Neil know Ed the way everyone else does—by his reputation as one of the greatest natural runners southern California has ever produced. So they are more than a little puzzled when they hit the roads with Ed and he is barely clicking off six-minute miles. Ed mentions the trouble with the stress fractures, how he wants to make sure he's healthy in August when the Balboa 8 rolls around and the season gets started. What he doesn't mention to them or to Larsen is that he is in the midst of his summer slowdown. He's at the car wash all day. That still wears him out. Put him on a starting line and fire a gun and Ed can go like few others in the country his age. But ask him to drag himself onto the roads or down to a track in the summer heat and he's probably going to take a pass. He will learn soon enough.

On Ed Mendoza's first day at Grossmont in August of 1971, he finds one of the lanes of the track covered with sawdust, just as Larsen told him he would. With the sawdust lane available, Ed really does never run alone. Tom or Neil or one or two of the other local studs, Larry Stone or Joe Stubbs, are always next to him when he needs to do his track work, or when he is warming up or cooling down from an afternoon of running the trails and empty dirt roads with his teammates. Now that he is with a coach who knows how to take care of his legs, Ed feels almost no pain.

Larsen also has these sheets of rippled rubber. He traces the soles of his runners' training shoes onto the sheets, cuts out matching pieces and has a cobbler glue them onto their shoes for extra cushioning. They're all wearing first-generation running shoes made of stiff leather and stiffer rubber. The added padding softens the pounding and cushions the impact. Ed increases his mileage, from about 35 miles a week to 70. Most of the rest of the crew is doing up to 100, beginning their mornings with four miles on the local roads. They are training for college races now, which are four miles on often rolling terrain, double the high school distance. Ed often skips this morning session for fear of another injury. He has never felt stronger. He feels like a real runner, especially as the wins start to pile up.

The Griffins roll through their season just like Larsen figured they would. Grossmont has seven dual meets in the Mission Conference and scores a perfect 15 points (taking the top five places) in all but one of them. Ed wins nearly every race. He takes first in the conference finals. Then, at the invitational competitions, the real races with all those top runners from all over the state, Ed emerges as a star. He takes first in the Hancock Invitational and first in the Mt. San Antonio College Invitational, known as "Mt. SAC." Branson is second at Mt. SAC and Tom is fourth. At Long Beach, Neil is third, with the rest of the team scoring high, too, making the Griffins largely untouchable. They are first at the Long Beach Invitational, and the Hancock, and Mt. SAC. Two more wins, at the Southern California Championship and the State Championship, and Larsen will have the titles he always believed his methods could produce—so long as he could find the right horses.

The Southern California Championship is set for Grossmont's home course in Santee, the fast, mostly flat trail through Santee Lakes. The planets are aligned. The team to beat is going to be

László Tábori's crew from Los Angeles Valley College. Their district is massive compared with Grossmont's, and Tábori, the Hungarian who held the world record in the 1,500 meters during the 1950s, has been pulling local gazelles onto his squad for years on the strength of his sterling reputation.

When the gun sounds, though, the Griffins take off. Tábori's crew from Los Angeles Valley knows almost instantly this will not be their day. A better team is going to beat them. And that is exactly what happens.

Now Bob Larsen really does have a state championship in his sights. He knows he has the best team, because of who they are and how they train. He just has to keep them from getting complacent during the two-week layover before the state championships, from believing that because they beat Tábori's boys in the Southern California Championship they can just show up at the state championships and pick up the trophy. He needs to find a way to keep the Griffins under pressure, to make them understand that whatever they have accomplished so far won't mean anything unless they win this last race.

When the Griffins gather for training the day after the Southern California Championship, he sits the boys down and makes sure they understand this is the most important race they have ever run. He tells them they can't just know that in their minds, they have to live it, to make each minute in training point toward those 20 minutes of racing that will happen in less than fourteen days at American River College near Sacramento.

Two days before the race the team boards a plane for Sacramento. If Tom Lux needed to feel any more gravity, he does now. He's never been on a plane before. When they arrive in Sacramento and check into a hotel, it's the first time Tom has ever checked into a hotel. This really is a pretty big deal, he thinks.

Like every other team they head out to the course the next day to study it, learn its contours, understand where the hills come. They search for the most likely spot for the break, that moment when the boys out front will decide it's time to go, where one of them, or maybe two, or three, but never more than that, will decide to take off.

They head back to the hotel, have a team dinner, then gather once more for one last team meeting. One last time they review the land mines that might await. He goes through all the nightmare scenarios that might mess up this important day.

The following morning, Larsen watches all those singlets stream by in a Technicolor blur. The four-mile race is maybe half over when Bob starts to do that thing that only veteran distance coaches can do. He is looking at the blur and counting, with frightening accuracy, where his boys are in relation to every other team. He has seen so many of these races he needs only to look for a moment or two before he can see the future. He can know how this will go.

For everyone but Ed, this will not end well. Ed is just off the lead. Well, a little more than just off the lead. More like 20 seconds back. But the leader, a horse from L.A. Valley named Dave Babirack, has opened it in just over nine minutes. Larsen knows there is no way he can keep that up. Ed, the natural, is doing just what he needs to do, running his own race, and he is going to be just fine. Three miles in, Ed is right on the leader's tail, and with a half mile to go he takes over the lead so quickly that the L.A. Valley horse won't think for a second that he will have a chance to catch Ed in the stretch. Ed Mendoza is the 1971 California cross country champion. No one else on the team is though. The rest of the Griffins lagged early. They fought to stay in the top 10, but slipped through the teens as they searched for the extra gear and couldn't find it. They finish in third place, behind both L.A. Valley and El Camino. Bob Larsen is sure this is all his fault.

The previous two days run through his mind. How different they were than anything else he has been through, so unlike the weeks leading up to any other big race, when Bob Larsen did everything he could to dial down the pressure on his runners. Somewhere along the line he forgot how exhausting it is for a distance runner to have to think for 20 straight minutes, while pushing his body to the edge and keeping it there. There are no timeouts in track, no chance to step out of the batter's box and think through the next pitch, no huddle after every four yards. He made his boys run this race while imagining every possible catastrophe every day for nearly two days. No wonder their tanks are empty. He has always had perspective, and he has long sought to pass that on to his runners, releasing tension instead of boosting it.

He has lost plenty of races and meets before, and made plenty of mistakes. All coaches do. But this is something new—blowing a championship, letting his boys down in such a monumental way. The boys are devastated, silent in the van after the race. Even Ed, as thrilled as he is to be the state champion, feels a strange emptiness. Bob Larsen will lose more races eventually, but he will never let it happen the way it did at this 1971 state championship again.

And certainly not with the most astonishing young runner he has ever seen on the way to Grossmont in a matter of months.

Schenectady, New York, 1991

Schenectady is a sad town. General Electric built manufacturing plants and turned it into a boomtown in the 1940s and 1950s. Then the company began abandoning the place in the 1960s, shipping jobs to cheaper locales. By the time I show up in 1987 to attend Union College, the city has all the trappings of twentieth-century misery—a mostly shuttered downtown, blocks of crack houses, frighteningly high rates of unemployment, poverty, and substance abuse.*

When I started running here in college, in the gray afternoons, after classes ended and before dinner began, I said I was playing defense against the beer, and the pizza, and all the other indulgences of undergraduate life. I am not nearly fast enough to run with the college team, which is fine. I get plenty of humiliation on the tennis team, where I regularly get smacked around by better players from Williams and Hamilton and Colgate. For a while I do this two-mile campus loop twice. Then I get bored and I venture to see what else is out there.

Head east from Union's hilltop campus and there is a neighborhood of stately homes known as the "GE Plots," because that's where General Electric acquired land and built houses for its executives. It makes for a good and safe area for running, even as the plots give way to the middle-class neighborhood that surrounds the local high school.

I'm there every day, sometime between three and seven. There's a loop I do that I can stretch from four to five to six miles, depending where I cut north for the trek back to campus. I'm there in the brittle cold, when the streets freeze over and don't unfreeze for weeks on end. I'm there on days when my friends are still sleeping off nights they don't want to remember

---

* Schenectady has made an attempt at a comeback in the twenty-first century. The downtown has been revived substantially, though unemployment remains high, as GE never brought its jobs back. Upstate New York needs tremendous help.

even if they could. I'm there after tennis practices, or one of the too many defeats, or even on the day once in a blue moon when I win. A run can be solace or a celebration.

Did I see you running the other day? a professor asks me one afternoon during her office hours. Probably, I say. Are you training for something? she asks. No, I say. I just like to run. Impressive, she says.

Maybe it is. I don't know when it became essential for me to be there, alone, every day. I just know that it is. On those roads, no one ever serves at match point against me. No professor tells me my paper is decent, but not "A" material. No girls tell me they just want to be friends.

I am not entirely alone, there's a girl I pass nearly every day. She runs the same loop but in the opposite direction. She's a year behind me. She's small, with short blond hair. She runs a bit like a medium-fast version of the Energizer Bunny. She looks like she will never stop. I don't know her name. She's friendly with some girls I'm friends with, but we have no classes together. We are never at the same parties. We only see each other on these streets. If we are on the same side of the street as we pass, we trade smiles, acknowledging our odd allegiance to this daily habit. I'm pretty sure she does not know my name either.

And then, I do see her one night. She's in the basement barroom of my fraternity house. I'm a few beers in and I've got a cigarette between two fingers. Smoking is something I do occasionally, especially when I am a few beers in and my friends are doing it, and because it's 1991 and I'm twenty-one years old and a college senior and it just feels good to stand around with a beer in one hand and a cigarette in the other at this moment in my life. There is a group of people around us, and then they are gone. It's just me and her, not passing on a frigid street in mid-stride but standing there face-to-face.

"You're a runner," she says. "How could you possibly be smoking?"

There is no good response here, other than to tell her she's right and to stub out my cigarette.

It's the first time anyone has ever called me "a runner." I like the sound of it.

The Outlier: Terry Cotton

The first time Bob Larsen sees Terry Cotton, he thinks the boy looks like he should be jumping off the pier at Pacific Beach. He is not. He is running. This is the fall of 1970. Larsen is thirty. He thinks he has seen just about everything that could happen in a running race. Then Terry Cotton takes a wrong turn down the stretch in Balboa Park.

Larsen is at Balboa Park that afternoon because word has made its way through San Diego's running circles that there's a special kid suddenly running for El Cajon High. No one knows all that much about him because Terry Cotton spent his formative years somewhere in northern California. Terry doesn't talk much, but among the folks Terry does speak to, and there aren't many, he's never very specific about where home was before he and his mother moved down the coast and settled in east San Diego County. She works odd jobs. He tries to do a little of that, too, to help make ends meet. There doesn't seem to be a father in the picture. There isn't much money either. Everyone knows only one thing about Terry Cotton—he sure can run.

Teammates, the ones he drives crazy by pushing the pace to turn every training run into a race, are the only people who come close to knowing Terry, because Terry only really talks when he is running, and he doesn't say all that much even then. Terry reveals himself in two ways. The first is through his art. He can turn doors and window frames into masterworks. He carves and etches and paints them with a complexity that removes all sense of them as normal, utilitarian objects. His specialty though is the three-dimensional works he creates with a piece of wood, finishing nails, and different color threads. He winds the thread around the nails in a way that evolves into rainbow-like beauty. When he is done with one of these, it looks as though the thread could not have been wound around those nails in any other way. It's as if nature had designed each piece. Friends and teammates go weeks and only hear a few words from Terry. Then he presents them with one of these works of art. There is nothing more he needs to say.

Terry's second form of expression is movement. His love and commitment to lead a team emerges when he is in motion, when he is running as fast as he can for as long as he can, urging his teammates to stay with him. He knows there will be moments when all this running at the edge will produce intense pain, and he will need them as badly as they need him. Then the run ends, and Terry goes quiet again. His face goes blank, almost expressionless, until he starts running once more, in the only gear he knows.

Terry's sun-bleached blond hair flows down below his shoulders and frames a face dominated by his light blue eyes. He has the kind of eyes that make it impossible to tell exactly what thoughts burn behind them. He rarely lets on. It's the face of a thousand surfers on San Diego's beaches on any weekend afternoon. His shoulders stretch away from his neck like an extra-wide coat hanger. The shoulders are so wide that they make Terry look like a bit of a freak. But then he runs and it all makes sense. Maybe that width creates plenty of room for what must be a massive set of lungs, lungs that appear to be puffing up the top part of his chest. His biceps look like soda cans. He has thighs the size of small tree trunks. He is neither tall nor short, but his legs are so long it's not exactly clear where his legs end and his torso begins. He is wiry but not scrawny, muscular but not bulky. This body is indeed meant to run, not surf. And when he does run, the running aficionados don't take their eyes off him, because no one has ever seen anyone run quite like Terry Cotton runs.

Terry Cotton is very fast. Even very fast people think of him that way. People who train with him, people who somehow manage to beat him sometimes, the coaches who watch him from the infields, all of them think of the word "fast" as soon as they hear his name. But fast is an unsatisfying adjective in Terry's case. Terry's brand of speed possesses a relentless ferocity. The voices of all those coaches and competitors rise when they talk about Terry's running. Their heads shake as if at the memory of a kind of violent act that causes those who witness it to wince.

It's been this way ever since Terry showed up at El Cajon. He is the runner others tell stories about, his wins ever more triumphant in each retelling. There is the dual meet against Monte Vista High School when Cotton is entered in three races—the two-mile, the 800, and the mile. He takes first in the two-mile in 9:05. Then he takes first in the 800, finishing in 1:56. Then he runs the mile in 4:20. First again. When the meet finishes, Terry blows off the team bus. He grabs his bag, throws it on his back, and runs another eight miles to get home. No one knows how long that takes. Everyone assumes it's not very long at all, because Terry Cotton only knows how to run one way.

Whether he is leading a pack through a series of quad-searing 5-minute miles, or setting out on a 20-mile run through the hills, Terry pushes to the edge from his first step. To watch Terry Cotton run is to watch someone hold his hand over a flame for too long. The instinctive reaction is to grab the daredevil's arm and pull it to safety. This is what coaches and teammates will always want to do for Terry when they are running with him. They will try to stop him, but they have to catch him first. That won't work most of the time. He has to be physically immobilized. Left on his own, he just goes—10 miles in the morning, another 10 in the afternoon. All the miles are as hard as he can make them. Terry runs as though he is being chased by a man with an axe.

So Bob Larsen wants to see for himself what all the fuss is about this kid. He heads to Balboa Park to watch what figures to be an unmemorable race with El Cajon and a few other high schools. Larsen positions himself about a half mile from the finish. That allows him to see a good-size chunk of the two-mile course. From the gun, Terry Cotton darts into the lead. He builds a cushion, stretching the margin more than he probably has to, Larsen thinks. It's clear after a few hundred yards that Cotton has far more talent than the rest of the field. All the other runners look like they are fighting their way across the course. Terry just seems to be gliding over it, in that effortless, quiet way. Great runners can seem to run so fast with so little effort. His heels nearly whack him in the ass with every step. The kid is very good, Larsen thinks.

As the race enters the final stretch, Terry is leading his closest competitor by 50 yards. He is cruising to another easy win. There is one last turn and then little more than a quarter mile to go. Perhaps 600 yards, not longer. At the turn though, there is confusion. Somehow, Terry goes the wrong way, right, instead of left. He disappears into the trees. Out of sight. Just like that, the race has a new leader, some kid who moments ago was trailing Terry by nearly 75 yards. He's run here before. He knows where the finish line is. He isn't about to follow Terry Cotton into the woods. Poor kid, Larsen thinks, probably skipped the usual pre-race review of the course with his coach. Lesson learned.

Then Terry comes flying out of the trees. It's as if he went in there to make things interesting, to give himself a challenge. Now the race is interesting. He's a good 50 yards behind with a few hundred yards to go. With every step he is reeling in the leader. Larsen is pretty sure there isn't enough race left for this to happen. Seconds later though, he is less sure of the outcome. Then the outcome becomes stunningly clear. Terry is burning through the stretch in a way Larsen has never seen. It's a full-on sprint, nearly 10 minutes into a cross country race over a hilly course. Every other runner he knows would have kicked himself after the wrong turn and lived to fight another day. Not this kid.

By the finish, Terry has the gap he needs. Terry's legs buckle when he breaks the tape. When Larsen gets to him, he is purple from oxygen deprivation. Agony appears to mean nothing to him. This is the kid I've been looking for all my life, Larsen thinks, because Terry Cotton is the perfect specimen to test every idea Larsen has about running on the edge. He can get Bob that much closer to the hidden truth. It isn't complicated, but it is difficult. Terry Cotton lives on the edge, and he invites his teammates there nearly every day. Almost no one will go to this place alone—it's too scary. But the group has power. Who knows where they might end up.

Sometimes the constant speed, the inability to do anything not at the edge of exhaustion, comes back to bite Terry, like in June of 1972 at the state high school championships. The meet is in Oroville, about an hour north of Sacramento, at the top of the Central Valley. Average temperatures for the month hover at 90 degrees. Cotton enters only one race. He chooses the mile. That surprises no one. Everyone knows he is among the fastest milers in the state, a threat to break the state record anytime he steps onto the track. And every distance runner with talent first wants to be a miler. The mile is the glamour distance. The pain of the race is gruesome, especially in that final lap, when the oxygen deprivation truly sets in. But then it's over, roughly four minutes after it begins. A good runner believes he can do anything for four minutes, and he loves the symmetry of the distance. Four laps, four minutes. Other races have records. The mile has a "barrier"—four minutes—one that used to be impenetrable until Roger Bannister smashed through it, but it remains one of those magic numbers.

The qualifying race for the mile final at the championship is on a Friday, the first day of the meet. Terry is supposed to breeze through this, win his heat and save his energy for Saturday's final. He hammers from the start, sprinting away, opening a yawning gap between him and his closest competition. He finishes in 4:10. A time 15 seconds slower would have easily gotten him into the final.

By race time Saturday afternoon, it's nearly 90 degrees. At the gun he takes off as usual, though he holds back ever so slightly, completing his first lap in 61 seconds instead of the usual 59. At the three-quarter mark he's still in the front but hasn't managed to shake a chaser, Mark Schilling of Garden Grove High School. Terry does not believe this is a problem. Schilling has never run faster than 4:10. He will put Schilling away over the final quarter. At the first turn of the last lap, Terry moves, but Schilling hangs right on him. He is just three yards back in the final straight. Cotton digs for a little more, but Schilling is still on his heels until, with 15 yards to go, Schilling finds a gear he has never found before. He finishes in 4:05.4 and beats Cotton by one tenth of a second, a half step. The time is good for a state high school record. The record, which should have been Terry Cotton's, stands for more than two decades.

Can a blistering mile the day before a final cost someone one tenth of a second the next day? That's one way to look at it. Terry Cotton probably thinks he should have tried to go out in 60 seconds, instead of 61.

It doesn't take much to convince Terry Cotton to enroll at Grossmont. There is interest from UCLA and USC and Oregon, but he barely has any money. The local junior college just happens to have the best distance running team in the state. It has a very good young coach and a lucky cluster of raw talent.

Districts the size of Grossmont's aren't supposed to have this many sets of fast feet and big lungs within their boundaries. Terry Cotton has had some bad luck in his life. Having Bob Larsen and the Grossmont Griffins within running distance from his home is a rare stroke of good fortune.

For Larsen, Terry will serve two very important purposes. First, he can score at multiple distances—the mile, the two-mile, distance relays. He seemingly never tires. Second, he is a running version of a crash test dummy. Larsen is still trying to understand the best way to train through each of his Grossmont Griffins. He will try to rein in Cotton, to explain the value of regulating effort, of slow boils and fast boils. It doesn't do a lot of good. So he watches Cotton and takes note of what happens to the runner whose volume is always turned up to "11," who is all about high speed at every workout. He will see the incredible results and know Terry is headed to an outstanding career, becoming a two-time All-American. He also sees the downside, the constant tendon tweaks and pulled muscles and stress fractures that often sideline him. The precipice between that peak state and breakdown is frighteningly brittle, far more so for some runners than for others. He understands that better because Terry Cotton joins his team and hears every day from Larsen about the dangers of always running on the precipice.

And yet, there Terry Cotton goes again, leading the pack into those quad-burning 5-minute miles early at the start of another 20-mile run through the hills of eastern San Diego. Most of his teammates have no earthly idea how or why Terry does this. There is no man with an axe chasing Terry. What in the world is he running from? A few yards back of Terry—that's generally where the pack trails when Terry is leading the way—Tom Lux thinks he might have a small clue as to why Terry always has to be running full tilt, why every day there is another race against ghosts.

Tom has known Terry since they began competing against one another in high school. They would see each other at races, nod, share a few words about a trail or a new shoe that one of them had discovered, then try to beat each other's brains out when the starter fired his pistol. That they both ended up in Grossmont, teammates, friends, is not a coincidence. Even with Tom, Terry still reveals little, but one day, as their friendship evolves, Terry does tell him a story from his childhood.

The details are vague. It's not clear where the story took place. Somewhere where Terry and his mother lived before they came to El Cajon. With his mother off working, he and his little brother entertain themselves. They are young, and playing in the water—a river or a canal, it isn't clear. They are not good swimmers. Terry's little brother falls in, and Terry can't save him. He watches him drown.

Tom often thinks of this story when he sees Terry running the way he does. Does the agony that exists on the edge suppress the other pain? Or is it that combination of pleasure and pain that brings on the confluence of white noise and meditative existence that soothes him? Perhaps the running is sustaining. No one will ever know for sure. They just know that once Terry signs on to attend Grossmont in the summer of 1972, he can make them nearly unbeatable.

Peace and War

The truth about running cannot be found without balance. Bob Larsen knows this.

Balance between the upper body and the lower body; between the right side and the left; between the head and the shoulders; the heart and the lungs; the body and the mind; between rest and overtraining; between what is expected from the team as a whole, and what each individual needs and can provide. This last tenet may be the one Bob works hardest to achieve. He prides himself on how well he knows his runners—their tendencies, their strengths, their weaknesses, what they love and what they hate. He knows them as well as he might know his own children. So how did he not know the most important thing anyone could know about Ed Mendoza?

On August 5, 1971, Ed Mendoza won the one lottery no one wants to win. On that day, six teenagers on the Selective Service Youth Advisory Committee spent more than two hours drawing birthdays and numbers from two drums on the stage at the Commerce Department auditorium in Washington, D.C. On the 310th pick, 108 minutes into the process, a committee member drew the number 1 and the date December 4, 1952, which means everyone born on that date will be first up for the draft. That is the day Ed Mendoza was born.

Months later, Ed Mendoza sees the return address on the envelope—"Selective Service" it says—and it tells him all he needs to know about the contents of the letter. He reads those words and he thinks the only thing that a nineteen-year-old can possibly think. He thinks he is headed to the jungles of Southeast Asia and isn't coming home.

But in one of the great feats of denial, Ed hasn't thought about the draft in nearly a year. He hasn't told his coach or anyone about his draft status. That's an astonishing thing, because the draft quota for 1972, a time when the military and President Nixon have promised to draw down troop levels in Vietnam, is 100,000 men. The previous year, the quota was 140,000. Kids, and they really are just kids, with draft numbers higher than 150 didn't get called up. The number crunchers now say no one born in 1952 with a draft number higher than 125 will be called to serve. All these numbers mean nothing to Ed Mendoza. If your draft number is 1, unless a meteor crashes into the planet, you are going to get called.

For months, Ed hasn't spent a minute pondering these numbers. He thinks about clicking off quarter-mile repeats in 65 seconds, running four miles in 20 minutes, crushing a 10-mile run in 57 or 58 minutes, crossing the line first in the state championship race. He doesn't think of the number that should haunt him, especially at a time when student deferments are being phased out. He has put his lottery number out of his mind. He hasn't spoken about it to anyone. All year long, no one knows what a bad spot Mendoza is in.

Ed grew up with that legend of his father lying about his age so he wouldn't miss action in World War II. Maybe it was true. Maybe it wasn't. Different time. Different war. Ed has never wanted to serve as cannon fodder in what has evolved into a hopeless battle in the jungle against God knows what. So for the longest time, he chose not to think about it. He can't do that anymore.

Ed takes the letter and heads over to see the one person he really wants to talk to about the situation—Bob Larsen. He knows there isn't anything Bob can do about it, but Larsen is the main adult in Ed's life at this point. He's a running coach, yes, but he also serves as a life guru to the boys who run for him. Got a problem with school or parents or a girlfriend? Bob is the one to talk to about it. He doesn't fix things but he is the ultimate listener. He does not judge, he observes, he listens, he simplifies.

Ed brings the letter ("Order to Report for Induction" it says at the top) to Larsen's office at Grossmont. He can barely talk as he hands it to him. Larsen takes a look at the letter and spends a minute or two reading through. There is a date in a few weeks when Ed has to report to a building in downtown Los Angeles. He is to bring documents, proof of identity, his Social Security card, proof of marriage if he has it (he doesn't, because he isn't), clothes for three days. About midway down, there is a sentence that says draftees may be rejected because of a mental or physical condition. Ed will be subject to a full examination when he arrives, but if he has medical records showing he suffers from anything that might prevent him from serving, he should bring them. Larsen reads that sentence again, and then he reads it once more. Then he's quiet for a bit.

Larsen considers himself a patriot. As a teenager in San Diego, he looked at all those naval officers in their white uniforms as local heroes. Bob did his six months of active duty in 1962. Then he spent many years in the reserves, training that one weekend each month. He very easily could have been called up for duty in Vietnam. His unit never got the call. He does not know why. He has friends who have died in Vietnam. One of his best friends, his fraternity brother from college, Mike Neil, the man who set him up with his wife and stood as his best man, went to Boalt Law School after he and Bob graduated from San Diego State, then enlisted in the Marines when he could have gotten started on a lucrative career.

Mike Neil served in the infantry and became a platoon commander with the 1st Battalion, 7th Marine Regiment. One night during his first six months in Vietnam, he battled through hand-to-hand combat and enemy fire to take out a machine gun nest. A third of the men in his unit died that night. Neil earns the Navy Cross for his valor. By the time Neil retires, he is a brigadier general. He returned to San Diego and set up a law practice. Larsen sees him often. There are few people Larsen loves and respects more than Mike Neil.

Larsen doesn't have much love for this war, though. It's the summer of 1972 and the whole situation seems so bleak. He's not going to be showing up at any protests. That's just not who he is, but he pays attention. This war isn't going well, and it's not going to end well. Even worse, it's not going to end anytime soon. It's been more than a year since one veteran, a former Navy lieutenant from Harvard named John Kerry, sat in front of the Senate Foreign Relations Committee and asked, "How do you ask a man to be the last man to die for a mistake?" Everyone saw that.

Larsen reads the letter again. Then he looks up at his runner. He tells Ed he wants him to go to every doctor he has ever seen about those stress fractures and shin splints. He needs to get a copy of every note they have ever written about him and every X-ray that has ever been taken of his lower limbs. He is going to take those notes and pictures with him when he goes to Los Angeles. He will show them to the military doctors.

Ed listens, of course. Everyone always listens to Coach Bob. But this might be the most ridiculous idea he has ever heard. Ed Mendoza is one of the best runners in the country. He won nearly every race he entered last season, a state champion. He's the favorite to win the state cross country championship in three months and he is a member of a team that is likely California's best. He runs somewhere between 50 and 75 miles every week. Not fit for military service? He's very likely the most fit candidate in his draft class. How are the doctors not going to see that?

Say nothing, Larsen tells him. Don't lie, but don't volunteer any information either. Can you do that, the coach asks the runner. Part of him hates giving these instructions. What would his friend Mike Neil with his Navy Cross and Purple Heart think of this? Nothing good, he is sure of that. But it really has become a miserable, pointless war, and he does not want Ed to be a part of it. Also, basic training does require a lot of miles in Army boots. He's pretty sure Ed will get hurt.

Ed tells his coach he thinks it's a ridiculous plan. Just do what I told you, Larsen says to him. These are facts, he says. You don't have to say you're an All-American runner. Show them these medical facts. Say no more.

Ed does what Bob tells him to do. He spends the next several days gathering every medical record and X-ray he can find, all those pictures of what the inside of his lower legs looked like when he felt like the nails and the screws were digging into them, when the kid who could run two miles in under nine minutes could barely complete one lap around his high school track. On the appointed morning, he tucks the envelope with the records and the films into a bag and holds them close to his body as he rides the bus up to a big concrete building in Los Angeles where he reports for duty.

The medical exams are among the first order of business. He sits in a room on a metal table. He hands a doctor his records. The doctor starts going through them, then excuses himself. He comes back with another doctor and the two begin to examine Ed. Then one of them leaves, only to return with another doctor. Before long there are five doctors surrounding Ed, poking and maneuvering his tibias to try to figure out what could be going on to make them look like such a mess in the film. One asks if he plays football. Another asks if he trips a lot. Another asks if he has a habit of banging his shins into wooden logs. All Ed says is that he runs a bit and when he runs this is what happens.

No one talks for a moment. Everyone just sort of looks at one another trying to figure out what to do next. Finally someone, not Ed, speaks. It's one of the doctors. "We call these march fractures," he says. "With boots on you wouldn't last a month in basic training."

Ed doesn't shout or smile or scream or cry. His coach told him to say nothing. So he says nothing. "I'm going to classify you as IV-F," the doctor says. Ed knows what this means. Every kid does in 1972. One of California's top collegiate distance runners, maybe its best, is not qualified for military service.

In the fall, Ed has company. In September, Tom Lux's number comes up. His birthday, February 11, has drawn number 26 in the lottery. Unlike Ed, Tom has been thinking about this and has a plan. He has terrible vision and wears thick glasses. He thinks all he needs is an eye doctor to sign the right form to let the military know he is blind as a bat. Unfortunately his eye doctor believes when the military calls you for duty you serve. In his office, he points to a six-inch letter on the wall a few feet away. He tells Tom to say what the letter is. It's impossible to get it wrong. Your eyes are fine, the eye doctor tells him, you are perfectly fit to serve.

So Tom turns to Plan B, the Mendoza plan. He's pretty sure it won't work. He has had three stress fractures in his legs and feet over the years. He has the records and the film to prove it. Still, they don't amount to the kind of file his buddy Ed presented over the summer. His fractures show up as calcium deposits and don't look nearly as severe as Ed's. They look like fuzzy white areas in the pictures, as if someone stuck a few cotton balls onto his shins before they put him in the X-ray machine. He's not going to fool anyone, he thinks. He's headed to the jungle.

He rides the bus to Los Angeles, follows directions to the big building downtown. Then he waits. When it's his turn to hop on the metal table for the exam, he gives his records to the doctor. The doctor looks at the records and looks at Tom. He brings in another physician for a consultation. They tell Tom he needs to come back the next day to see an orthopedist. All the kids who have some kind of out-of-the-ordinary medical condition that requires a follow-up exam have to do the same thing. The military puts them up in a hotel. It's the second hotel Tom Lux has ever been in. The other one was with the team at the state championships the year before. What he wouldn't give for another shot at something so simple as a state championship race right now.

The next morning he heads back to the big concrete building and soon he is called to see the orthopedist. The doctor looks at the records. He examines the X-rays, then plays around with Tom's shins a bit. Not good, he says. Tom says nothing about Arthur Lydiard, the Kiwi coach whose 100-mile-a-week training regimen he followed for much of the summer. He barely has time to. Before he knows it, the doctor has classified him IV-F, too.

The reprieve comes so quickly, it's almost anticlimactic. Tom finds it strange that the biggest moments of his life, the ones where his existence can head in one direction or go the opposite way, can feel so small. Like Ed Mendoza, Tom Lux is free to carry on with the rest of his days however he chooses. In the years since Larry Lux brought Tom to that basketball court and made his little brother run home, Tom has come to believe running saved his life. Now he knows it to be true.

With the core of the team intact, Grossmont's cross country season gets back on track in the fall of 1972. Terry Cotton brings that competitive tension to the group, just as Larsen knew he would. Once high school rivals, Ed and Tom and Terry train together every day. Or rather, Ed and Tom try to keep up with Terry, which is often hopeless. Always, they are chasing him. When they ask Terry why he runs like this, he explains that he simply can't run any other way. They warn him that if he doesn't ease up, those little tweaks in his

Achilles and his calves are going to turn into serious injuries, but it does no good.

With Terry on the team, Bob Larsen can count to eight: Terry, Ed, and Tom, plus Bob Wilson, Larry Stone, Joe Stubbs, Ed Kuehne, and Steve Israel. They go undefeated in their conference. In seven of eight races they score 15 points, sweeping the first five places. In three of those meets they take the first seven spots. Terry Cotton wins every race.

Cross country is a bit like golf. Even Tiger Woods at his best can only win one of every three tournaments he enters. Certain terrain, like certain golf courses, is more suited to certain runners. Not everything can click every day. The body is so frail, the margins so thin, a sniffle, a bad night's sleep, a nagging tweak in a tendon can lead to a slight drop-off that causes even the best runner to slip from first to fourth on any given day. And yet, Terry runs the table at the big races, too. He finishes first at the Long Beach Invitational, where he and Tom Lux are neck and neck at the end and decide to cross the finish line together. Then he wins the Moorpark Invitational, the Hancock Invitational, and the Mt. SAC Invitational.

It's not just Terry shining at these meets. Grossmont runs the table, too, taking first at Moorpark, Hancock, Long Beach, and Mt. SAC. They are making a mockery of the junior college competition. As always, at the end of every meet, Larsen wanders over to the scoreboard to study the times of the top four-year universities. Grossmont would have beaten all of them, too. His little junior college, which essentially collects kids from eight high schools, is the best distance team in California, and California is just about the biggest state in the country, with arguably the greatest collection of athletes in the land. Top to bottom, the Grossmont Griffins may be one of the best college cross country teams in the U.S.

With three weeks to go before the state championships, Larsen brings his boys to the track. He tells them it's time to sharpen their weapons. After months of grueling miles on the roads and through the canyons, they have all the endurance they need. It's time to focus on speed. Terry, Tom, and Ed have a quick huddle. They want to do twelve 400s, each in 60 seconds. Larsen gives his blessing. One after another they begin to grind them out, their legs and lungs on fire. Each day they come closer and closer to the goal. At first they can sustain the roughly 60-second pace for three 400s, then it's five, then seven, then eleven. Well, Terry can. Ed and Tom don't quite have that speed.

Ed is amazed. He has no idea that a body can get that much faster in such a short amount of time. His jet-black hair bounces off his shoulders with every step. Terry has been the better runner all season, but Ed has no intention of giving up his state championship without a fight. He is also beginning to experience what he thinks Terry experiences, that state of beautiful transcendence that exists just beyond the edge of total exhaustion, that place where Bob wants them to get to. That moment when the body feels as though it has nothing left to give, when everything is depleted, and then it discovers just a little more.

For the Southern California Championship, the team heads to the College of the Canyons, on the edge of the Angeles National Forest, seventy miles north of Los Angeles. Fall rains pound the region all week and the day before the race officials have to scrap the usual course through the hills and design another one that loops around the school. There are no tricks, no sudden hills or crazy turns. It's all there in front of them and the boys know this one is theirs. Ed and Tom and Terry push the pace from the start. By the final mile they have an 80-yard cushion. There is only one thing left to do. They all want to win, and they all will. No one has to say anything. They know they will cross the line together. They break the tape in 17:46. A kid from Bakersfield finishes next in 18:01. With Larry Stone in 7th and Ed Kuehne in 12th, the team finishes with 25 points. Bakersfield is 2nd with 75, and El Camino is 3rd with 77. It's a wipeout.

Once more, Larsen can see a state championship within his grasp. He knows his mistake from a year ago. His runners are so much more fit than everyone else. His task this year is to keep them loose, psyche them down rather than psyche them up. His usual string of "what-ifs"—those questions that force the boys to think about Plan B and Plan C—become a string of absurdities. What if Terry can't break seven minutes for the first mile? What if Ed forgets how to put one foot in front of the other midway through the race? What if Tom decides to run the final mile backwards? The questions leave no doubt about their message—relax guys, we've got this.

As they head out for the training run, Terry, who is usually so quiet, goes on and on about some bad apples he ate that caused him to tie his teammates in the league championship. Larsen likes this. He has no doubt that Terry and Ed are the two best runners in the state. If they are going at each other from the gun, watching for each other's surges, making sure to cover each other's moves, there is no way they can lose. One of them will, but only to the other, and if Grossmont goes 1-2 it's going to be very hard for another school to win this championship.

As the weekend approaches the team heads back north. Coincidentally, the state championships are also scheduled for the College of the Canyons, so two weeks after its triumph over southern California, the team is back in Santa Clarita. The rains have subsided. The race will take place on the traditional rolling cross country course. The night before, Larsen reminds the boys this won't be the speed chase that the Southern California Championship was. Go ahead, push the pace he says, but no need to go crazy.

In the back of the room, Terry Cotton sounds like he is coughing up half his lung. He's been fighting a cold for days. Larsen scans the eyes of every one of his runners to see if they are thinking what he is—that they have worked so hard all season, beaten all comers only to arrive at the state championships with the star of their team battling a nasty cold. Will they all wake up the next morning with hacking coughs and mucus spewing from their lungs? How can he fix this? Should he quarantine Terry? He scans the room again. To a man, the runners seem to be barely noticing Terry's hacks. Terry sleeps with the rest of the team.

The only time Larsen senses any nerves with this crew is the next morning in the van over to the race. The razzing and verbal jousting that usually fill the bus rides are missing. An uncomfortable silence fills the room. Larsen knew this was coming. The Griffins run and compete like grown men but they are eighteen- and nineteen-year-old boys, susceptible to all the frailties befitting those late teen years, when a person can seem twenty-five one moment and twelve the next. He is ready for this.

As the boys pile out of the van, Larsen tells them to hold up before they head over to the officials' tent to check in. Get in a line, we've got one more drill, he says. The boys do as they are told, leaving their bags that hold water bottles and Vaseline and rolls of tape by the van's tires. When they are in a line Larsen tells them they need to practice exactly what they are going to do if things don't go their way today.

"Watch," Larsen says. He leans one hand on the side of the van. He swings back his right foot ever so slowly. Then he brings it forward, as though he is giving a rock the lightest of kicks. As the foot grazes the dirt, he lets out an almost sarcastic "Aw, shucks." He turns back to his team. He asks them if they got it. A few nod at him. The rest think he's cracked. Are you sure, he asks? Let me show you again. The leg swings back, then forward. "Awww, shucks," he says. "Now come on. Everyone over here by the van. We need to practice this."

This is not the time to start questioning the man's methods. One by one, they take a few steps over to the van and kick the dirt together. "Come on now, say the words," Larsen tells them, "Awwww shucks." This goes on for a full minute or two. The boys are hoping no one can see them. No doubt they look like goofs. That is the point, to not take themselves or this race, or any race for that matter, too seriously. Don't make it more than what it is. As they kick the dirt over and over, the pre-race banter returns. Time to run, Larsen tells them. We're ready.

As they walk over to the start area, Larsen has one more message to deliver. Like he always does, Ed is trailing the group. He's small, and as he walks his short legs don't cover as much ground as the rest of the team. That gives Larsen the chance to sidle up next to him. Larsen knows Terry will bring everything he has. He wants to make sure the reigning state champion does, too. "Remember Ed," he says, "in the last half mile, no one passes you."

Ed tells Larsen not to worry. That last half mile is dead flat. "No one is going to pass me," he says.

On the start line, Ed is pretty certain a kid named Granillo from Bakersfield will bring the biggest challenge. Granillo finished fourth at the Southern California Championship behind the Grossmont threesome. Like any competitive runner would be, Granillo wasn't really happy about how they turned that race into their own party. He assumes Granillo has placed a target on Ed's and Terry's backs.

He is not wrong. Granillo is there at the end of the first mile and at the halfway mark of the four-mile race, too, as Ed and Terry push the pace across the rolling course. The third mile is where Ed is supposed to go, to build that cushion he needs to hold off the speed he knows Terry and maybe Granillo will bring to the finish. When he does go though, they go with him. Then, in the last mile, Granillo slips from Ed's peripheral vision. Ed knows it's coming down to him and Terry. With a half mile to go, it's now or never because he doesn't have a prayer against Terry if this comes down to the last 150 yards. He starts a final surge, a furious blast that will last for 800 meters, or it won't. The arms pump, the quads push and bang. He goes, and Terry doesn't go with him. Ed stretches his lead over Terry to three and five and seven then finally nine seconds as he breaks the tape in 19:25. Ed Mendoza is a state champion once again.

On the grass near the finish, Larsen barely bothers to do the math. He sees all those green and yellow Grossmont singlets so close to the front and he knows the championship is his. Griffins finish in places 1, 2, 11, 14, and 18 for 46 points. Second-place Mt. SAC is next at 102. L.A. Valley, with all those runners from all those high schools doing all those intervals all fall, doesn't even crack the top five. Larsen's Griffins, from those eight high schools in east San Diego, are so much better than everyone else it's almost silly.

Larsen wants to enjoy this moment for all it is. His top runner is the best in the state and so is his team. Terry won't be happy. He will blame the loss—amazingly his first of his college career—on his bad-luck cold. That's fine. He will get a chance to avenge it next season. Larsen's team has won and he wants to be present, to be here taking in the decade-long journey to a collegiate championship. He knows there are going to be more, many more likely, until the rest of the world figures out the true value of running at the edge, of holding your hand over the candle and letting it begin to burn. There it is, the essence of Larsen's way. Take that journey to a moment that feels dangerous. Then stay there. Make it last. Learn to find comfort in that space. Go there with a like-minded soul, so you are not afraid to push the edge out a little further on the next journey, to stay there a little longer, and then longer still. And faster. In this way, every mile, every second, becomes meaningful, because the longer you are there, the longer you believe you can stay, perhaps forever.

He does enjoy the moment, but before very long Larsen's mind will drift to next season's challenges and then to something far bigger. Something preposterous but not beyond the realm of possibility. Larsen's secret sauce has finally come together after a decade of pursuit. Eventually, he is going to want to take aim at something larger, maybe even one of the biggest races his fledgling sport has—the Amateur Athletic Union's Cross Country National Championships. Other than that marathon in Boston, it's the one race the country's top runners circle on their calendars. (The New York Marathon is still in its infancy—a small group of runners circling Central Park four times.) The fancy clubs in New York and Boston and Colorado and Florida pull in the ringers for it. It may seem whimsical here at this junior college championship, but there will come a time when, in his mind's eye, he will be able to see a group that would include the best guys on this team, the core of his little group from the Jamul A.C., going for the national crown.

This isn't something that gets talked about. Everyone who has doubted him all these years would probably say he's really cracked. Junior college championships are one thing. A nice little achievement for him and his kids. But a national championship against the fastest men in the country? That's just silly.

Or is it? Bob's got Ed and Terry and Tom. All he might need down the line is a few more horses.

Or maybe some Toads.

Fayetteville, Arkansas, 1992

When I first move here from New York, to a land that feels far more foreign than the handful of foreign countries I have been to, I run because it's the only time during the day when I feel like myself.

Every other waking minute I am an alien in what is for me a very strange land. Here, the only way to get a copy of the Sunday New York Times is to line up at the drugstore on Dickson Street around two in the afternoon, when the guy in the pickup truck brings the fifty copies that get flown in from Little Rock. But the sweet tea and chicken-fried steak are magical. (Who knew there were people who pound and bread and then deep-fry steak?) The bagels are awful and the pizza is terrible. I came here after graduating from Union College for grad school in creative writing and to make myself uncomfortable. For better or worse, mission accomplished.

I learn that sometimes the day grows hotter at twilight, something about the way the humidity surges as the sun drops that I will never understand, though my sweat glands do. Have you ever had the sensation of sweat pooling in your eyeballs at 8:45 in the evening?

I learn what it means to run hills. Real abductor-crushing hills. The tree-covered Ozark Mountains this city is nestled into are no joke. They are long and high, and the higher they go the steeper they get. I also learn, although this I kind of knew, that there are plenty of runners here. The University of Arkansas is home to one of the great track programs. That runner who passes you on your way up the hill, or zips by you on the track? Take a mental snapshot. You may very well see him or her on the Olympic telecast from Barcelona this summer.

Sometimes I end my runs down at the college track, because that's where the folks going to the Olympic trials in June always end up. As I stretch on the infield, I notice a triple jumper who looks like he is flying as he practices that ballet-like hop-skip-and-jump. This is Mike Conley, the world's top triple jumper, a few months before he takes the gold medal in Barcelona.

There is another reason I end at the track. It begins to happen more often than not as the year goes on, after I've looped back from West Mt. Comfort Road where, when no cars are buzzing by, you can hear the Hamestring Creek trickling through the trees. It's the same reason why my runs are stretching longer here, going from 6 to 8, to 10 or 11 miles. It's why sometimes, on days when I am done with classes by mid-morning, I might head out for a short run before lunch, and then for another later in the afternoon.

Yes, I have an idea that I want to run my first marathon in the fall, in New York or Washington, D.C. But the real reason is the running keeps me away from my studio apartment, up on the hill above the track and the rest of the athletic facilities. There, things aren't so good. It's where my girlfriend-of-the time is whiling away the days and weeks and months before she starts graduate school back east in the summer.

It's my fault that things with us are crappy as much as it is hers. We're not near ready for this cohabitation thing. We don't know this before it's too late, but we are not much more than a security blanket for a couple of early twenty-somethings who are lost and lonely after college. It's a relationship that should have ended a few nights after graduation. Instead, we're nine months past that, and disliking each other more and more each day.

There's no good guy or bad guy here. We're both just young and stupid and careless and not old enough to know how precious the time is. I'm supposed to be spending my free time writing the great American novel. Instead I run. She's supposed to be catching up on some education research. Instead she smokes a lot of pot. She's stoned from mid-morning, pretty much straight through the night, probably trying to escape the same stuff I am, just through another means.

There's a day when I confront her, tell her it looks like she's addicted to a bunch of chemicals. So, she says, you're addicted to running, and all those chemicals that get released in your body when you do it, those endorphins. Isn't that the same thing?

I don't think it is, but I also don't know what I don't know—that she's likely more right than wrong here. We go back and forth for a while on this one. At some point there's a lull. She rolls a joint. I lace up my shoes. Another couple months like this. Then we're done.

The Birth of the Toads

Bob Larsen has a coach's wandering eye.

There are runners in and around San Diego that he would love to bring into his fold but can't. Rules are rules. If they are out of his district he can't bring them in. That doesn't mean he can't look at them and think about what might be if, by some stroke of luck, they moved across the district lines, or if he ever got the chance to pull together a team that represented this whole San Diego area, with its odd cluster of raw material, of guys who just keep popping up out of the woodwork with fast legs and big sets of lungs. These are guys like Dale Fleet and Dave Harper and Kirk Pfeffer. The names aren't even all that important. It's what they represent—that idea, that willingness to run united by a single principle of seeking out the edge of what might be possible, peering over it, and then taking a fearless leap.

Two years earlier

University City, San Diego, Summer 1970

Dale

The breaking point comes in the shower, with the hot water flowing down over Dale Fleet's linebacker-sized shoulders. Dale is a big kid. Legs up to his rib cage, pushing 6'4", big face, big forehead, soon a big mustache. He's also got his daily, massive headache from all the noise carrying up the stairs from the living room of his mom and stepdad's too-small house six miles inland from the peaceful ocean breezes of Pacific Beach. The noise of the fights between his mother and stepfather is becoming unbearable.

It's like this every night. Has been for a while now. Dale's stepdad is not a bad guy. Carlton Pippin is his name. Dale's mother met him four years before, after she returned to San Diego with Dale from their four-year sojourn in Washington. The venture north followed the breakup of her first marriage, to Dale's dad. That one happened when Dale was a small boy. His memories of it are dim, though he does recall all the noise that came before it. It sounded a lot like it does now.

On the other hand, Dale's father is lucky to have made it to that marriage. Drafted for Korea, he was assigned to a Marine division that was scheduled to head across the Pacific during the first year of the war. Just before those orders came through, someone noticed Private Fleet was just about the best swimmer around. He'd been a lifeguard on San Diego's beaches and part of a group of early scuba divers. The "San Diego Bottom Scratchers Club," they called themselves. They were famous for swimming far offshore and emerging from the waters with abalone, broomtail grouper, and the occasional 150-pound giant sea bass. So instead of shipping out to Korea, Private Fleet became a drill instructor responsible for teaching marines how to swim. Lucky for him. The rest of his platoon got wiped out in the Battle of the Chosin Reservoir in the fall of 1950.

When the Marines were done with him, he joined the local fire department and lived in Pacific Beach. By 1953 he had a wife and a son.

Dale's mother had plenty of positive qualities, but she was tough on her men. The ability to accept their shortcomings was not one of her redeeming traits. By the time Dale was seven, the booze his dad was drinking to numb the criticism no longer did the job. He was finished. So was the marriage.

Now Dale is hearing history repeat itself. His mom and Carlton Pippin get into it when Pippin comes home with his 99-cent six-pack. He drinks Brew 102, the proud, crap lager out of Los Angeles. It never gets physical, but for Dale, the noise is so loud, so disconcerting, it feels like an assault, even when he is upstairs, in the shower, with the water pounding on his back. That's when he realizes he's got to get out of here. He's got to get a track scholarship to some college far away.

There is one big problem. Dale Fleet is nowhere near fast enough to earn a track scholarship. Sophomore year he was no better than the seventh-fastest guy on his high school cross country team. Junior year he was maybe the fourth-best on a team that came in third in the regional championships. His best mile time is 4:26. His best two-mile time is 10:03. Pretty good, but to get a college scholarship Dale is going to need to convince college coaches he can run even faster over a longer distance, since collegiate cross country races are at least four miles. Also, something happens to Dale in the second half of a second mile. His chest tightens. His legs turn to rubber, no longer able to spring across the trails or dirt and clay running tracks. San Diego's other top high school distance runners pass him by. He feels as if he is running backwards.

He's never been all that big on training. The rest of the guys on the team live in Clairemont, several miles west. They run together there sometimes. He's up in University City, a hike away from the group. For Dale, there is no easy solution. One guy on his team, Mark Novak, never runs a step in the off-season. Yet, he's somehow always in front of Dale at the finish. Fletcher Thorton spends summers on his surfboard. Dale has a view of his backside during races, too. Dale knows he is not a natural. He knows he's got to train like he has never trained before to escape. Then, maybe he can get fast enough to get the hell out of San Diego and away from his mom and stepdad's miserable marriage.

There, in the shower he begins to think about numbers. The times for his splits, the distances of each workout, his mile time, his two-mile time. Then he comes upon the big number—800. That's how far he is going to run this summer, because he has decided that if he logs at least 800 miles in the dry, breezy heat of a San Diego summer then he is going to be able to run fast enough during one final glorious high school year to get a track scholarship and get the hell away from home.

That's about 90 miles a week, for nine weeks, anywhere from 5 to 15 miles a day. He will figure out some routes on the hot pavement that surrounds him. It's 8 miles from his house to Clairemont High and back. That's a decent loop. If he wants to go long, he can stretch it out to Mission Bay and loop around the water. There's a dusty, man-made landmass in the middle of Mission Bay named Fiesta Island. The handful of folks that do run in San Diego can often be found there, trudging around its three-mile circular roadway.

This will be a lonely endeavor though. Fiesta Island is roughly two miles but a world away from Pacific Beach, where the rest of Clairemont High School's rising seniors are whiling away the summer. Few will understand what Dale Fleet is doing. Kids have run track for decades, but train in the off-season, and through the summer? Is this really the way a seventeen-year-old is supposed to be spending his time?

It will have to be. To be considered for a scholarship Dale is going to have to get close to nine minutes for two miles, more than a minute faster than he has ever run. At his pace, that means he's going to have to be roughly four football fields faster over those two miles than he is right now. That's a lot of yardage to make up. He's going to have to knock 10 or 15 seconds off his mile time, too. He really has no right to believe he can do this, but he does, if only because he still possesses the occasionally valuable stupidity of youth, and he can remember not so long ago, in middle school, what it felt like to be faster than just about anyone else.

He has run regularly ever since he began winning races in gym class at Taft Middle School. The only break came during his sophomore year when he pulled a D in algebra and his stepdad yanked him off the track team. No racing, no training, until he got his grades up. It was a brutal period. All he wanted to do was run. That's how he feels now, standing there in the shower, the noise from downstairs still rising through the house. He can't wait to run.

Over the next weeks, Dale pushes to his limits on the roads of University City and Clairemont, on Fiesta Island, and around Mission Bay. It's brutal work, but that is the point, and as the summer progresses his feet begin to lighten. He is getting faster. He knows this. He wears a watch, and watches never lie. The blessing of youth also provides seemingly endless powers of recovery. He runs midmorning and in the evening after dinner. Dale Fleet has happened on the discovery that every talented runner needs to arrive at if he wants to race with the strongest competition—to run far fast, he needs to practice running far fast.

He needs to learn how to run fast when his lungs tighten and tell him to stop. Ignoring the pain from exhaustion is impossible. It will always be there, but it needs to not matter. It needs to become a signal that he has reached the edge and it's time to push even faster. Sometimes, when it really hurts, he thinks of the noise that sounds like it's going to bust the walls in his house. That helps. He also knows that when this summer of solitary torture ends, he will not have to run alone. He'll get to run with his buddy Dave Harper. That helps, too.

Dave

Dale Fleet knows no matter how hard he trains there is one runner he may never catch. Dave Harper is the closest thing there is to a prodigy at Clairemont High. Running has always come so easily to him. He was the fastest kid in his neighborhood when he and his buddies timed one another's laps around the block. He was the fastest kid in his elementary school on those 600-yard heats that were part of the Presidential Physical Fitness Test. In junior high, his father, a no-nonsense medic who served in the 1st Marine Division on Guadalcanal, entered him in an open mile race for his age group. Dave ran away from the field and won that race in 4:53. Dave's mother and siblings never came to watch him run. His father was always there, looking on from the bleachers. He never said much when the races were over, even when Dave won, which he almost always did.

Dave's father favors structure, demands punctuality, and is not easily impressed. For his son, the long and lanky and prodigiously fast David Harper, running is not complicated—it's a desperate battle to impress his father. The desperation is never closer to the surface than when Dave is a sophomore in high school. His track coach is Art Anderson. Anderson played college football at Idaho and did stints in the NFL for the Pittsburgh Steelers and Chicago Bears. Anderson becomes Dave's torturer-in-chief.

The practice schedule for the rest of the team goes like this: Monday is endless 400s. Wednesday is endless 200s (200s are the Kansas phenom Jim Ryun's favorites and in 1968 nearly every amateur track coach is making his kids do exactly what Jim Ryun is doing). Tuesday and Thursday are easy road runs. Fridays and Saturdays are for rest or races.

For Dave Harper, Anderson schedules a 6:15 a.m. pickup in his beat-up Volvo. He wants Harper running four miles before school each morning under his supervision. He also keeps a close watch on his afternoon intervals. When the rest of the team is merely trying to complete their twenty-eight 200s, Anderson is clocking Dave's, making sure each of his are under 30 seconds. It works. In a dual meet against Kearny High School Dave's sophomore year, he goes up against a senior named Chuck Ledbetter. Ledbetter carries the reputation as the best distance runner in the region. Dave sits on Ledbetter's tail during a slow first mile, then jumps him on a straightaway in the second. He runs his second mile in 4:30 and holds off big-time competition for the first time. This is when Dave Harper realizes he just might impress his father one day.

As juniors, Fleet and Harper and their teammates finish third in the regional cross country championships. When it ends, they promise one another they will finish first next year. So while Dale Fleet spends the summer counting to 800, hunting for those precious seconds to knock off his times, Dave and the rest of the team, who all live near each other in Clairemont, bang out miles through their own neighborhood. They're a motley crew with long hair and mustaches, not like those straitlaced guys from the military or the San Diego Track Club. When they come together as school begins in the fall of 1970, there isn't a team of high school runners around more ready to accomplish what they want.

They still listen to Anderson and follow his workouts to a T (they have little choice). But they begin freelancing, too. They decide they want to hit 70 miles each week. Before school, they strap on 10-pound weighted vests and head out on the four-mile runs Anderson set up for Dave. They whip off five three-quarter-mile loops around the upper fields of their high school. They map out a 10-mile loop from their high school, down over the bridge that leads to the bay, around the bay and back. They make a pact to run it faster than 56 minutes every time. They run that loop three days a week. Some Saturdays they do it twice. Dale and Dave nearly always take the lead.

They are perfect training partners. Dave, the miler, is lightning on the track intervals. Dale, who is morphing into a true distance specialist, hammers on the roads. On the track Dave leads, with Dale right on his tail. On the roads, it's Dale in front with Dave just off his shoulder. On those 10-mile bay loops, their goal is to go out so hard that they drop the rest of the pack as they hit the Hilton Hotel on the waterfront roughly halfway through.

They win the large-school team championship with little trouble. Dale knows this title doesn't help him much. Dave, whose mile time hovers just above four minutes, has plenty of come-ons from top colleges. John Chaplin from Washington State has hooked him. Dale still needs to get to nine minutes.

He enters an open meet at Balboa Stadium where he thinks he can run fast enough to qualify for the San Diego Indoor Championship, a winter race where Fleet believes he will be in top form. It doesn't make a lot of sense. A big kid like him should struggle on the tight turns of an indoor track. But running in front of a crowd of more than 10,000 fans that will be on top of him at the cozy San Diego Sports Arena should bring him home. That's what he believes, anyway, and belief is what matters.

Before the qualifying race at Balboa Stadium, teammate Mark Novak, the guy who never runs a step unless Anderson tells him he has to, asks Dale how fast he plans to run. Dale tells him 9:10. Novak rolls his eyes. He doesn't say the words, but he might as well. *A boy can dream.*

The next time Dale hears Novak's voice it's coming from the infield as he burns through the first mile in 4:34. Novak and the rest of the team are beside themselves. Dale's lost his mind, and gone out too fast, they're telling each other. As far as they know, Dale is still the guy who lumbers through a two-mile race on a track in 10 minutes. Those are high school tracks though. He's at Balboa Stadium in front of a crowd that numbers in the thousands. He is flying. He's never felt this fast in his life. He crosses in 9:11. That's good enough to qualify for the San Diego Indoors, and it's close enough to let him believe, really believe, that a sub-nine two-mile time can be his, that he will escape his home.

This is where Dave's speed becomes vital. Needing those last seconds, Dale spends one more month hammering intervals and

10-mile bay loops with Dave. Dave knows his job here—to make Dale work as hard as he has ever worked, to stay with him to make his legs turn over faster than they ever have.

When Dale arrives at the starting line at the San Diego Sports Arena for the indoor championship, there are 12,000 people in the building. They are so close and so loud, the noise feels like a blanket. It's the kind of noise that lifts you up instead of weighing you down. It isn't at all like the noise he's been trying to escape at home this past year, though it is one last reminder of what's on the line—a ticket out. The track is 160 yards around. That's 11 laps to a mile. Dale hears the sound of the gun, and then everything goes quiet. Over the next 22 laps, that silence breaks only twice. A runner nearly crashes midway through and there is one of those decibel-crushing roars of fear that nearly breaks Dale's concentration. Then, leading in the final straightaway, he hears the public address announcer scream, "He's going to break nine minutes!" A step after the finish line, Dale turns to glance at the scoreboard—8:58.6. Dale Fleet is free.

Before the week is out, John Chaplin, from Washington State, reaches out to him. Then Chaplin flies down to San Diego and offers Dale an escape hatch. Chaplin isn't the only one. Kansas invites Dale to visit. Every young runner leaps at the chance to visit Jim Ryun's alma mater. Dale wants to stick with Dave, though, and heads to Washington State.

As school ends and summer begins, Dale and Dave and the rest of the Clairemont crew do not relent. With two teammates heading to Washington State they feel real. Chaplin had made it clear to them they are going to be a part of something big and new. Chaplin has connections in East Africa. He's got Kenyans like Henry Rono and John Ngeno on the way. No one in the U.S. has ever heard of them but soon everyone will know who they are. Dale and Dave don't know a lot about African running, but they know enough about champions like Abebe Bikila and Kip Keino, the reigning Olympic 1,500 gold medalist to know that Chaplin isn't messing around. So every day, they gather at one of their buddies' houses to head out on those loops around the bay. When the running is done, they nap in the sun and shoot pool and enjoy the simplicity of being eighteen and fast.

There is one last local race before they head off to college, the Balboa 8, the day when all the runners in the region try to show off the work they've put in all summer. The race has its individual winners but also a team competition, scored like any other cross country race, where the few clubs that exist go against each other. There's a bunch of guys with the San Diego Track Club who want the Clairemont crew to run with them from here on out. Dale and Dave and the rest of them don't want to do that though. They've got two top Division I recruits and enough firepower to give the runners from the SDTC, and the military team and that cocky crew from Jamul A.C. that Bob Larsen coaches, a run for their money one day. They want their own club.

So what the hell should we call ourselves? they wonder. For this crew, running is equal parts competition and rebellion, a way to excel but also the thing they do because just about everyone else believes it's nuts. Their name has to embody that. Once they reach that conclusion, there really is only one possible name. At every meet, their guy Novak, the guy who disdained training miles but somehow always managed to score near the top, would survey the competition. Then he'd pick out a target and declare, "That guy is slow as a toad." There it is, they decide. This group from Clairemont becomes the "Toads."

On race day it doesn't matter what Dale and his buddies call themselves. With a mile to go in the race, he passes this runner with dark, closely cropped hair. The guy has that stride that looks like it's been through a few races before. He's familiar, and for just one moment Dale thinks of something other than the finish line. A year ago Dale couldn't break 10 minutes for two miles. Now he knows he's got this race in the bag. He's on his way to breaking the tape in 41:55 on a brutal, hilly course. The highlight, though, happens roughly four minutes before the finish as he passes that guy with the dark hair and sweet, but slowing stride. "Holy shit," he says to himself as he realizes that guy he just blew by has the 10,000-meter gold medal from the 1964 Olympics in his sock drawer, "I just passed Billy Mills."

The next time he races he will be 1,500 miles from home.

Kirk

No matter his age, or what stage of his life he is in, when Kirk Pfeffer ties his shoes and takes his first steps on a run in the first light of the day, he is an eight-year-old boy once again.

As a little boy Kirk is an early riser, always up by six in the morning, well before anyone else in his childhood home in San Diego's East County. He can hear the birds chirping outside. And that smell, the blossoms. There is always something blooming in San Diego, something new that mixes with the scents of eucalyptus and the salty sea air—sagebrush, juniper, hibiscus. As soon as he is out of bed he wants to be in it, running through the scents. So he laces up his tennis shoes, quietly steps out his door, and he begins to run. Just down and around the block on Ridgeview Drive, enough to become immersed in the dewy morning blossoms. He does not run far. He's only eight, after all.

The running comes so easily to him. He doesn't tire. At John Marshall Elementary School one afternoon he hears students boasting about a boy who ran 20 laps around the schoolyard without stopping. The next day at lunch, he runs 40 laps around that same yard. He is still running when the bell signaling the end of lunch rings. He ignores it and keeps on running as the yard empties. Several minutes later, a teacher comes out to fetch him. It's time for class. Bummer. He would have run all afternoon.

Kirk's father is a parts buyer for an airplane manufacturer. There isn't much extra money for summertime activities. There is a world-famous zoo in San Diego though. The zoo is Kirk Pfeffer's favorite place in the world. He is at peace there, walking anonymously among the panda bears and the flamingos and the tourists from all across the country.

Even better, during the summers kids get in for free. It's not very close to the Pfeffer home. It's about four miles, but Kirk doesn't see this as a problem. He can run there. He takes a quarter from a jar of change. That will get him a bag of peanuts that will sate him for the day. He sets off and a little more than half an hour later he cruises through Balboa Park and into the gates of the zoo. He wanders, stares at the birds and the bears and the monkeys for a few hours. He eats his bag of peanuts. In the afternoon, he sets off for home, running once again.

Just like Bob Larsen when he was a boy in northern Minnesota, Kirk Pfeffer learns that running is a very good way to get from here to there. In middle school, a friend tells him if he shows up at Jack Murphy Stadium during the second half of Chargers football games, the ushers will let him in for free. He tries this one Sunday afternoon, running three miles from his home to the stadium. He watches the fourth quarter, then runs home. He has neglected to tell his family about this plan, and as Sunday evening rolls in the Pfeffers have no idea where their son is. When Kirk finally sprints up Ridgeview Drive, his father is waiting on the porch for him. He's not happy, though he realizes his son is going to do what he is going to do. He's going to run. Let us know where you are going next time, he tells him. And please be careful.

At first Pfeffer runs because he is good at it and it does get him from point A to point B. He knows he can keep going fast when others falter. Then, even as a child, he begins to understand it as an expression of who he is. Just like the rest of those who found their way to Bob Larsen—misfits and Toads alike—before he even realizes, Kirk defines himself by the miles in motion. His quest *becomes* his identity. Other boys are loud and rambunctious, always yelling and pushing each other. Kirk finds comfort in quiet. He rarely feels a need to be social. He plays Pop Warner football for two years. He's not a bad defensive back. But the laps around the field at the end of practice, the thing the other boys dread, is the part of the game he likes most.

Kirk's father actually thinks his son's running fetish is pretty cool, if a bit weird. He doesn't discourage it. To show his support, he takes Kirk down to Crosswalk Sporting Goods, across from Hoover High School, and he buys Kirk a pair of adidas, the white ones with the black stripes. Given the mileage Kirk piles up and his tendency to pronate, he goes through shoes about every three weeks. Before very long, Kirk will have tried out nearly every model of adidas running shoe that exists, even one that is made of kangaroo hide. They are all basically the same boxy thing, without much in the way of arch technology or padding. No matter.

When Kirk is a sophomore at Crawford High School, he tells his dad he wants to give this race called the Mission Bay Marathon a go. His father drives him to the start line near the water. Kirk thinks running a marathon will be a cool adventure. He's never actually been real tired at the end of a run, so who knows how far he can go. The course travels two laps around Mission Bay and ends near the beach. Twenty miles in, like every first-time marathoner, Kirk wonders what he has gotten himself into. The sun is relentless. He can feel the blisters forming on his feet. He trudges on, finishes in 3:01. He doesn't see his father at the finish line, so he wanders around, then decides to collapse on the beach, on the other side of the seawall and boardwalk. His father finds him sleeping there an hour later. Time to go home.

His family's home backs up onto a canyon and a dry riverbed. He runs alongside it as far as it goes, far beyond where the new housing developments of the sprawling city give way to the brown and green hills that lead out to the Capitan Grande Reservation. He finds a steep, 50-yard incline behind his house. When he is bored in the late afternoons, he laces up his track spikes and sprints up the hill over and over. He runs back and forth to school, three miles each way, wearing his backpack.

He joins the track team at Crawford High and finds a kindred spirit in an assistant track coach named Dan Matheny. Matheny and his brother ran for Bob Larsen during Larsen's early years. He likes to take small groups of runners to the hidden parts of the city. One Friday, he tells them to meet in late afternoon in Balboa Park. He tells them to bring a flashlight. When they arrive they learn why. Matheny leads them on a descent into an oversized sewer pipe. He tells them to turn on their flashlights and run. They have to hunch down to avoid banging their heads.

Pfeffer, who is long and lean, with wiry limbs and a birdlike neck, has to hunch more than the others. He doesn't care. They can't run very quickly even though they want to. The lights show the cockroaches and other creatures crawling on the walls of the pipe. The pipe runs for more than a mile under downtown San Diego. Eventually, they arrive at a manhole cover. Matheny pushes it open and the runners emerge into the evening light. They can see diners sitting on the deck at Anthony's Fish Grotto on the waterfront. Kirk thinks this is one of the greatest runs he has ever been on.

When he isn't leading them through sewers, Matheny drags them into the eastern hills and has them run from one water tower to the next. There is no cut trail to follow. Just spot your destination and get there. He sends them up mountains and across golf courses, through the flumes and over the old stagecoach roads near Jamul where Bob Larsen once took him. Matheny has one rule on these runs—no shoes. The Mexican Indians who first ran this landscape didn't wear shoes, so why should Kirk Pfeffer and the boys from Crawford.

In 1973, the summer after his junior year in high school, when Kirk is sixteen, he meets a runner named Richard Bernard at an all-comers meet he paid $3 to get into. Bernard is a few years older and lives near the beach. He tells Pfeffer about a group of hard-core runners in the neighborhood who call themselves the Toads. They run mornings on the weekends and evenings during the week. The two big guns on the Toads are a couple of guys from Washington State named Dave Harper and Dale Fleet.

By this time, Dale and Dave have spent two mostly frustrating years in Pullman, Washington. Things started badly when they showed up with their long hair and Dale sporting a mustache. The athletic department told them to shave and find a barber. They refused, and thanks to a similarly shaggy teammate named Tim "Hawk" Robinson, who took the fight to the school administration, they didn't have to. Dale and Dave kept their hair the way they wanted, but they soon realize there are really two track teams at Washington State, one for Africans and one for Americans.

The Africans get coach John Chaplin's attention. They are the Kenyan and Ethiopian transplants that Chaplin has convinced to come to the U.S. to attend school. He believes they are the future of distance running, though no one is exactly sure how old they are or what academic credentials they may or may not have. The Americans are left largely on their own and told to pound out miles in the spirit of the former Cougar phenom Gerry Lindgren. Lindgren was famous for his 150-mile weeks and for setting a series of American and college records in the mid-1960s at distances that ranged from 3,000 to 10,000 meters.

Do what Gerry did, Dale and Dave are told. It's also bitter cold out there near the Idaho border. There are really only two decent loops—northeast along Airport Road or south down Johnson Avenue. Dale and Dave helped the Cougars to top-three finishes at cross country nationals in 1971 and 1973, but they spend many months in Pullman looking forward to their ventures home to San Diego, a return to those warm loops around Mission Bay with their beloved Toads.

Pfeffer joins the Toads one night, and for the first time he learns what it means to really hammer a training run, to spend three or four miles warming up and then to bear down and raise the pace for the next five or six or eight miles, to use every ounce of strength to stay with or even push the pack, help the group get to the edge. As bad luck would have it, the Pfeffers have just moved thirteen miles northeast that summer to Santee. No matter. Kirk gets a bicycle, rides to the beach to meet the Toads, hammers out a 10-mile run, and rides home.

Dale and Dave and their buddy Mike Breen and the rest of the Toads have never encountered anyone quite like Kirk before. He is a metronome in motion, an absolute machine. The farther he goes, the stronger he gets. One night, after a workout, after Kirk has hopped on his bike to head home, the Toads gather to discuss whether Kirk is a guy who runs with them or whether he is a true Toad. Traditionally, only Clairemont High School guys have been full-fledged Toads. But here's Kirk, as dedicated a runner as any of them. He's also got a spirit that sends them hammering miles for hours around the bay or barefoot on the beach or through the hills as hard as they ever have. He's also riding his bike some 30 miles a day to do it.

With the Balboa 8 mere weeks away, the Toads desperately want to beat those Jamul A.C. guys from the East County—Mendoza and Lux and Cotton and the rest of them. They sure could use Kirk. He's a true original. He's a Toad, they agree. End of discussion.

August 1973, Balboa Park

Dale and Dave have a plan. It's pretty simple. They are going out hard on this Balboa 8. They know those boys from Jamul A.C. are flying high. They've got their state championship. Mendoza is headed to Arizona. Lux has a ride to Oregon. Terry Cotton runs angry. If the Toads are going to take this thing, they have to send a message early. They are going out strong and building the kind of lead that demoralizes the competition, a lead that makes the guys behind you wonder early in the race if they are going to simply lose or if the competition will humiliate them.

Those boys from the Jamul A.C., they are thinking about something else. This is their race. These guys with their fancy scholarships at Washington State aren't going to beat them on their territory. Not today.

Who any of these guys are, their specific backgrounds, won't eventually matter all that much—and certainly not to the local running guru watching from the side that day. What matters is their service to the principle that Bob Larsen has been trying to manifest, the idea that what is truly possible is somewhere in the neighborhood of what most people believe is impossible. That's what gets them out on this starting line this morning and onto the streets or the trails or the track on every other one. They are chasing victory, but also the primal idea of doing what the body was meant to do, doing it beautifully and to its fullest extent, which are really the same thing.

When the pistol sounds, Dale and Dave sprint to the front. It's a tricky course. The roughly 150 runners cover the roads and paths and grass fields and up and down the aptly named Zig-Zag Hill near the eastern edge of the park. All those turns give a leader an opportunity to disappear, to "run-and-hide" in runner speak. That's exactly what Dale and Dave plan to do.

For 30 minutes the plan works. Dale and Dave are so far in front, they begin to wonder if the Jamul boys decided this is hopeless and dropped out. Kirk falls off first, and with two miles to go, Dale drops Dave and edges into the lead. When he feels like his cushion has grown comfortable, he steals a quick glance over his shoulder. That's when he sees them, back there in the distance, those yellow and green singlets of the Jamul A.C. He realizes Mendoza and Lux are in pursuit.

Dale knows what to do here. Stay cool. Hold your form. Don't panic. Only, he does panic. He turns back to Dave and screams as loud as he can, "They're coming!"

With a half mile left, they come over the Cabrillo Bridge—nicknamed "Suicide Bridge" for its popularity as a death jump spot among so many San Diegans. Dave becomes its next victim. He's done himself in with the too-fast start. Mendoza and Lux chew him up and spit him out. Passing the rococo, Spanish Colonial landmark known as the Museum of Man, Dale can feel the finish line edging closer, but he knows he's got nothing left. This plan that he and Dave worked out, it's all gone to shit.

With 300 yards to go Mendoza and Lux do the deed and pass him by. They even do that celebratory gentleman's-tie thing, joining hands and finishing together in 41:12, shattering Billy Mills's course record. Dale and Dave finish third and fourth. Their teammates are seventh and ninth, but it's no consolation. They lost to Lux and Mendoza and they're as bitter as runners can be.

Taking all this in, not far from the finish, is Bob Larsen. At the start of the day he was pretty sure this was the way this race would go. When summer began, and Tom was getting ready to go to Oregon and Ed was preparing to ship out to Arizona, Tom showed Ed a copy of the famous Lydiard book that touts the value of volume. In addition to all the threshold runs Larsen has been putting them through, Ed and Tom are well over more than 100 miles a week. They are in the best shape of their lives and they know it. No one was going to put them away early in this race.

What no one, not even Bob Larsen, realizes is that what has just transpired carries a larger meaning than just another win for the triumphant Tom and Ed and a dispiriting loss for Dale and Dave. Dale and Dave are the same age as Tom and Ed. They are only going to get faster. Then there's Kirk Pfeffer, who now lives in Santee, a stone's throw from Grossmont. Kirk runs with the Toads. If Larsen has anything to say about it, Kirk will be at Grossmont. The way he runs, that easy rhythm, Larsen is dead-certain the farther he goes the better he will be. Larsen has the freakish Terry Cotton for another year, too. Right there, in a ten-mile radius, are six of the best young runners in the country. One more would make seven—a full cross country team that chases the spirit of running in the manner of a dream.

Their times track to about 31 minutes for a 10K race, not all that far behind where the top guys finish at the Cross Country National Championships. These guys have work to do, the kind of work that very few others in the running game in 1973 are familiar with—pushing the pace the way Larsen would want them to. But maybe putting together a local collection of runners to take on the fancy athletic clubs at a national meet isn't all that nutty after all.

September 7, 1996, Central Park, New York

I'm getting married at 6:30 tonight in North Salem, New York, about fifty miles north. Being the groom, there is not all that much for me to do before then. Even if there was, on this day of days, there is no way I am not going to run.

I don't overdo it. Just the usual six-mile loop around Central Park. I live four blocks from the West 72nd Street entrance, the one across from the Dakota and next to Strawberry Fields. It's always clogged with tourists trying to breathe the air where John Lennon took his last peaceful breaths. I don't mind them at all. If I didn't live here, I'd visit this spot, too.

It's a little after nine in the morning when I turn south onto the Park Drive. Wouldn't you know I am a little nervous and can't sleep. The park is already hopping. The running lanes are filled with packs of training groups setting out on medium-long runs in preparation for the New York Marathon two months away. I'm running that one, too. It will be my first New York Marathon, and my fourth overall. In other words, I know enough to have gotten my long run out of the way earlier in the week, before the day I have to walk down an aisle and say "I do."

I curl around the south end of the park, cruise past the Boathouse, fight my way up the hill behind the Metropolitan Museum of Art. Is it me or does it feel a little harder than usual today? I'm looking all around as I run, trying to take in the color of the sky (yellow-gray), the quality of the air (kind of heavy and sweaty), and all the people who pass me along the way (the most beautiful in the world, always). I keep telling myself when I next run this route I will be a married man.

I keep an eye out for Madonna. She runs in the opposite direction, wearing sunglasses and a hat and next to her bodyguard, though usually a little later in the morning. It's also probably too early for a John Kennedy Jr. sighting. The unofficial prince of the city is usually zipping around here on his roller blades on the weekends. Even with the sunglasses, you know that hair and that jawline anywhere. There's no bodyguard around him. No one ever bothers. He's just another New Yorker out enjoying the park.

The Park Drive descends after it passes the reservoir on the East Side, winding into the edge of Harlem before turning sharply uphill for a quarter of a mile, just long enough to make the hill feel like real work, like preparation for something, like the ascents of the five bridges connecting the boroughs in the NYC 26.2. The Columbia cross country team is out here in the afternoons, running this hill over and over. It never looks fun. Then the road rolls up and down to the south edge of the reservoir, and from there it's a straight three-quarter-mile shot down and flat back to where I started. I'm drippy and winded, but far looser and less nervous than when I started.

There's a wooden fence around the edge of the Park Drive at 72nd Street. I use it to stretch sometimes after I am done running. Nothing too intense. I lean over and push against it to stretch my hamstrings. I use it for balance when I pick my foot up and put my heel in my pocket to stretch my quads. I do some of that, and then, just because I am not in a rush and I want to take another minute to take in sights and sounds and smells on my last morning as a single guy, I take a seat. I'm there for a minute or two when I realize there's a growing group of men about my age (twenty-seven) and a little older gathering around me. They seem to know one another. They are gathering here, I assume, for a pre-marathon training run.

I do a few more stretches, take in a few more sights. I trade smiles with a guy who does a little of the same next to me. When I sit back down, he sits and he asks me how I'm feeling and says something about it being a nice morning. I tell him I'm doing just fine, and yes it is a pretty good morning for running. We trade a few more friendly words about nothing important—miles this week, whether we are both running New York. There are some self-deprecating jokes about our respective shortcomings as runners, some chatter about where we live and what we do.

He asks me how long I've lived in New York. I tell him four years in the city, but I grew up not far away, and I'm thinking this is one of the friendliest guys I've met in a while. I generally find New Yorkers friendly and helpful and endlessly generous, but I don't end up talking to a lot of folks while stretching and running in the park. Just doesn't happen. Then he asks if this is my first time running with the group, and what I'm doing after the run, and that's when, finally, I realize what's going on here. I see a few of the members of his group wearing the blue "Front Runners" singlet, and I realize what this is. "Front Runners" is a running club mostly for the LGBT community.

His life is going one way. My life is going the other.

Well, I say, I actually just finished my loop. I'm not with the group. I'm just stretching here. And since you asked, I'm actually getting married later.

This being 1996, saying you're getting married is a pretty clear declaration of what side of the fence you play on.

Ohhhh, he says, and we are both smiling at each other. Well, good luck with that he tells me. I hope it goes well.

I tell him I hope it does, too.

It's the first time in my life a stranger has tried to pick me up. I don't care a whit that the come-on came from a man. It counts. I will pass that bench on thousands of runs, through decades of marriage and the births of multiple children. I will think of that sweet man who runs like I do nearly every time.

The Jamul Toads

"Talk to your guys. Ask them what they think."

This is the message Bob Larsen gives to scrawny nineteen-year-old Mike Breen, on an early-summer morning in 1974.

Mike Breen is what happens when a coach like Bob Larsen, from a school in a tiny district, wins a state championship and dominates the bigger schools. Word gets around fast that there's a coach who has a magic touch, a kind of running whisperer who surfaces where no one expects him to surface, mysteriously and with little warning. In running circles, no matter how small and concentric they still are, Bob Larsen is becoming a thing. And Mike Breen is the connective thread that is about to create a dream for Bob Larsen.

Mike has stringy, light brown hair, two Bugs Bunny–like front teeth, and a cheesy mustache in the spirit of everyone's hero—Steve Prefontaine, one of America's current running rock stars. In June 1972, Frank Shorter is still a largely unknown Yale graduate and law student three months shy of an Olympic marathon gold. Prefontaine is already "Pre"—the future, even the present, of American running. He made the cover of *Sports Illustrated* in 1970 at nineteen. He looks like a fifth Beatle from the Sgt. Pepper era. Most importantly, he races from the front with a terrifying aggression, and he never loses a college race between three miles and 10,000 meters. Not one.

Clairemont High School, where Breen attended, running a couple years behind Dale Fleet and Dave Harper, is in the western part of San Diego County, by the beach. Grossmont is in the east, inland, toward the desert. Clairemont is not in the Grossmont district. Remember, community colleges have zones, like public high schools do. Mike Breen is not supposed to go to college there. He's supposed to go to San Diego City College. But there is no running whisperer at San Diego City College. So Mike Breen does what the best runners in the region will eventually do—he gets an address in the Grossmont district and registers for school there. Luckily, he's at the apartment the afternoon an inspector from the school district shows up.

"Yes, this is where I live," he tells the inspector, half truthfully. When school starts he runs for Bob Larsen.

In his first year he does everything Larsen can ask of a runner who doesn't have the innate gifts of a Terry Cotton or an Ed Mendoza. Mike is a brawler. A 4:20 miler and 9:19 two-miler in high school, he was champion of the region's Western League and a member of a youth team that toured Europe. He makes all-conference his first year at Grossmont. He helps the Griffins sweep the Long Beach Invitational, the Southern California finals and capture a second straight state championship. They will win seven more championships before Larsen moves to his next job. Since summer began though, he's been splitting time. He trains with Larsen and his college boys from the Jamul A.C. on certain days, and with his old posse of Toads in the west county on others. Dale and Dave are back from Washington State. Kirk Pfeffer, who is set to start Grossmont in the fall, has been coming around. They hammer out loops around the bay and up along the coastal hills like they always do when they are together. They swear this summer the Toads will reign supreme at the Balboa 8.

Sometimes Mike and Bob Larsen get to talking about these two different sets of runners, the Jamul A.C. guys in the East County and the Clairemont guys in the West. As they philosophize about running and speed and life, the conversation casually wanders to its logical conclusion—that there isn't any good reason why this much talent, so close in age and geography and spirit, battles against itself. Why are they not running as one club, united. The things that they could do together.

This is the message Bob asks Mike to deliver to Dale and Dave and Kirk and everyone else who has caught this running bug in the fiercest way. These are the guys who can cite every race and PR Prefontaine has run up in Oregon. They are junkies, and running is their heroin.

Let's get together, let's talk about this, Bob suggests to Mike. Larsen knows how good they all want to be. Mike knows that Dale and Dave are essentially training on their own, and Larsen can help get them where they want to go.

Mike Breen does as he is told. He doesn't know how this is going to go over with the Toads. All he knows is Bob Larsen is as good a coach as there is. Any runner worth his spikes ought to run over mountains for the chance to work with him. And yet the Toads have this thing, this special, organic, independent thing. They're just a bunch of young guys from the beach (or close to it) who like to hammer together. No one tells them what to do or where or when to run.

This is one of those inherent tensions every dedicated runner confronts at some point. When runners find their tribe—when they find a brotherhood made real through shared sweat, miles, and sacrifice—they organically create a shared language and shared sense of ritual. To add outsiders into that in-group, or to yield control of the working dynamic to a coach, this is not a small ask. And yet every high-performing runner knows his pilgrimage requires finding a guide, and then maybe another one, too, and figuring out how to bring more brothers and sisters into the fold. New legs. New life. Whoever those people are they must understand that the quest is not merely about an athletic goal. It is a vision quest.

Maybe just listen to what Larsen has to say, Mike tells his guys when they gather next. Fine, we'll listen, they say, but no promises.

The summit happens on Sunday morning, July 28. On the grass just south of the Hilton Hotel on Mission Bay. Larsen's crew is there, including Mendoza and Lux. They are home for the summer and training with Bob and the rest of the Jamul A.C. The Toads bring everyone who has ever touched their club, even some shot putters and discus throwers and high jumpers they competed with in high school who want to be a part of a certified club to compete at certain meets. They believe there is power in numbers. They want to show they are real. There are about thirty of them in all.

Larsen asks them, Do you all understand how good we can be, the things we can accomplish together? But then Bill Gookin, the old-timer from the San Diego Track Club, chimes in. Gookin complains about this group and its amphibious name. "Toads" suggests a lack of seriousness and direction, he says. None of this sounds good to Dale Fleet, who really wants Larsen to help guide him and Dave, but is growing more annoyed by the minute. That's the point of the name, he says. He doesn't have the energy to explain the concept of irony to Gookin, how showing up at a race with a cartoon of a toad on your singlet, then running the daylights out of the competition is like sticking up your middle finger to the establishment in the greatest way. The name will not disappear, Fleet says.

Larsen says he really doesn't care what the club is called. All he has ever wanted was the chance to guide the most talented collection of young runners the region has ever produced, and if the Toads are looking for help, he's willing to give it. He doesn't bother explaining the science of the threshold run, or that he knows how to get runners from the start to the finish faster than they have ever done so before, or that he knows how to win. He doesn't have to. They know this. They have lived it. Let's come together and surprise the hell out of some people, show them what it means to run the way we run out here, pushing the pace to the edge, he says.

Since Dale and Dave are the Toads' best runners, what they want is going to carry the day. They don't really have a coach of their own. They largely supervise themselves, and know that Larsen offering his services is a godsend to them. Dave has had it with Washington State. He's done with school, done with the cold, done with Coach John Chaplin and his African imports. He's dropping out and moving home to start working maintenance for the San Diego School District, but he wants to keep running. Bob Larsen is his lifeline. Dale isn't sure whether he's going back to Pullman. He might take a semester off after the cross country season. He's about done with Chaplin, too.

Look, we'll do this, Dale and Dave say. But they want one thing to be very clear—this is a merger and not a takeover. The Toad name has to remain.

Yes, the name should stay, they all agree. The Jamul Toads are born. Who knows if anything will come of it.

—

The crew that gathers on Saturday and Sunday mornings in Larsen's front yard is larger now. Larsen's wife, Sue, has to increase her lemonade production. She's glad to do it.

The pack heads out nice and easy. Larsen still leads the first few miles. He is thirty-four years old and he's never stopped running the warm-up miles with his crew. He can keep up a pretty decent clip, but everyone has to stay behind him. Rules are rules. Then, three or four or five miles in, depending on the day, he releases the reins. The boys are off, beating the path through the next six or eight or 10 miles, taking turns at the front. They fight not to get dropped, make cars stop, pedestrians part, and beachgoers gawk when they are tearing across the sand.

They go as Larsen has told them how to go, hard and then harder. They know that the longer they stay together, the more likely it is that they will stay out there on the threshold where the magic happens. It's the same message when they show up at the Grossmont track for workouts during the week. Get loose, and then go, and keep going, and bring your fellow Toads with you to the edge.

They plan their debut for the Balboa 8 on August 17. They want to get it right, especially the singlet. That takes some fast work by Kirk Pfeffer, who it turns out is a pretty good artist in addition to being a unicorn of a distance runner. Larsen has to make two trips to Los Angeles to get the right paint for the silk-screening, but once he has it and Kirk has the design finalized, the singlet that emerges from the Pfeffer garage nails it. The snarkiest of toads is in mid-stride, wearing the yellow singlet of the Jamul Toads. He's got two dimples. He is barefoot.

When the Balboa 8 rolls around, the toad is the perfect mascot for chasing down Danny Morris of the Marine Corps team in the final miles of the race. Dale and Dave spot Morris a 20-yard lead at the halfway mark. They pass the midpoint of the eight-mile race in 20:45, seven seconds behind Morris. As they come up the steep incline known as Powderpuff Hill near the six-mile mark though, Dale is on Morris's shoulder. In a flash he is by him. Dale wins by a commanding 16 seconds with a time of 40:36.5. His time breaks Billy Mills's course record, and he bettered Larsen's own winning time from 1958 by almost three and a half minutes. Fleet is the first runner ever to go under 41 minutes on the course. Dave

Harper is third. Toads account for nine of the first 12 spots. It's not a bad start.

It's good enough to convince Dale the timing is right to take off a semester. He'll get back to Washington State at some point to finish his degree, but right now he's going to work at a golf club and run with Dave—five miles in the morning, 10 miles in the evenings after they knock off.

The Toads are back at it in late September at the Aztec Invitational, an open meet that draws teams and runners from across the Southwest. Ed is there, but he's with his mates from Arizona and has to run for them. Larsen brings Dale and Dave, plus Terry Cotton and a few others from his Grossmont team. Ed sets the pace from the start of the six-mile race. He's got runners on his tail through the first four miles, when the race disappears onto a bridle trail near the freeway.

By the time Ed is off the trail with a mile to go, he's 200 yards ahead and cruising to a 37-second win in a course-record time of 29:19. Ed is barely breathing hard at the end. Dave runs well enough to take eighth place, and Terry takes 16th, even though it's the first race he's run in months. Nagging leg injuries sidelined him for much of the summer. Arizona wins the meet with 83 points. Larsen's Toads finish with 111. It doesn't take a genius to do the math. Put Ed Mendoza in a Toad singlet and allow the Toads to use his score, and the guys with the funny amphibious name would have finished on top.

Larsen leaves the race greedy. He has been in charge of the Jamul Toads for a month. By coincidence, the AAU has scheduled the national championships for late November near San Francisco. Driving distance. Maybe there is some magic in that singlet with the snarky toad.

After a few more decent showings, Larsen tells the Toads they are going to the big dance. He's got Kirk Pfeffer in his stable now and the kid is as mad for running as anyone he's ever coached. Pfeffer is desperate to go over 120 miles a week—hard. "That's what Shorter does," Kirk tells Coach Bob. Larsen tries to explain that Shorter is a twenty-seven-year-old man with big-boy muscles. Pfeffer is an eighteen-year-old kid still developing the strength to protect his joints from injury. He tells Kirk he can run eight miles in the morning and eight in the afternoon. That includes his warm-ups and cool-downs. Sometimes Kirk even listens. Kirk's big problem is college races end after 4 miles and 20 minutes, when Kirk still has so much left in the tank. To Larsen's thinking, maybe the national championship distance of 6.2 miles will allow Kirk to capitalize on the endurance that makes him exceptional. (By January he will hold the junior world record in the marathon, after he runs 2:17:44 at Mission Bay as an eighteen-year-old, some 45 minutes faster than his first shot at the distance.)

Larsen doesn't care that the field is going to include some of the world's great collegiate and post-college distance runners. Frank Shorter will be there. So will Kenya's John Ngeno, the Washington State runner, whose epic battles with Oregon's Pre were can't-miss events in the Northwest.* Ireland's Neil Cusack, that year's Boston Marathon champion, England's Nick Rose, the soon-to-be NCAA champion, and Colombia's Domingo Tibaduiza, a 1972 Olympian, are also showing up. Rose caused a stir at the NCAA championships in 1973, leading for the first four miles, sending a message to Prefontaine that he had no intention of handing him the race. Pre would have to work if he wanted to win this one. Of course Pre took the lead with a mile and a half to go and cruised to a six-second win. An injury will keep Prefontaine away from the nationals, but everyone else will be there. Larsen believes his Toads are ready.

The first signal that things might not go as planned comes in mid-November. Tom Lux calls Larsen to tell him that he's going to be running for the Oregon Track Club rather than the Toads. Oregon? Really? Why? Bob asks. Nothing against Oregon coach Bill Bowerman and the rest of the Ducks, current and former, who mostly account for the OTC, but what about the Toads, Larsen

* The rumor was Ngeno and the rest of the African runners Chaplin recruited to WSU were actually significantly older than American college students, giving them a clear advantage since the leg musculature required for elite distance running generally takes roughly a decade to develop.

asks? Tom says he's pretty sure the Toads don't have any money to cover his travel expenses and Oregon does. Larsen tells him he's right. Phil Knight, the former Oregon runner and Nike founder, is based 110 miles up I-5 from Eugene, where Knight had a solid career running for Bowerman in the late 1950s. That might help explain the OTC's largesse.

Undaunted, Larsen plows ahead. On the morning of November 29, Larsen and eight Toads pile into his Volkswagen bus and Larry Stone's 1965 Plymouth Valiant, a four-door, steel boat nicknamed "Betsy." Betsy has a hood that stretches farther than the entire length of some sports cars. Ed Mendoza, flying in from Arizona, is spared the journey. So are Dale and Dave and two other teammates, George Pullen and Tom Smith. They have other commitments and will fly up later in the day.

The second signal of trouble ahead comes on the roads. Betsy isn't quite the force she once was. Her lights and power are on the edge of failure throughout the trip north. Larsen's VW stays close in case of a breakdown. There are stops to try to figure out why Betsy isn't cruising like she usually does. Then the mystery, and the caravan, rolls on unsolved. There is a race to be run. Trouble is, an arrival after dark messes with Larsen's pre-race plan. He had wanted to go over the winding, up-and-down course through the green foothills above the Crystal Springs Reservoir. Those hills provide the scenic landscape for drivers cruising up the Junipero Serra Freeway to San Francisco. They will wreak plenty of havoc with the country's best distance runners, who will race on four-foot-wide trails and try not to end up tripping and losing their teeth to tree roots.

The fourteen Toads, including Coach Bob, pile into two nearby motel rooms. Ed Mendoza, fresh off his ninth-place, All-America finish at the NCAAs, rolls in late. Ngeno and Rose, who just went 1-2 at NCAAs, are no joke he reports.

"A" guys get the beds. "B" guys hit the floor with their sleeping bags. There are attempts at sleep, but seven to a room does not exactly lend itself to peaceful, pre-race slumber. There are no discussions about strategy, or the usual "what-if" talks of Plans A and B and C. The journey here has sapped the group, including Larsen. The best plan seems to be to run hard, stay cool, and try to be there at the end.

When the Toads arrive at the start, all they see is the open field that leads up over the first, gopher-hole-covered hill of the race. They think they know the drill with a course like this. Get out fast over that quarter-mile incline, but not too fast. No one wins a distance race in the first mile, but plenty have lost them there by heading out too quickly, especially against a field unlike any they have ever faced. They don't notice the 200-yard descent that follows, leading into a tight path into the woods. They aren't the only ones. When the gun sounds, Ngeno and Cusack sprint to the front. Too many others do not.

Less than two minutes into the race, the middle of the pack reaches a standstill for several seconds as the course funnels onto the trail, like three car lanes merging into one on the freeway. Even Shorter gets stuck about 100 runners back. It's a mess of congestion all the way to the end. Ed fights his way up to seventh place by the time he crosses the finish line. He's four spots ahead of Shorter, which feels good. No other Toad finishes higher than 58th though. Two of Larsen's college boys, Breen and Gary Close, finish ahead of Dave Harper. Kirk Pfeffer, a Grossmont freshman, finishes six spots ahead of Dale Fleet. Maybe sleeping on the floor wasn't so bad after all.

Wandering around the finish area, the Toads are humbled. They know they were ill-prepared and in over their heads, many of them still boys, or very close to it, racing against men. They have done the work. They believe, and Larsen knows, they are as fit as anyone. There is a difference between running and racing, though. Anyone can run, and many, with the right training, can run fast. But racing, competing at this level, is something else.

Arriving the night before, heading into a race without knowing how to beat the field to the key spot, that is not competing. "Plan the race, and race the plan" is the mantra of every experienced runner. Even if every so often the competition forces you to abandon your plan, to cover an opponent's move, there has to be a plan.

As the final scores go up, Larsen sees the numbers that tell a story he already knows. The Toads finish eighth, with 215 points. Ahead of the Toads are all those fancy clubs he wanted to knock off. Colorado, New York, Philadelphia, Florida, Oregon. Maybe this was a dim idea, he thinks. Those clubs pull guys from all over the country. He's pulling kids from an eight-mile radius in California's third city. At the end of the day, they were largely inexperienced kids racing against men. All the threshold runs in the world might not be able to overcome that. But Larsen is not giving up. He and the Toads might need nothing more than time and more racing. He will be able to think this all through more clearly when he gets home later and gets some rest. That will happen soon enough.

Then, just when it doesn't seem like things can get much worse, Betsy breaks down on the way home, turning what should be a nine-hour adventure into a thirty-two-hour journey from hell.

When Bob Larsen finally climbs into bed, it's just before 2 a.m. Monday. He is reminded that in elite sports, sometimes, but only rarely, everything comes together in a moment of pure symmetry. The results are a kind of magic and alchemy. Even in something seemingly as basic as running fast, there is science, but there is also art, and there is fortune. Strokes of luck and cosmic timing are often required for the perfect moment. Winging it and hope are not substitutes for planning for success. Now he knows. This wasn't the right moment for the Toads. He will search for one.

Hamptons Marathon, the Last 13.1,
September 2015

Finally, I have company.

I passed someone in the 14th mile, after I hit my split at the halfway mark and made the turn past Lazy Point to begin the trek home. I've come back along Cranberry Hole Road, where I pass people running an hour slower than me. They still have miles to cover that I have already tread. We trade nods as we pass. We're in the same race, but not really competitors any more than I am against whoever is at the front. For most of us, and especially for me, there is only one rival—the relentless digits of a ticking clock.

It's been nothing but the silent swooshing of my own feet across the pavement for a while now, but then there are steady steps coming behind me. I peek over my shoulder. I do the quick marathoner's size-up—much younger than me, taller than me, longer legs than mine. He's also been smart enough to pin his number to his shorts and go shirtless on what's becoming a warmish day. He's ripped, too. Use him, I tell myself. When he gets up to my shoulder I ease into his pace. Not more than 100 yards pass before we are chatting. Where are you from? What brings you here? How many of these have you done? What time are you aiming for?

He's twenty-two, a resident of Troy, New York, and a recent graduate of Rensselaer Polytechnic Institute. He's running his first marathon. He feels strong, a whole lot stronger than I felt when I ran my first marathon at twenty-three and slogged home in 4:10.

We stay in lockstep as we approach the 16-mile mark, both of us glad for the company on a lonely quiet course. I pass the marker in 1:59, a minute ahead of the two-hour mark I wanted to hit at this distance. I tell him I am aiming for under 3:25. I explain that at my age that will get me to Boston. He asks me how old I am. I tell him forty-six.

Forty-six and still running like you are, that's incredible, he says.

If he means this as a compliment, it doesn't sound like one.

Shit, he says, *you're going way under 3:25. You're going to be under 3:20.*

I don't tell him I'm not. I don't tell him the ugliest part of the race lies ahead in the final miles, for me at least, and probably for him. It's impossible to really know this until you have survived those last miles at least once.

What do I have to run to qualify for Boston? he asks me.

Not sure, I tell him, but fast. (Faster than you are going now, I want to say, but I don't. Let's just get him across the finish line.)

All right, he says, and then, in seconds, he's 2 and 4 and 8 and 15 steps ahead. Then he's 50 and 75 and 100 yards beyond me, until the course begins to wind onto a dirt road through the woods. But I'm pretty sure I'm going to see him again.

At the 20-mile mark I glance at my watch. It says 2:29. I wanted to be there at 2:30. This is working. If I can't run the last 10K in 55 minutes, six sub-nine-minute miles, with enough seconds left over for the final 385 yards, I don't deserve to be in Boston. My legs are fine, though getting slightly heavier. I have this, I think. I just need to keep my shit together and get the math right. That can be easier said than done after 20-plus miles of running. I learned that the hard way six months ago, at a small marathon in Connecticut. That day I had 26 minutes to run the last 3.2 miles. I decided I could take it easy on the first of those, then stay steady on the way in for the final two. Just run three 8:30s and you'll be fine, I said. I hit the 26-mile mark at 3:24.30. Usain Bolt can't run one fifth of a mile in 30 seconds. Neither can I. I missed Boston that day by 28 ticks.

And so I trudge on, counting off 21, 22, 23, and 24 essentially alone. There's one last venture into a seaside windstorm at Louise Point, but I laugh it off and head toward the elementary school where this all started. As I look up ahead of me in that final straight, my shirtless buddy comes into sight, laboring, his feet barely lifting off the ground during these last few hundred strides. I'm not going to catch him, but trying to get close keeps me on the clock. With 100 yards to go my watch hits 3:22. It won't get to 3:23.

When I cross the finish, I bring my hands to my face and look at the sky. A lovely older woman hands me a medal and says congratulations as my legs stiffen and I begin to limp around. There's no one cheering, nor should there be. I didn't make my family trek all the way out here to indulge me in this silly quest. This triumph is mine and mine alone. *You're okay?* the woman asks.

I'm going to Boston, I tell her. I'm sure she has no idea what I mean. A quarter century after I decided that yes, not only am I going to run a marathon but I am going to find a way to qualify for the biggest one of all, I am officially elite (lowercase "e," of course).

Now I want only one thing—faster.

1976

Ed Mendoza can't breathe.

He is in a dormitory at the University of Oregon, sharing hall-ways with the fastest men and women in the country. It is June of an Olympic year, which means one thing to an elite American runner: the Olympic Trials at Hayward Field in Eugene, "Track Town, USA," as it is known. The U.S. trials are the most difficult track meet on the planet. The U.S. is so big, and there are so many fast people. Yet, for each event, there are a maximum of three spots on the Olympic team, even though in several races, especially the sprints, the fourth or fifth best American in the event would likely contend for an Olympic medal on any given day.

Complicating matters further, the U.S. trials are a do-or-die event. You can be a world record holder and a defending Olympic champion. Fail to finish in the top three at the U.S. trials, and you stay home to watch the Olympics on television with everyone else. This is what Ed Mendoza is thinking about as he lies in bed in his dorm room the night before the trials for the 10,000 meters, wheezing from an asthma attack, gasping for oxygen. If he can't breathe, he can't run. If he can't run, he will not be going to the Olympics in Montreal next month.

Ed being Ed, he somehow missed the memo that Oregon's Willamette Valley is home to some of the most hazardous pollen counts in the country. This is not unusual for Ed, who seems to float through life in a way that is unique among elite runners. As a group, they are decidedly Type A personalities, obsessed with achievement, anal about routines, and splits and preparations. Ed showed up to the 25-kilometer national championship race in San Diego in December of 1974 thinking it was a half marathon, rather than 15.5 miles. He ran a 4:48 opening mile and averaged 4:59s the rest of the way. At the 13-mile mark, with no finish in sight, he realized he still had another two and a half miles to go. No matter, he finished in 1:17.30, setting a new American record in the process. After, Larsen told him if he kept up that pace he would run a 2:11 marathon.

"I want to go fast, not far," Ed said that day.

"Ed," Larsen told him, "you're going to be a great marathoner whether you like it or not."

A month later, Ed is leading the Mission Bay Marathon after 24 miles. It's his first marathon. He ran the first 20 miles on pace to finish at 2:12. Over the last six though he develops blisters on his feet the size of egg yolks. Near what he hopes is the end, he sees Coach Bob at the side of the road. "How much farther?" he asks his coach. Another mile and a half, Coach Bob tells him, pick it up a little. Ed does as he is told and crosses the line in 2:16. Is that good? he asks Coach Bob. He has no idea that in 1972, Kenny Moore and Frank Shorter won the U.S. marathon trials in 2:15:57. Jack Bacheler was third in 2:20:29.

"It's pretty good, Ed," Larsen tells him. "You run that time in an Olympic year you qualify."

One month after that, Ed comes back from Arizona to San Diego and cruises to a win in the 2-mile race at the San Diego Indoor Games. He runs an 8:33 and is so excited to see his fellow Toads that he can't resist accepting an invitation to hammer 10 miles with them the next morning. This is a terrible idea the morning after an intense, 2-mile race. They head out doing their usual 5:30s. Six miles in, Ed feels like a knife is slicing through his Achilles tendon. The Achilles tendinitis that develops that morning will cost him the spring track season.

So it is not all that surprising that Ed had done little research on the pollen situation in the Willamette Valley. All that rain combined with all that damp cool air and the varied vegetation can make life a wheezing mess for allergy sufferers like Ed. Cedar and pine pollinate in December, then in January, hazelnut, juniper, and cypress take their turn. February, it's alder, birch, and elm. Then spring rolls around, bringing out pollen from oak, sweetgum, sycamore, cottonwood, maple, ash, hickory-pecan, beech, locust, and walnut. Now it's June, which means the peak of grass season, an especially dangerous witches' brew because the valley has more than a half-million acres used for the commercial production of grass seed. A pollen count of 200 parts per cubic meter is considered high. In June in Eugene, pollen counts can run as high as 750.

Ed has been in Eugene a little more than twenty-four hours. He went for a six-mile run through the woods the day he arrived. He took it easy for most of his second one. As night falls his bronchial tubes begin to seize up. Now it feels like he's breathing through a tiny straw. He drags himself out of bed to find a phone. He needs a ride to the emergency room.

At the hospital he gets shots of adrenaline and cortisone, an inhaler and the necessary paperwork to show that he's not taking the drugs to gain a competitive advantage. A doctor gives him a paper surgical mask and tells him to wear it until the start of the race. Ed asks him if this is really going to work. The doctor shrugs. Try not to think about it, the doctor tells him. Nerves and obsession can exacerbate asthma symptoms. Fortunately, Ed is very good at not thinking.

The problem is, as Ed gets to Hayward Field the next day, he realizes this version of the U.S. trials in the 10,000 meters demands more thought than perhaps any race of its kind that has taken place. The ghost of Prefontaine hangs over the competition. This was supposed to be Pre's race, or one of them anyway, since he is the American record holder in both the 5,000 and the 10,000 (and the 2,000, and the 3,000, and at 2 miles and 3 miles and 6 miles). This is his home track, the oval where his legend formed the spiritual template for every American distance runner.

The year before, Prefontaine organized a professional meet here at Hayward Field for the country's top runners. The meet was not sanctioned by the Amateur Athletic Union, which oversees track in the U.S. Anyone who participated risked his eligibility for the Olympic Games, which were still supposedly an amateur-only affair. The top runners are taking money under the table and have been for years, much of it from officials at the AAU and their counterparts overseas, who own and organize and profit from the track meets. Challenging the supremacy of the AAU, tearing down this exploitative and hypocritical system, was the whole point of this meet. It was Pre's mission. That spirit of rebellion that drove him to run like a warrior now had him declaring war on the kingdom. He knew that being the best was basically a full-time job. Prefontaine couldn't understand why after college, athletes in Olympic sports are essentially put out to pasture. No sports medicine, no camps, nothing. He didn't want to be subsidized. He just wanted to earn his keep. "To hell with love of country," he declared. "I compete for myself. People say I should be running for a gold medal for the old red, white and blue and all that bull, but it's not going to be that way. I'm the one who has made all the sacrifices. Those are my American records, not the country's."

In that meet a year earlier, the Finnish star Lasse Virén was supposed to come for a 3.1-mile race against Pre, the competition's featured event. But Virén pulled out with an injury, so Pre flew in his friend Frank Shorter to substitute. With Shorter pushing him, Pre came within 1.5 seconds of breaking his American record.

The night after the race, they attended a mellow party in the hills above Eugene for the athletes. When it got late, Shorter climbed into Pre's MG convertible for a ride to Kenny Moore's house, where he was spending the night. When they arrived, they spent a few extra minutes in the car, plotting the coming battle with the AAU. They were underdogs, and they knew that an underdog's only viable strategy was to attack. They said good night and Pre drove off. Minutes later, he lost control of the MG and flipped it into the side of the mountain on Skyline Drive. He died instantly. The spot, which became hallowed ground in running circles, would forever be known as "Pre's Rock."

Now, a year later, Shorter is here again to run this U.S. trial 10,000, partly in honor of Pre. The reigning Olympic champion in the marathon won the U.S. trials at that distance the month before. Ed dropped out of that race after 21 miles, when he realized the leaders were too far ahead of him. It was his first marathon against world-class competition, and his lack of experience—and having a day that wasn't quite right—doomed him. In dropping out before the end Ed was trying to save his energy for the 10,000.

Bill Rodgers—"Boston Billy" is how everyone knows him—is here, too. He has the face of a regal bird and runs like a deer. He came in second in the marathon trials to Shorter. A bronze medalist at the international cross country championships the previous year, he's a proven beast at this distance. He juggles a running career while teaching special education at a suburban Boston middle school. Then there is Craig Virgin of Illinois, last year's NCAA cross country champion, a nine-time All-American. And everyone knows Garry Bjorklund, the former Minnesota star who likely would have qualified in 1972 if not for an injured foot. He has come with something to prove.

On the start line, no longer wheezing, Ed reminds himself of what Larsen has always told him. Push the pace. Trust your training. Know you are the guy who wears out the field and wins races long before the home stretch. It's a good plan, the only plan, only it doesn't quite work when those four beasts run 4:30s for the first four miles. Ed stays with them into the fifth mile, but then he fades, not far but far enough. He watches with awe as Bjorklund loses a shoe in the 14th lap, then, with one unshod foot, somehow musters the strength to make up a 30-meter gap between him and Rodgers and finishes third behind Shorter and Virgin. Ed plows home in fifth at 28:25, 20 seconds behind Rodgers.

He's still heaving on the infield, feeling dizzy and sad, when Rodgers approaches. Keep yourself in shape Ed, Rodgers says, you're going to Montreal. Ed has no idea what Boston Billy is talking about, but Rodgers keeps at it. Shorter is going to pull out of the 10,000 and focus on defending the marathon gold. Rodgers, the fourth-place finisher, says he's going to turn down the alternate spot and concentrate on the marathon, too. That's his best distance and best shot at a medal. That moves Ed to third. Stay in shape, Rodgers says. Stay in shape.

Ed takes it all in and returns to Arizona despondent. Focused on that fifth-place finish, he can't believe anyone would ever drop out of an Olympic race. Each morning he thinks about taking a run, and then doesn't. He's not sure when he will run again, or at what distance, or if there is a point to it. He spent all spring tailing his Arizona teammate Terry Cotton on those runs at the edge through the Arizona desert and still came up short. Allergies, pollen, the emotions of Pre, and Hayward Field. The planets just weren't aligned for him. Maybe they never will be.

And then, ten days after the Olympic Trials, the phone rings in his Tucson apartment. On the other end is Sam Bell, distance coach for the U.S. track team. Shorter is out. Rodgers doesn't want the alternate spot. Ed is next on the list, just as Boston Billy told him he would be. The spot is his if he wants it. Bell has a question though. Have you been training, because if you have let yourself slip there are some other guys who finished behind you that have a little more experience at the international level.

Then it's Ed's turn to ask a question. "If they had so much experience, why didn't they beat me?"

Point taken, Bell says. Now get your ass to the Olympic training camp in Plattsburgh, New York.

Ed hangs up the phone. Then he picks it up again. He wants to call Coach Bob to tell him the news. He puts the phone down again. He knows Larsen will ask him what he has been doing since the trials. It's a question he doesn't want to answer. Ten days without running is enough to let your fitness slip critically, especially if being prepared for the biggest track meet in the world is the goal.

Ed decides his fitness will not be an issue. Putting on a pair of sweats and a singlet that says "USA" will provide enough adrenaline to make up for any deficits in lung capacity. He will put in ten days of hard work at the camp. That should get him back to speed.

When he arrives at the track in Plattsburgh, he sees a familiar face. It's Mihály Iglói, the Hungarian who was mentor to Coach Tábori at Los Angeles Valley College (the old Grossmont nemesis). Iglói is overseeing the distance team through its workouts. Ed knows that Larsen had studied Iglói and decided long ago that his methods were missing something crucial. Yet Iglói is the man in charge. Larsen is currently back in California, getting ready to watch the Olympics on television.

What would Coach Bob do with a week to go before the race of his life? Coach Bob would have him and the rest of the Toads hammering quarter-mile intervals at 65 seconds and lower, adding in leg speed to the base of endurance. Iglói is telling them to run laps at "60 percent," then "70 percent," then, every once in a while, "80 percent." What does that mean anyway, Ed wonders? He's just happy to be here though. And this guy is an Olympic coach, so he must know what he is doing. By the end of the week, Ed's legs feel fresh. He loads onto a bus to head over the border to Montreal.

Ed marches in the Opening Ceremony, not quite believing he

has really come as far as he has since those days roughly a decade ago when he believed he was slow. In the Olympic Village, at the dining hall, he gazes at the other athletes. The best of the best, all with one goal in mind. The same one he has. It's the craziest thing. Yet he believes this is meant to be.

Halfway through his preliminary heat, he realizes it isn't. Ed's best time in a 5,000 is 13:55. When he passes the midpoint of this 10,000-meter race to get into the final he hears the race official yell "13:56." These guys mean business, Ed thinks. It doesn't take a genius to do the math. They're going to run a little over 28 flat in a prelim, which is supposed to be slow and tactical. At the four-mile mark, Ed's lungs seize up and he can't hold the pace anymore. It isn't about leg speed. It's about oxygen debt. His cardio fitness just isn't there. He finishes 10th in 29:02, 40 seconds out of a spot in the final. Always though, he is an Olympian.

A few nights later, Ed is at a party thrown by Nike for the track athletes. A young Nike executive named Geoff Hollister approaches him. Nike, the company formed by former Oregon runner Phil Knight and his old Oregon coach, Bill Bowerman, wants to embody the rebel spirit of Prefontaine. They are starting a running group called Athletics West. We'll sponsor you, you won't have to worry about making ends meet, Hollister says. Come to Oregon and run. Thanks, Ed tells him, but there is a problem. I can't breathe in Oregon. Plus, there's a job as a physical education teacher at a local elementary school waiting for him in Arizona. He's going to squeeze some running in with that, kind of like Boston Billy.

Montreal wasn't what he thought it would be. But the rest of his life awaits.

Watching Ed trudge through his heat in Montreal, Bob Larsen knew midway through the race it just wasn't Ed's day. He was laboring too hard to keep up. That smooth, easy, effortless stride wasn't there. Disappointing, yes, but Larsen is a coach whose mind is always tuned to what's next. It would have been nice to make the final, but he knew Ed was probably a few years away from contending for a medal, a medal that is most likely to come from the marathon. Also, he will always have the thrill of watching a kid he first coached when he was a seventeen-year-old boy, a boy who struggled with stress fractures from his toes to his knees, line up for a race in the Olympic Games. So many coaches out there. Only a precious few can say they developed an Olympian.

Larsen has one other thought after Ed runs in Montreal. Maybe this is the year.

Ed may not have been able to crack 29 minutes for 10,000 meters today, but three weeks ago he was flirting with the low 28s. Those times translate very nicely to a cross country race, where the thoroughbreds have to battle tree roots and divots and winding trails and hills and descents. Ed is also a little more than two months removed from all that training for the U.S. marathon trials. During the winter, just a few months before the trials, Ed dropped his marathon time to 2:14 at the Fiesta Bowl race. In Montreal, everyone else sees Ed struggling over the finish line in 10th place. Coach Bob sees a base of endurance that will set Ed up very nicely for races in the fall.

Now it's time to take inventory of the rest of the Toads. Bob watches Dave Harper and Tom Lux finish 1-2 in the Balboa 8 in mid-August. Harper, even though he's holding down a full-time job doing maintenance for the San Diego schools, has become one of Larsen's most devout disciples. He's at his house each weekend morning for those long runs. There are 10–15 of them hammering together now in a fast-moving clump, ready for what has become the favored route of the moment, Bob's house to Mission Beach Bird Rock—about eighteen miles from the dry hills to the sea. Drivers on San Diego's roadways wonder what the hell is going on. When the Toads arrive on the jagged coast of Bird Rock, named for a pelican-covered rock formation in the shape of a bird, just off the coast, Sue Larsen is always there, waiting with the van and that lemonade that keeps them coming back and wanting to get to the coast as quick as they can.

What is going on is America is catching the running bug. Regular folks with potbellies are buying shoes and taking to the roads. But the sight of twenty-five incredibly fast humans cruising west on San Diego's big boulevards like they own the road makes drivers slam on the brakes and think, who the hell are these dudes and what are they doing? It also makes many of them want to run. There's been word of a coming running boom ever since Shorter won that gold medal in the marathon in Munich in 1972, then a silver* in Montreal this year. Maybe this is it.

Dave Harper has also been showing up in the afternoons to do workouts on the track with the Grossmont crew. He tries not to wonder what might have been had he found a way to work with Bob before heading out to Washington State. Tom Lux, meanwhile, is back from Oregon, back into the fold of the Toads, back doing whatever Coach Bob tells him to do. He's as committed now as he was when he was at Grossmont, and so are the rest of the Toads. One weekend morning, leading the Toads through the final miles of a threshold run Lux sees a wallet lying on the ground. He doesn't dare stop to pick it up. No one else does either—this training run isn't a race but sure feels like it.

As the college season begins, Bob makes a mental note to keep an eye on what Terry Cotton is up to in Arizona. Terry is the wild card, always either masterful or hobbled, chatty or silent. Injuries sidelined him for much of the 1976 spring season. After doing his time with the Toads on some summer weekend jaunts, he's been back at Arizona since August, and it's anyone's guess what kind of form he might be in. He's not the sort that really keeps in touch.

Larsen's first clue about Terry comes in late September, when he notices that he took second in a multi-team meet up at UCLA. Larsen knows the 6.2-mile course. It's not the hardest, but also not the easiest, and Terry bangs it out in 31:04. Then in mid-October, Terry returns to San Diego with the rest of the Arizona team for the Aztec Invitational in Balboa Park. Coach Bob is there with his Toads. It's a six-mile race, but Terry being Terry, he flies from the start and the race is basically over midway through. Terry breaks the tape in 29:02, crushing the course record, a half minute ahead of his Arizona

---

* There is little doubt that Frank Shorter deserved to win the gold medal in Montreal in 1976. He was beaten in the final miles by the East German runner Waldemar Cierpinski. The East Germans are now known to have operated a vast performance-enhancing drug operation from 1968 to 1988. Files related to the operation became public after the collapse of the Iron Curtain. Cierpinski's name is listed in those files, though he has never acknowledged that he cheated to win.

teammate, another San Diegan, the freshman phenom Thom Hunt. Lux and Harper are fifth and sixth, some 45 seconds and a good 300 yards back of their training partner.

Larsen sees more than the numbers though. What he sees is the Terry he first saw at that high school race five years before, the kid who blazed back after the wrong turn. His form is gentle and fluid and fierce all at once. At the end of the race, he looks as though he's got six more miles in him. He's Arizona's top runner by a long way. Everyone wonders what has been going on with Terry to produce this burst of success. The answer is fairly straightforward. The answer is his new teammate, Thom Hunt—one last piece of Larsen's seven-piece puzzle, one last guy who is never happier than when he is running to the edge, and is moving frighteningly fast when he gets there.

Thom Hunt does not remember a time when he didn't run or hang around people who do. Or when he wasn't the fastest kid around. Or when he didn't win nearly every race against kids his own age. Thom's father ran at San Diego State in the 1950s. He set the school record in the mile there, then helped his teammate Bill Gookin start the San Diego Track Club. After college, he became a gym teacher and a coach. When he isn't coaching, he's working as a race official at local meets.

As a young child Thom tags along with his father to the meets. He's the coach's kid, the little guy helping the adults check runners into their races. He loves all the different colors of singlets, a whole rainbow out there speeding around an oval in a colorful blur. By middle school, he's going out for the occasional run with his father around their neighborhood in San Carlos, a quick jog from Bob Larsen's haunt at Grossmont College. He's jumping into junior races. If there isn't anyone too much older than Thom, he is always first to the finish—by a lot. He's perfectly fine at other sports, a decent little baseball player. But there is no doubt what his sport will be when he enters high school. He's going to run track, and he's going to be a star.

By his sophomore year he's beating Kirk Pfeffer, who is two years older than he is, in cross country races and the mile. When he is a junior he gets connected with two Swedish transplants in their twenties who are training to go low in the Boston Marathon. Thom, this kid with spiky hair and sinewy arms and big eyes, joins them for their long runs of 18–20 miles at race pace. Thom stays with them step-for-step.

In his senior year, he wins the Mt. SAC Invitational cross country race. That helps get him a spot on the U.S. national cross country team that wins the world championship. It includes a kid from Wayland, Massachusetts, named Alberto Salazar. Nothing, though, matches the night at the Jack in the Box Indoor Games in San Diego, when he gets put in the race with the senior men to take a shot at the national indoor high school mile record. With 12,000 people cheering him on, he shatters it, running a 4:02 on the boards. No one touches the mark for twenty-five years. All this is happening in Bob Larsen's backyard. Larsen tells Hunt he'd love to have him run for Grossmont but someone at his level probably doesn't need any seasoning in junior college. He also doesn't live in the district. So Thom Hunt heads to Tucson to be a Wildcat, just like Ed Mendoza and Terry Cotton did.

Thom makes the adjustment to running and living in the desert just fine. He wakes up a little earlier to get the morning run out of the way before the sun begins to roast. Other than that, he's got no complaints. He's religious about getting his two daily runs in. Nothing is going to get in the way of that. Then, just weeks after he starts as a Wildcat, his stepfather dies. Thom is worried about his mother. He doesn't want her to be alone. The family owns a travel trailer, so Thom tells his mother to drive the trailer down to Tucson. He finds parking and a utilities hook-up spot for $75 a month, and he moves out of the dorm and into the trailer.

When Terry Cotton hears about this, it gets him thinking. Terry is a fifth-year senior. He has financial aid to help with tuition, but he still doesn't have two extra nickels to rub together. He's just broken up with his girlfriend and needs a place to live. A rent-free existence would come in very handy. Thom doesn't know exactly what to think when Terry asks to stay with him and his mom so Terry and his own broken family can save some bucks. Terry tells Thom not to worry about space. He's going to sleep outside. No one will know he's there. Within days, Terry has rigged a setup attached to the outside of the trailer that includes an awning, drawers, and cupboards. He needs nothing else, though there is an added perk in the deal for him.

Thom Hunt did not blast that indoor mile record or become a world junior cross country champion by accident. He did it by being perhaps the most disciplined young runner in the country. He knew what the guys up at Grossmont were doing. Hard, long threshold runs combined with some speed work as big races approached. In high school, he arranged his schedule so he could have first period off each morning. That gave him time to bang out six miles on the route that led out from his high school and around Lake Murray before each school day. That way, when his high school coach made him do all those intervals like every other high school coach did back in those days, Hunt could follow the orders knowing he'd gotten his long runs in already.

Nothing changes when he begins at Arizona. He is all about doubles. Each morning when he exits the trailer to head out for a run, Terry Cotton wakes up, too, crawls out of his makeshift living space, and goes with him. Terry knows that Hunt may be five years his junior, but he is very, very fast and he trains like a beast. For the first time in his life, Terry is on a true regimen. Hard distance in the morning. Speed in the afternoon. With Thom on his shoulder, setting the pace, he doesn't feel the need to turn every session into a death race. He goes hard, twice every day, with Thom. That's enough. And he doesn't get hurt, and he wins darn near every race he enters for Arizona—by a lot.

Bob Larsen gets brought up to speed on all this after Terry's breathtaking win at Balboa Park. Then he can't help but start to count again. Dave Harper and Tom Lux, and a steadily improving Dale Fleet make three. Terry Cotton gets him to four. Thom Hunt grew up in the shadow of Grossmont and is a San Diegan through and through. He did the occasional run with the Toads in high school. Bringing him on gets Larsen to five. He's got some good prospects at Grossmont this season, but if he's going to take another run at the cross country national championships, he's going to do it with seven of his biggest and best guns or he isn't going to do it at all. He's got two more slots. Two more calls to make.

Kirk Pfeffer has a ritual. At some point every day, sometimes on the way to class, sometimes on his way to track practice, sometimes during practice, he likes to take a glance at his hero. Frank Shorter is never hard to find. He trains at 11:30 each morning and at 3:30 every afternoon. Right there in Boulder. In good weather he's out on the streets or in the trails under the Flatirons, or on the outdoor track at the university. In bad weather he's on one of the highest indoor tracks in the country. The 1972 Olympic marathon champion is out there, effortlessly clicking through his road miles, or churning out his half-mile intervals. He is the apotheosis of efficiency. If running is a small but growing cult religion, Shorter is its prophet, especially now that Pre is gone. Shorter is why Pfeffer is here in Boulder.

After two years of running for Bob Larsen at Grossmont, he had the times to write his own ticket at a major college program. Pfeffer wanted Boulder for one reason—Shorter had settled there. Shorter had grown addicted to the cool, dry weather and the mile-high altitude, ideal for training. If it was good enough for Shorter, it was good enough for Pfeffer. Since showing up in August not a day has passed when he felt like he made the wrong decision, even if Colorado's coach is an old-school interval guy, and Kirk is all about those thresholds on the roads. Kirk trains often on his own. In early mornings. At night when he is antsy. It makes no difference. He's even got the wavy brown hair and the Shorter mustache. Boulder is his spot, has been since he first landed here.

Then in mid-October, Bob Larsen calls and asks Kirk if he wants to be a part of the Toads team going to the AAU Cross Country National Championships in Philadelphia the next month. Pfeffer doesn't take a minute to think. Of course he does. Once a Toad always a Toad, he tells Larsen. That's exactly what Larsen wants to hear. Also, Larsen has been reading up on some of the early studies about altitude training. He's beginning to believe that it can make a pretty big difference. Hearing Kirk say he's ready to sign on makes him even surer that this really might be the year of the Toad. Kirk was a demon running at sea level. Train him a mile above sea level, and perhaps there's no telling how far and fast he can go.

When Kirk arrives at track practice a few days after his chat with Larsen, he is told that Colorado athletic director Eddie Crowder needs to have a word with him. Pfeffer has no earthly idea why Crowder might be interested in him. Crowder spent eleven years as the football coach in Boulder. Like most athletic directors with football roots, that's mainly what he cares about. He's got nothing against the track guys. It's just not his thing. He has a chiseled jaw and chin. He wears square, wire-rimmed glasses and has hair only on the sides of his head. Colorado athletics is his domain, the place where everyone listens to him.

When Kirk sees Crowder, the athletic director wants to know what's with this rumor that Pfeffer plans to run in the Cross Country National Championships with some team from San Diego named the Frogs or the Toads or something. Yes, the Toads, Pfeffer says. He explains that the name of the club is the Jamul Toads. It's a Mexican-Indian word for bad water, he explains. The Toads part, well that's kind of an ironic joke, because no one who is not a member of the Jamul Toads takes this group seriously, which can play to their advantage at races, and nothing else would live in the bad water but a toad. That's who we are, he says.

Crowder doesn't do irony, and he doesn't care about any of this. He can't understand why Pfeffer doesn't know that when runners at the University of Colorado compete outside the NCAA they run with the Colorado Track Club. This, of course, has been explained to Pfeffer many times of late, mainly by members of the aforementioned CTC, who have caught wind of his plan to run for the Toads. The CTC is the two-time defending national champion. Shorter runs with them on occasion, though they are mostly Colorado alums and anyone else they can grab from the big mountains in the West. The athletic director poses a question: Is the club that is occasionally joined by the only American with an Olympic gold and silver medal in the marathon somehow not good enough for Kirk Pfeffer?

Pfeffer explains this has nothing to do with any dissatisfaction with CTC. CTC is a fine club that he would be proud to run with if he were not a Toad. But he's been training with his pals from San Diego for going on four years. They have made him the runner he is today, and he wants to run this race as part of their team. Crowder takes this all in, considers it, then strongly encourages Pfeffer to consider running for the CTC. Pfeffer tells him the recruitment is flattering, but he is a Toad. Then Crowder decides to up the ante. Let me explain this to you, he says. If you run for a club based outside the state of Colorado you will cease to be a member of the track team at the University of Colorado.

Kirk Pfeffer is not prone to anger. He is the pensive, artistic sort, machinelike when he runs, meditative almost. There is no screaming confrontation with Crowder, no doors are slammed. He simply gets up and leaves. The national championships are still several weeks away. He has plenty to think about, and plenty of time to think, which is one of the benefits of being a long distance runner. He will think, but his mind won't change. The Toads turned him into a junior college champion, an object of desire for the track team in Boulder. This is what running is to Pfeffer. It's San Diego. It's the Toads, no matter what some former football coach in Boulder tells him. His mind is made up. He will spend the weekend before Thanksgiving running for the University of Colorado Buffaloes in the NCAA cross country championships. The following weekend he will join Larsen and the Toads at the AAU National Championships in Philadelphia, where he will try to run the tar out of his friends on the Colorado Track Club. It's not clear what will happen after that. He will find somewhere to run. He always does.

Now Larsen has one last call to make. He needs to reach Ed in Tucson. He has no idea how this will go. He asked Thom and Terry if they had seen him much in the months since the Olympics. They have not. When runners don't see other runners, it's never a good sign.

When Larsen finally reaches Ed, he tells him of his plan—to take another shot, a real serious shot, at nationals this year. Ed is all in. Couldn't be more excited in fact. The Olympics are behind him. He's ready for the next challenge. This is how runners are. A race ends, usually not the way they want it to. It hurts for a time, though often not for very long. It's not like stick and ball sports, where a blown throw or a double-fault haunts a career. Running is elemental. You show up on the start line, and either your best that day is better than everyone else's or it isn't. You run to win, always, but often don't finish first. When it's over, time moves on, to the next race on the calendar.

Larsen then has one other question. Ed being Ed, he has to ask it. Ed had that base of endurance through the Games, and if the Toads are to have a shot, Ed's training needs to be there. Thom and Terry have barely seen him on the roads. Ed, he says, have you been running at all?

In fact, he has. About eight miles a day, on his own, no set schedule as he gets used to the teaching life and being a real person. Not crazy hard, but hard enough to feel good and easy enough to stay healthy until the time comes to step it up and get ready for the next race. He has nothing on his calendar because he hasn't decided what distance he wants to focus on. Now he has a target. Six weeks hence in Philadelphia. Thresholds and repeats until then, he tells Coach Bob. Not on the streets where the stress fractures can return, but on the grass beside the roads and in the local parks.

Good for him, Larsen thinks. His Olympian is on board. He can count to seven. This just might be the year.

With roughly six weeks to prepare for nationals, Larsen knows he has a team to be reckoned with. He knows how to put them in the best possible position to succeed in Philadelphia. He does not know where the hell he's going to get the money to get them there. He's got to get airfare, food, and two nights lodging in Philadelphia for eight. It's going to run a couple thousand dollars at least. He doesn't have that kind of money. He's got to find someone who does.

Larsen's first thought is that shoe company up in Oregon—Nike. Their roots are in distance running. Nike founder Phil Knight ran cross country at Oregon, then started his business selling running shoes from Japan out of his trunk. They believe in the sport as a way of life and a form of self-expression. He even knows Geoff Hollister, Nike's chief promoter. If Nike truly believes that distance running represents that underdog spirit of rebellion, that the spirit of Pre that espouses this sport is at its roots the ultimate countercultural activity, then there isn't a group that better embodies that than the Toads.

Larsen knows Hollister from his occasional trips to Oregon to check in with the coaches there, Bill Bowerman and Bill Dellinger, for clinics that are helping to make him as smart a coach as he can possibly be. Ahead of the 1972 U.S. Olympic Trials in Eugene, they handed Larsen the stopwatch and had him oversee Prefontaine's workouts in the days leading up to the event because he was too busy organizing the meet. Hollister ran at Oregon through the mid-1960s.

In 1968, at a campus Dairy Queen, he took up Phil Knight's offer to start selling and marketing those Japanese running shoes, back when Nike was Blue Ribbon Sports. That made Hollister Nike employee number three. In 1972 he was charged with getting the waffle-soled Nikes on as many runners as possible at those U.S. Olympic Trials and all the other big races. Larsen can see where all this is going. The shoe companies like Nike are going to create their own clubs and take over the sport. They will understand that the best way to sell shoes isn't to explain the technical attributes of those shoes but to get them on the feet of the best runners in the world. If money to finance the sport flows from that, so be it. It's got to come from somewhere.

Knowing Hollister's zeal and his missionary-like belief in his product, Larsen calls him in the fall of 1976 to tell him about the Toads. They train like beasts, he says. They are going to Philadelphia and they are going to be tough to beat. He thinks they can win.

Who's on the team, Hollister wants to know. Larsen runs down the roster. It's a local crew from San Diego. Hollister knows Ed Mendoza from the Olympics. A few of the others are vaguely familiar to him. He knows Lux from Tom's time at Oregon. He wasn't any great shakes there, though. Overall Hollister isn't impressed. Colorado, Florida, Boston, Oregon, New York Athletic Club, that's where the quality is right now, he says. Not San Diego.

I'm going to pass, he says. "You have to understand Bob," he adds, "Colorado knows how to peak."

Bob Larsen hears those words and he can't help but smile. Hollister has left him empty-handed financially but he has given him something far more valuable.

"Colorado knows how to peak."

It's the perfect line. He's getting fired up just playing it back, over and over in his head. Time and again over the next six weeks the Toads will hear what Geoff Hollister and, by extension, everyone else in the running world thinks of their quixotic little venture.

"Colorado knows how to peak," he tells the Toads with that wry smile whose meaning they all know so well. And he knows it's lines like these, the little digs and challenges, that fire up distance runners best. The rah-rah speeches are for football. This game is too long, too taxing, too nonstop. It's a long, slow burn, and the motivation has to work that way as well.

Coach Bob still needs some cash, though. He's got another idea. Local team, local sponsors. He tracks down Jack Goodall, a top executive of Jack in the Box, the burger chain that began in San Diego in 1951. Goodall is a big believer in servicing your community and he's a sports nut. He's happy to kick in the bulk of what's needed, he tells Larsen. Whew. Big relief.

Larsen isn't the only one dialing for dollars though. Dale and Dave start spending late afternoons knocking on the doors of businesses up and down Mission Boulevard. They tell their story. They plead for funding. A local realtor and some car dealers agree to help out. When they get close enough, within a few hundred dollars, Larsen tells them not to worry about the rest. He'll cover it. He's invested plenty more than that in this bunch of Toads over the years. He has no doubt it will pay off.

In the final weeks before Philadelphia, Larsen tweaks the training regimen, for Dale and Dave and Tom who are training with him, and for Kirk and Ed and Tom and Terry, who are in Arizona and Colorado. He relays word to them by phone. He knows they are all plenty fit. He needs them fast. He remembers well what happened in San Francisco two years ago. That wide start line and the race to the funnel into the woods. The narrowing in Philadelphia might not be as severe, but there will be a funnel, and a sprint to the opening. That's the nature of the sport, the only way several hundred runners cram into a narrow wooded trail.

We're going to need to get out fast and put up low first miles, he tells them. We need speed. So in addition to those lung-searing 6- and 8- and 10-mile tears out on the roads and the trails of San Diego and Tucson and Boulder, there are quarter-mile repeats to gets the legs turning over as fast as they can. Instead of 6 or 8 800s at 2:15, there are sets of 10 and 12 400s at 60–65 seconds. Concrete times. We're going to get out in that first mile and we're going to be bold, he says.

In early November, there is a bump in the road. Terry Cotton needs emergency surgery to have his wisdom teeth removed. His cheeks swell to the size of softballs. He loads up on the painkillers, spends most of the next few days sleeping at the trailer. Ten days after the surgery, he heads up to Tempe for the regional championships. He runs with Thom. They finish seventh and eighth, good enough to qualify for nationals. Five of the six guys in front of them are Africans. They look much older than college students.

When Coach Bob hears about the wisdom teeth, he gets a little nervous. There's a freshman at Grossmont, a newly christened Toad named Glenn Best. He's heard about this plan to go to nationals. He wants in. He isn't the natural talent the rest of the Toads are, he doesn't have that last turbocharged gear, but he is strong and reliable and the senior Toads who are headed east are the guys he worshipped growing up. Larsen tells him he's got to pay his own way. There isn't enough money for an eighth man. And he'll definitely be one of the guys sleeping on the floor of the hotel room. He's a quasi-alternate. Deal, Best says. He's headed to Philly. They all are.

The journey east is not easy. They leave on Thanksgiving. Ed and Tom and Dale and Dave and Kirk and Bob and Glenn come from San Diego. There are two connections, one is made, one is missed, and the journey grows to nearly twenty hours before they finally end up in the Ben Franklin Hotel off Independence Park. Thom Hunt and Terry Cotton have been there since Tuesday. They came from Denton, Texas, where Thom finished 13th at the NCAA Championships, and Terry, his gums still swollen, is five spots behind in 18th. That makes both of them All-Americans. Not too shabby.

The Africans are at the top of the leaderboard, and in several of the spots ahead of them. Henry Rono, Samson Kimobwa of Washington State. Wilson Waigwa and Joshua Kimeto of Texas–

El Paso. It's a cruel foreshadowing of what is to come, though they don't know that yet. The Toads pile into the beds and the cots and the sleeping bags in the two rooms their budget allows and grab a few hours of sleep.

In the morning, it's time to head out to Fairmount Park to go over the course, something they never had the chance to do the last time they were at nationals. This is when Bob realizes he's messed up the math. He rented the biggest sedan he could find to get the Toads from the airport to the hotel and back and forth to the park. He figured four in the front and four in the back. A cross country team of seven, plus a coach. But Glenn . . . he's forgotten about Glenn, his quasi-backup for Terry. They all look at the sedan and look at each other, wondering what to do. The solution becomes obvious. Glenn is low man on the totem pole. He's going in the trunk. Larsen promises Glenn he will drive carefully. Plenty of air back there, he assures him, and it's just a fifteen-minute ride anyway.

At Fairmont Park they jog easily over the 10,000-meter course on the part of the park known as the Belmont Plateau. Just like Larsen assumed, a broad start leads to a narrow path through the woods that hikers indulge in because of its rises and descents. The four hills are large enough to have names, with three of those names suggesting unforgivingly steep gradients—Flagpole, Parachute, Nursery, and Surekill, which doesn't sound like the sort of hill that any runner wants to confront. There are rocks sticking up from the trail, and divots and gullies hidden beneath the foliage. It's what they call a "billy-goat course"—lots of hops and half steps. So much more than a boring, rubberized track for speedsters. Careful where you put your foot, but we can do damage here they think. It's cool and gray, the Northeast in late November. They aren't in San Diego anymore. That is the point.

When they are done, they grab some food and spend most of the rest of the day bumming around the hotel, staying off their feet. There's a venture to a cheap, nearby restaurant for dinner, a burger and pasta place that could be anywhere, and then it's back into the hotel. Center City Philadelphia in 1976 is something of a no-man's-land, not the place to go wandering around at night. Thom and Terry tried this earlier in the week when they went hunting for a place to go bowling, anything to ease the boredom. Within minutes they'd beaten a path back to the hotel, chased by an unruly gang that didn't realize just who they were chasing.

There is light chatter in the rooms, the kind of razzing and ribbing that young men who have competed with and against each other for years are prone to. It feels like a reunion of sorts. The Toads are just so happy to be here, together, running as one. Larsen doesn't bother with any pre-race manifestos. The Toads know why they are here and what they have come to do. Larsen knows at this point his job is to psyche them down, not psyche them up. They're ready. So is he.

The morning breaks gray and a little on the warm side for this time of year—60 degrees. Not bad at all. They pile back into the sedan. Four in the front, four in the back, Glenn in the trunk. They wouldn't have it any other way. As they pull into the lot at Fairmont Park and pile out, the Toads gaze around at the competition. All around them are running teams in designer-brand matching sweats. Everyone's got some version of a Nike or adidas or New Balance racing flat. No doubt the fancier clubs got these for free.

The Toads' eyes turn to each other. They are all wearing whatever they could cobble together from their drawers. Beneath their unmatched sweats they wear dark green and yellow striped shorts and the yellow singlet with Kirk Pfeffer's silkscreen of that wise-ass Toad. The budget couldn't stretch far enough for warm-up gear. That's just fine with them. They know the first lesson of this sport— that it's the runners in the uniforms that make the team, not the uniforms, not even the shoes.

They stretch on the dewy grass, run some warm-up sprints on the open plateau, then gather in close with Larsen for one last chat. The clouds are hanging low. It's not so different than morning in San Diego, he tells them, before the sun burns off the early gray. Larsen tells them not to worry about reputations, to enjoy the day. Remember, head out fast, get to the narrow trail as quickly as possible. Passing won't be easy in that part of the course. Get a position, hold it, push the pace. Make them understand you are not going anywhere. Become their problem.

The Toads head to the start. They crush toward the front, jockeying for position among these few hundred pioneers of long distance. A month has passed since the first five-borough New York Marathon, when some 2,000 runners—lunatics, in the eyes of most—bounded over the Verrazzano-Narrows Bridge, sounding a sort of unofficial start to the mass running movement that for years has been populated by few others than the elite few hundred on this start line today and their brethren.

The Toads have collectively spent decades hammering the pavement in San Diego under the baking southern California sun, running mile after mile to escape from nasty fights between moms and stepfathers and wars that should never have been fought and lonely summers and tragic childhood loss. Together, they ran away from what made them different and toward an ideal that would make them all the same.

Then the haunting, quiet moment that all races produce finally arrives—the moment when there is nothing left to do but wait for the sound of the gun.

Standing on that start line with the Toads, a few feet away, as ready as anyone to win that race is a twenty-four-year-old Harvard graduate from New Mexico named Ric Rojas. He has a poofy, brown afro and a thick mustache. He wears the yellow T-shirt of the Colorado Track Club with red and white candy-stripe shorts. Rojas was born and raised in Los Alamos, New Mexico, where he is a computer analyst at the Scientific Laboratory. He is 5'9" and 135 pounds. As a teenager he desperately wanted to play stick and ball sports but didn't have the skills. In tenth grade he tries out for cross country. This he has the skills for. His father works at the National Laboratory, but most of the kids on the cross country team are Native Americans, who spend their weekends running through the high desert surrounding Los Alamos.

They invite him to come along. Running up and down those hills like a mountain goat, grabbing the trail with your toes, then pushing off an instant later, this is where Ric really learns how to run. He sets a New Mexico high school record for the mile, running a 4:12 at 6,000 feet. Like every fast kid at the time, he desperately wants to go to Oregon to run with Prefontaine and Bowerman. When he visits, Bowerman asks him about his grades. Ric is a straight-A student. Who else is looking at you, Bowerman asks? Harvard and Yale, Ric tells him. Go there, Bowerman says. Ric explains that he wants to run at Oregon with Pre. Bowerman says he's sorry, but he's not going to offer a scholarship to Oregon to a kid who can go to Harvard.

So Ric goes to Harvard, where he is far and away the best runner but basically left to train himself. His coach has him racing every weekend. By the time the big conference and regional meets roll around, he's burned out. After graduation though, he moves back to Los Alamos and decides to get serious about running again. He's doing 100 miles a week, repetition workouts of 5 times a mile at a 4:25 pace. He's doing ladder workouts—400, then 800, then 1,200, then 1,600 and all the way back down. It works. He wins the Pan American Games trials marathon in 1975, running a 2:25 at altitude in Flagstaff, Arizona. He beats Shorter by 55 seconds in a 15-kilometer race in Denver. He meets some of the guys from the Colorado Track Club there. They ask him if he wants to run with them sometime, maybe be a part of the club. So once a month, Rojas makes the seven-hour drive from Los Alamos to run with the CTC crew. They have their sights on this national cross country championship that they have no intention of giving up. He's got the race circled on his calendar, too. He cuts back his work schedule to six hours a day and hits the hills hard.

Ric Rojas is a fine runner, one of the country's best, but on this day, in this race, running with a team that is nearly 400 miles from where he lives, with guys he has little connection to, it is very clear what his purpose is. Ric Rojas is a ringer. He is that thing that the Toads, who all grew up in homes that are in jogging distance from each other, do not have. Colorado's rivals from the Florida Track Club and the New York Athletic Club have even more.

They are the reason Larsen wants to win this race so badly, with a group of local guys who share something more than laundry. They are far from the most talented collection here, or at any race. But they have been training a certain way, his way, running on that edge, for years. This is the moment he gets to show the world where that can get you—all the way from a farm with no running water in northern Minnesota. And he just might be able to do it with a bunch of Toads.

Get out fast, he thinks in the instant before the pistol fires. Just get out fast.

Then comes the gun.

It takes a millisecond for a near-disaster to strike. On his second step, Tom Lux's planted foot gives way. He's on his way down, halfway to a faceplant in the mud, when he feels a tug at the back of his singlet. Dale, next to him, has somehow gotten ahold of Tom. He yanks as hard as he can and gets his fellow Toad upright. Barely missing a beat, Tom is back running. A fall at the start, with 9,998 meters left, may seem like a small thing. But a tumble there is 2 or 3 seconds, and 2 or 3 seconds is 20 meters, and 20 meters is 80 runners. That doesn't happen though, and the Toads are off, Thom Hunt leading the way to the opening, just like Larsen prayed he would.

Hunt can't make it stick though. A mile into the race, his eighteen-year-old legs are feeling every meter of his All-American performance at the national championships one week ago. He drops back. But Kirk is right up there, and so is Cotton.

Ed, on the other hand, isn't feeling so good. From the moment he woke up, he's been thinking about all the great runners who are here. The last time he lined up in a race at the Olympic Games, everyone seemed so much faster, as though they had something he did not. Why will this day be different? He hasn't been able to shake the doubts all morning. Since the gun sounded, he's been trying to think his way through this race, trying to figure out how, on a day when he might not be at his best, when his legs haven't felt the tension of competition since the summer, he can best help his team. He's worked himself into a kind of trance. He's holding himself back, waiting, but for what?

Where the hell is Ed, Larsen is thinking as they come to a clearing. He begins that instinctual counting of the colors. He sees some yellow up front, but he doesn't see Ed, that shock of black, shoulder-length hair streaming behind the littlest guy out there. He knows he needs to see Ed. Then, there he is, maybe 50 or 60 places off the lead. It could even be 80. He's running like his feet are sinking deep into the mud on each step while everyone else's are flitting across the trail. This is fixable, Larsen thinks, but it has to be fixed now. Larsen is going to have to do something he's never done before, something that normally makes Larsen different from every other coach out here today. He edges up to the trail. Ed is ten yards away and about to fly past when Larsen cuts loose, for literally the first time in his career, and maybe the last. "Ed," he hollers, "you have *got* to get up there!"

The voice hits Ed like a slap across his cheeks. He knows Coach Bob is not a screamer, but he sure is screaming now, and Ed is damn sure going to listen. He gets one quick glance at Coach Bob and sees his eyes are nearly coming out of his head. Time to stop thinking, he tells himself. Time to go.

Now Ed is picking off runners by the bunch. Plenty of them are even wearing the same singlet as he is. First Dale, then Hunt, then Dave. Push, keep pushing. Be passing people, he keeps telling himself. Don't think, just run and pass. Climb the ladder, move up.

Ric Rojas has been doing plenty of passing himself. He was 100 spots back after the first mile, but now he's near the front. At the Surekill hill, three and a half miles in, he makes his move and flies past a slowing Pfeffer. Pfeffer took the lead on a long downhill heading into the halfway mark, but now he's feeling the NCAA race, too. Terry is moving up, though. He's been fourth or fifth for the last mile or so, but now he is breaking with the pack and trying to keep Rojas in his sights. With a mile to go, Rojas is 50 yards ahead. Terry starts to think it's over. Time to play defense and hang on to second place. But the more he stays steady, the bigger Rojas looks.

Son of a gun, he's getting tired, and coming back to me, Cotton thinks as they come into that last stretch. He begins to hear the chatter from the crowd of onlookers and curiosity seekers gathered near the finish. Cotton gives one last furious push but Ric Rojas has just enough gas to make it over the line, in 30:23.8, 2.2 seconds ahead of Terry. It was a ballsy effort by Rojas—run away and make everyone believe you are never coming back. He fooled Terry for just long enough. Three seconds back is a Penn State alum named Jeff Bradley and nine seconds back is Kirk.

A few feet away, Bob Larsen is doing the math. Two and four

makes six. Where the hell is Ed? There, there he is. Bang. Seventh, 17 seconds off the lead. The Toads are at 13 points. Larsen's seeing so many other colors, trying to keep some semblance of a running tally in his head. Please God, show me two more yellow singlets, two more Toads. Then, there's Dave, out-sprinting some guy from Colorado for 12th. That's three in the top 10 and four in the top 15. And before he can even figure out that 15 and 15 makes 30, there's Tom Lux, all big teeth and big eyes and curly, bouncing, blond hair streaming across the line a whole lot faster than anyone figured he would. Tom is 20th.

Larsen is done counting. The Toads are at 45. Colorado, the only other team with a shot at this, isn't done yet. That takes another 10 seconds and 5 places. Too little too late.

Larsen doesn't move. He stays away as he sees his Toads gather with the rest of the runners in a clump behind the finish line. They are gazing at each other, gasping for air after completing as tough a cross country course as there is. He can read their lips and see they are trading times and finishing spots. They have spent the past half hour running to the edge. They have no idea what they have just pulled off. It's likely only Bob and maybe Colorado's coach know what has just happened. He likes it that way. Everyone else will know everything soon enough. For this moment, the victory is his alone.

After a few more minutes, when everyone has made it through the chute, he wanders over to his boys. There are only two words left to say. "You won," he tells them.

At first they don't believe him, but as they look at each other and look at Larsen, they realize there is no way coach would be pulling their legs on this one. The hugs and hand-slaps and whooping and hollering begin. Ed, always a little removed from the situation, takes a second to look around. He notices the other runners beginning to look at them. It's not with the usual expressions of respectful envy ("all credit to them, we'll get them next time") that runners who lose usually gaze at runners who win. Everyone seems to be asking everyone else some version of, who are these guys, where are they from, what are they called? These guys, with the funny little frog on their singlet, they actually won? And who are they again?

The Toads, yes, the Toads. They run, each one, for reasons that are their own. They run like few others have ever run before. For most of them, this will be the best day of their running lives, the day they become, after all those miles on the edge, the best collection of runners around, the ones everyone should follow.

Bob Larsen believes he will not be some small character in a narrative that is a closely held secret anymore. The secret is out. He should become a phenomenon of the running boom that is about to explode. He knows better than just about anyone how to run far fast. You practice running as far and as fast as you can. And then you try running farther, faster to that place where every next step becomes an act of faith, a conquering of fear. You share it with others, with brothers and sisters who understand that to take the next step is to believe that even though it hurts, the only way to ease the pain is to run faster, to push. Like the yogis say, the only way out is through.

But Bob Larsen does not become a phenomenon. He does not become anything more than well known to those who know him well. For the next eight years, as America produces two of the best distance runners in the world, a few road warriors at the top follow the Larsen way, running to the edge, over and over. And then, somehow, everyone decides not to do this anymore. The running cognoscenti start to believe there is a better, easier way. The results of all this will break Bob Larsen's heart, burn him even, in a way that nothing before has. Surely others would understand what he had done, what the Toads had done, how they ran and why it worked.

No, not yet at least. As far as that rebellious world where the oddballs of running chase great speed and life's truths over great distances was concerned, Bob Larsen was headed back to the edge of the unknown, that odd, almost obscure place where there is just one advantage—no one ever sees you coming. Maybe this will all be for the best.

TWO

TWO

Can We Be Fast Again?

Spring 1993, Drake Stadium, UCLA

These are the days Bob Larsen loves most, when the high school kids descend on the powder blue track at his college. The chance to run in the footsteps of legends just a few years older inspires them to run as they have never run before. They take on the best competition around, and Bob Larsen, now one of the esteemed minds in running, sits in a corner of the stands under his Panama hat and watches the past and the future blaze in front of his eyes all at once.

He watches these fifteen- and sixteen- and seventeen-year-old boys, still finding their stride. There are plenty of girls now, too, thanks to Title IX. They are just beginning to grow into their bodies, to realize who they can one day be. As he watches, his mind drifts back to Monte Vista High School, three decades ago. He is telling that first collection of misfit toys that if they want to run far fast they have to practice running far fast. They even listened to him back then, when they weren't pausing in the middle of training to take a rock to the head of a rattlesnake along the trail.

Then, inevitably, he watches the best of this new generation accelerate into a back straightaway on the red rubber of the UCLA track, or explode out of a starting block and pull away from the group. Instantly, Bob's focus shifts to the years ahead, when the kid breaking away, the one taking off like he's got batteries in his shoes, has put in so many more miles and has learned how to race and how to win. The stopwatch tells part of the story. Numbers can explain only so much, though. They say almost nothing about heart and character and aura, the stuff that separates the talented runner from the champion, the stuff that allows Bob Larsen to see into the future. In this way, Bob lives his life through a series of races. He has never wanted it any other way.

—

For the past fourteen years, no one has done this better than Coach Bob. In 1979, after he won eight consecutive state championships at Grossmont, the phone calls from the big four-year schools became too difficult to ignore. The opportunity for which he had been waiting two decades finally arose. Back in high school, those nagging, senior year injuries made Larsen miss his chance to convince track coaches at UCLA he was worthy. Twenty-two years later, the college of Jackie Robinson and John Wooden wants him to take over a once great program.

The opportunity to coach at UCLA is everything Coach Bob hasn't done. Since he started down this road in the early 1960s, he has always led the life of the scrappy underdog. He knows there is nothing better in sports than winning when you are not supposed to, when everyone says you can't. It's like coming from the back of the pack when no one expects it. He would not trade what he has forged for anything. But he has always wondered what he might be able to pull off if he had everything a coach could ever desire—a school with world-class facilities, top-notch academics, a reputation in athletics no other school can match. With the wind at his back, how far can he go?

As it turns out, very far. He has done just about everything there is to do. He arrives at UCLA men's track and field program in 1979. Eight years later, in 1987, he wins his first NCAA championship. The next year he and his assistants, John Smith and Art Venegas, coach what is considered one of history's greatest college teams, in any sport. Those teams won the national meet by 53 points in 1987 and 41 in 1988. Those are bloodbath-level beatdowns.

His UCLA runners are among the fastest people on the planet. So many of them now have Olympic medals. Steve Lewis, one of his star quarter-milers, was all of nineteen when he captured the gold medal in the 400 meters in Seoul in 1988. Danny Everett took the bronze in that race and won a gold alongside him a few days later in the 4x400 relay. Michael Marsh, a sprinter, won the gold medal in 1992 in the 200 and a gold in the 4x100 relay. Kevin Young took the gold in the 400-meter hurdles in 1992, when Steve Lewis took the silver in the 400. Young's world record, 46.78, still stands.

In 1976 Coach Bob watched the Olympics from a television set in San Diego. He had just a single horse in the field, Ed Mendoza. Ed had that off-day and failed to make the final of his event. Now he watches whole bunches of his guys ascend to the top step of the Olympic podium every four years.

It's different though. The Olympic champions Coach Bob helps develop are not the sort of men who put his name on the map during that Bicentennial fall nearly two decades before. They are nothing like those anonymous Toads who, after that perfect day in Philadelphia, created all that chatter among what was then the fringe set of distance fiends. What are those guys doing out there in San Diego, everyone asked?

The answers were fairly straightforward—run long and hard, run on the edge, then wake up the next day and do it again, and again, and again. Find your threshold, and stay there.

They needed a new vocabulary for this. That small but quickly expanding collection of elite runners began to talk about "thresholds" and "tempo runs" or simply "running on the edge." It didn't matter to Bob Larsen what they called it, only that, finally, the world had come around to his way of thinking, his understanding that running fast over a great distance was really not so different than sprinting a short distance. Keep the legs churning, the feet under the body, the knees driving forward. The speed comes from reducing contact time and getting that foot back in the air as quickly as possible. Just like on that beach in Mexico at Christmas in 1963. And after months of long, hard threshold runs, don't forget about sharpening the speed in the final weeks, because in the end nearly every race becomes a sprint to the finish.

Shorter practiced a version of this by himself when he was at his best in the early 1970s. He'd head out on a cool Boulder morning and run three six-mile loops around his neighborhood. The first loop was an easy 5:30 pace. The next one at 5:00. Then Shorter would turn on the jets and reel off six 4:30s to finish up the morning. Few knew what Shorter was up to. He ran alone. No one else could keep up.

As Shorter faded, Bill Rodgers took over in the late 1970s as the world's top marathoner. Boston Billy, with that loping stride and floppy blond hair under his trademark painter's cap, captured his three Boston Marathon wins and four more in New York until another guy from Massachusetts, Alberto Salazar, took his place.

Both Salazar and Rodgers learned from Bill Squires, who'd been a miler at Notre Dame, then returned to The Hub to teach and coach at Boston State College. Squires often liked to ply his trade over cheap beers and other fine spirits in Boston bars. Two nights each week he oversaw the Greater Boston Track Club's training sessions at the indoor track at Tufts University. In the mid-1970s, Squires caught on to what Larsen had been teaching for a decade—that magic mix of speed and distance, running long and hard and hard for long. That beat the tar out of all comers, produced the champions, and helped to accelerate the running boom that turned every other lawyer and banker and schoolteacher into a wannabe Boston Billy.

For Bob Larsen, this all felt like a kind of dream. The fringe sport he loves hits the big time, in large part because the best Americans train the way he's been telling everyone they should for the better part of twenty years. Now he's the guy behind the lectern and on the dais at the coaching clinics and seminars. He passes out copies of workouts and training logs and explains the elementary physiology behind the theory so they can understand why this works. Few are skeptical. People believe results. When the guys capturing all the state championships and the Americans winning the biggest races are training the same way, that's about all anyone needs to know. Coach Bob and his ways have traction.

He knows his work is hardly done, but when he moves up the coast to Westwood and shifts his focus to a different sort of runner, he doesn't worry about his country losing its perch atop the distance world, even if most of the boys he brings in to wear those iconic light-blue-and-yellow UCLA singlets aren't the hippie gazelles and mountain goats he gathered around San Diego.

They are true stars, thoroughbreds in every sense. Coach Bob still cares about the gazelles and the mountain goats, but the move to UCLA forces a shift in focus, from endurance to speed. His job is to bring track and field national championships to Westwood. He has twelve scholarships to give out in total for track and cross-country runners. No one wins national championships with distance runners, who can score only in one or two events. Coaches win national championships with quarter-milers, those crazily versatile, freakishly athletic specimens who can drop down from the 400 to the 200 or stretch to the 800 when the team needs them to. They hog points in relays. Some of them can even pull off near-record long jumps and triple jumps with little practice.

Bob also likes to nab a thrower or two, a guy like John Godina, a house-sized boy from Wyoming who can throw a discus like a Frisbee and put a shot like a baseball. Occasionally Bob's got a half scholarship or some money for free books to give to a distance guy. There isn't much more than that. This is how the game is played. He also knows the best distance guys don't want to come to Westwood to train anyway. The neighborhood is beautiful but filled with concrete and cars. The closest trails are miles away. The gazelles and the mountain goats want to go train with Dellinger up in Oregon or at a place that's got some altitude, like Wyoming, or northern Arizona, in Flagstaff. Bob Larsen's path to glory at UCLA is with the thoroughbreds. Coach Bob follows it. He barely gives it a second thought.

The mountain goats have their charm, though. Coach Bob still loves to keep his eye on the up-and-coming distance kids. He loves to take in the occasional race, even if he isn't evaluating any prospects, like this two-miler he is settling in for in the stands at Drake Stadium. These races are almost entirely for pleasure, events that hark back to his roots, those first days of running on the farm in Minnesota, those warm summer evenings in San Diego years ago, when his body, limp with exhaustion from a day at the gas station, would magically come to life. The glory may live with the speed demons, but the long race is where Bob Larsen's soul endures.

That's what he's thinking as he watches this small kid with a funny name duel for the lead as the race approaches its final laps. He's got a smooth stride. He arches his back a little too far. The kid with the odd name is pushing hard, forcing his only competition to pick up the pace a little sooner than he wants to. What's his name? "Kefleggy?" Something like that. Larsen thinks he's going to fade. He's working too hard too early.

Then, with two laps to go, the kid with the funny name takes off. Larsen can't figure out how, because he swears this kid doesn't look like he's moving very quickly at all. He's rumbling around the track more than running, but he's got a motor. There is only one other kid in the race with a shot at winning. He stays on the shoulder of the kid with the funny name, and yet it's that kid, the one with the funny name, who is dictating the terms of this race.

Coach Bob is pretty sure he knows why. The kid with the funny name understands who he is. He knows what he has, and what he lacks—which is to say, top-class speed. And yet he knows what he has to do to have a shot at winning. Son of a gun, Coach Bob thinks, sitting there in his Panama hat, am I watching the second coming of Ed Mendoza? Just like that he is back in San Diego in the early 1970s, watching those gazelles and mountain goats and dreaming of what they can achieve.

He wasn't wrong back then. Those boys-who-would-be-Toads had gotten him his first national championship. A couple of them had gone on to individual glory, too. After 1976, Ed won four more marathons in Arizona and California. Then in Boston in 1983 he ran a 2:10 and finished fourth, just a minute back of the winner, on a warmish day.

Kirk Pfeffer should have won the New York City Marathon in 1979. Kirk was living in Boulder after graduating from college. He had no plans to run the New York race that year. The Friday before New York he did two 10-mile runs and never felt better. He woke up the next morning and called the New York race director, Fred Lebow. Kirk told Lebow who he was and that he wanted to race. Lebow told Kirk he knew who he was. Pfeffer had won the Enschede Marathon in the Netherlands that August. He ran a solid 2:11:50 that day. Lebow paid attention to these things. He told Kirk to head to the airport; a ticket would be waiting for him.

Pfeffer got to his hotel around midnight. He grabbed a few hours of sleep, then woke at dawn to head to the starting line on Staten Island. At the gun he took off, feeding off the energy of the hundreds of thousands of New Yorkers lining the streets for the 26-mile block party that few knew existed a few years before. Seventeen miles in, he ran alone up First Avenue. The drunk yuppies screamed for the Colorado hippie and wondered where the hell the three-time winner

Bill Rodgers might be. Sure enough, Boston Billy was lurking, waiting to pounce during those final miles in the hills of Central Park. As Pfeffer inevitably slowed, Rodgers zipped past him in a blur and won by 87 seconds. Pfeffer would set the world record in the half marathon six weeks later, but he never stopped kicking himself for going out too fast in New York that day.

Bob Larsen had made those guys. They always said their wins belonged to him, as well. Could he do that again?

As the kid with the funny name comes around the final turn, Larsen can see that he isn't going to win. Larsen doesn't care. The little kid is maybe five and a half feet tall but he's got a chest like a fire hydrant. More importantly, he races the way Coach Bob loves. None of this sitting and kicking crap. He pushes the pace, daring the field to go with him. Stay with me if you can. With the right training, would anyone be able to?

It's kind of a stupid thought. Larsen knows this. While he's been up in Westwood, winning collegiate championships and honing those thoroughbred world champions, American distance running has all but collapsed. The supremacy of the 1970s and early 1980s has given way to foreign champions. So many of them are Africans, for whom the sport is a national religion. Americans barely register on the world stage at any distance longer than 800 meters. Everyone just assumes those rising Kenyans and Ethiopians have some sort of unique genetic advantage.

What the hell happened? Where have all the Shorters and Rodgerses and Salazars or even the next generation of Toads gone?

After the race, Larsen sees the kid with the funny name shaking the hand of the boy who has just beaten him. He looks fresh as a daisy, not like someone who has battled for two miles as hard as he could and come up just short. Then Bob Larsen silently asks himself the only question that someone like him would ask. He is, after all, the running version of the music producer, the guy who gets paid to listen to a tune on an acoustic guitar and imagine how it might sound accompanied by drums and a bass and a horn section and all the other bells and whistles that might make it as good as it can be. This is what he hears himself ask—can we be fast again?

He doesn't know the answer, but he thinks he does. He knows as well as anyone how fast we once were, and he's pretty sure of one possible place where it all began to go off the rails, with that strange misunderstood tale of Alberto Salazar.

The son of an anti-Castro Cuban freedom fighter, Alberto Salazar runs angry. He runs as though he is chasing someone he wants to kill. He grows up just west of Boston in the 1960s and 1970s, only a few miles from the start of the Boston Marathon. Alberto starts to run because his older brother, Ricardo, his hero, is a star high school runner who later attends the Naval Academy and runs a 4:07 mile. When Alberto is fifteen, he starts hitching rides to local races and competing against adults.

Alberto Salazar knows how to run only one way— to the edge of complete exhaustion. It's how he runs during the summer of 1977, when he rises at five in the morning and works all day surveying at his father's construction sites. At the end of the day, his father pulls the truck over to the side of the road seven miles from home. Alberto hops out and races the truck back to the house. It's how he has run all this summer leading up to the seven-mile Falmouth Road Race in August 1978, where he runs the first three miles in 13:43 on a hot, sticky morning and ends up in the medical tent with a temperature of 107. At a hospital, a priest administers Last Rites. He survives, but the near-death experience does not make him cautious. Quite the opposite. Peering into the abyss, he felt only the peace of his deep Catholic faith. He has no fear of what might await him on the other side.

After college, where he wins the NCAA cross country championship, he stays in Eugene, Oregon, to train and makes the 1980 Olympic team. He misses the Olympics because of the U.S. boycott, but signs on for the New York City Marathon that October at the last minute.

Most runners approach their first marathon as a learning experience. The muscles and bones have to get used to roughly two hours of pounding, and the body's nutritional system has to figure out how to process enough fuel to survive as glycogen stores become depleted. Salazar looks at the expected field in New York and thinks something else. He thinks he is faster than anyone. He decides he can win. Never mind Boston Billy, who has won this race four years in a row. Alberto understands the marathon as twenty miles of transportation and a six-mile race. Rodgers does nearly all his training on the roads. He can't match Alberto's speed. Also, Alberto knows Rodgers doesn't train as hard as he does. No one does.

In New York, he tells the media he is the man to beat. Then he runs like he means it. He stays at or near the front of the pack. During the eighteenth mile, he gets a stitch in his side. It lasts for three more miles, and when it goes away, so does he. He breaks from the field and cruises in for the victory in 2:09:41.

The win begins a run of dominance that few runners have ever experienced. The next year he has twelve weeks to prepare for New York. He wants to follow up his breakout win with a world record. He knows the record will be his when, amid a series of very long and very hard runs on wood-chip trails around Eugene, he reels off six one-mile repeats at a sub-4:30 pace. When he gets to New York, wearing a leather jacket and acting like James Dean in running shoes, he tells the media he expects to break the world record. Then he does, running the race in a then-blistering 2:08.13.*

He also delivers times that place him among the best ever in the 5,000 and 10,000 meters. The year after that he pulls off the magic double. He wins Boston in a race that will come to be known as the "Duel in the Sun," in which he runs neck-and-neck with Dick Beardsley for the second half of the race and edges him by a few yards on an 80-degree day. Then, on a temperate October morning in New York, he tries a different strategy. Instead of hanging behind the leaders at first, he goes out fast, leading the way at the front of the first pack. About a dozen runners stay with him through the first half of the race.

They begin to trail off in the next miles, as the race makes its way over the 59th Street Bridge into Manhattan. When Salazar surges

---

* This world record was actually removed two years later. After a re-measurement of the course using stricter regulations that accounted for elite runners who know how to take the shortest route on every turn, the New York City Marathon was determined to be 148 meters short of the world standard. Salazar was not pleased.

after the 18-mile mark, on the Upper East Side, only one runner dares to go with him, Rodolfo Gomez of Mexico. Salazar throws down a few 4:30 miles, but Gomez stays right on his shoulder, into and then through Central Park. With a little more than a quarter mile to go, they cross a dirt path in the park. The motorcycles leading the way kick up a cloud of dust. Salazar chooses this moment to make one last push. When he emerges from the dust cloud, he has a seven-yard lead. He stretches it to 10 and then 12 yards up the final rise to the finish line. He glances back over his left shoulder in the last moments. He sees Gomez trailing behind, hopelessly. He turns back around to prepare to break the tape. He is going to win again, and the next year, and the one after that, he thinks. He is certain in two years he will rise to the top of the podium in the Olympic Games.

At this moment in 1982, American sports fans don't really know much about distance running, but they know one name. They know Alberto Salazar. They know he is the best. His timing is perfect, too. His glory comes just as the massive wave of that first running boom in the United States is cresting. He becomes one of those athletes who singularly define the sport in which he performs, like Mark Spitz in swimming or John McEnroe in tennis. When a third-grader runs a flashy mile time, adults will ask, "Who do you think you are, Alberto Salazar?" Alberto Salazar is running. Salazar knows this, too. He has one final goal—winning an Olympic gold medal. If he does that, rather, when he does that, immortality will be his.

As he crosses the finish line in New York, there is no way he can possibly know that once he breaks this tape he will never win a big race like this again.

Just as quickly as the glory came, it starts to slip away. In the spring of 1983, he strains a groin muscle while training for a marathon in Rotterdam. He shuts out the pain, trains as hard as he ever has. He can't do better than fifth. It's the first marathon he enters but does not win.

He gets colds and sore throats and respiratory infections. A miserable cough and cold sends him to a last-place finish in the 10,000 at the World Championships. Bronchitis keeps him out of the

Falmouth race. He finishes sixth in the Fukuoka Marathon in Japan in December 1983. More bad luck comes the following March. In New Jersey, at the World Cross Country Championships, he twists his knee and finishes seventh. Still, he doesn't rest. There is a gold medal he needs to win. He keeps training and develops a stress fracture in his foot. Altering his stride to compensate for the balky toe and knee, he strains his right hamstring at a 10,000 in Europe.

On the day of the Olympics, when he is supposed to transform into a legend, he is never more mortal. He slogs to a fifteenth-place finish in 2:14.19. Within a year, he will lie on an operating table twice, as surgeons try to repair the tendons in his knee by scraping away scar tissue. They try to relieve pressure on his hamstring by releasing a fatty lining they are sure is constricting it. The procedures and the continuing injuries further disrupt his stride. They do nothing for the lingering and exhausting respiratory illnesses that he simply cannot shake. He tells himself he just has to wait until the 1988 Games to get that elusive medal. Yet when '88 arrives, he won't even make it to the U.S. Olympic Trials. On his way to running immortality, Alberto Salazar has run into a wall.

Bob Larsen watches all this from a distance. He doesn't know Salazar personally, so he is as mystified as anyone about his collapse. The rise and fall of Alberto Salazar becomes the mysterious terror tale of American running. At twenty-four, he is the greatest distance runner on the planet. At twenty-six, he is washed up. The crash is so sudden and seemingly so inexplicable. Larsen assumes there must be a reason, but whatever that reason is, he is fairly certain over-aggressive training is not solely to blame. He will be fully certain of this before too long. This idea that soon takes hold, that Salazar ran himself ragged and out of a career that might have been so great for so long, Bob Larsen just doesn't buy it. The human body he knows doesn't work that way.

There are several reasons for Salazar's collapse, though even Alberto won't know many of them for another decade. He suffered from exercise-induced asthma and depression. In his thirties, he takes Prozac, and his world goes from black and white to color.

He even manages to win the 1994 Comrades Marathon in South Africa, a 56-mile footrace that is a favorite among ultra-runners. In retrospect, given that Salazar suffered from these two physical ailments, it's a wonder he won any races at all.

No one, though, knows about any of this when Salazar is crashing and burning in 1984 and 1985 and 1986, when he is disappearing from the rarefied world of elite running when he should be peaking. The best distance runners often run their fastest marathons in their late twenties and early thirties. Salazar is long done by then, unable to overcome the stress fractures in his feet and the tendinitis in his knee and the severity of the strained hamstring. These are all perfectly normal problems that anyone trying to be the fastest marathoner in the world has to face from time to time. Usually, a period of rest does wonders. Alberto Salazar never learned how to rest.

What most elite runners do know about Salazar is this—no one ever ran harder, or more intensely, than he did. In races and in training, he ran with an unrelenting ferocity. If Terry Cotton always ran as though he was being chased by a man with an axe, then Salazar ran as though he was the man holding the axe, chasing down anyone who dared to get across the finish line more quickly than he could, or even just complete a workout. He never bothered to try to hide any of this. *Stay with me if you can, because I know you can't.*

So when the fastest distance runners in mid-1980s America talk about Alberto Salazar, this is what they talk about—be careful, or else you, too, might run into a wall. Perhaps, some of them come to believe, all of us are born with only so many miles in our legs. They are like the physicians of the 1950s, who believe the human heart is born with only so many ticks, rather than understanding it as a muscle that can grow stronger, or weaker, depending on how it is used. You want your running career to be finished by age twenty-five, they say? Then run yourself ragged like Alberto Salazar. Want a long and fruitful career? Ease back on the mileage and the intensity. That way you will avoid burnout and injury.

Bob Larsen knows something else—it's the surest way to avoid winning as well.

—

The decline of Salazar coincides with the rise of the British middle distance specialist, Sebastian Coe. Coe, the son of an aristocratic English family, takes the middle distance world by storm in 1979, when he sets three world records in forty-one days to become, without a doubt, the fastest 800- and 1,500-meter runner on the planet. Handsome and learned, with a degree in economics and social history from Loughborough University, Coe is everything the mythical British gentleman athlete is supposed to be. He is the worthiest of heirs to Oxford's Dr. Roger Bannister, the legend who broke the four-minute mile. Before his career is through, Coe will win consecutive Olympic gold (1,500) and silver (800) medals at the 1980 and 1984 Games. He will still be at the top of his game at the end of 1986.

Coe is largely coached by his father, Peter Coe, an engineer who guides his career from the time he is a schoolboy champion. In 1981, he brings aboard an American physiologist named David Martin to help. In 1991, Coe and Martin publish a book called *Training Distance Runners: The Art and Science of Optimal Training by Two of the World's Leading Experts*. The book becomes something of a bible among coaches and researchers in the blossoming world of sports science because it's supposed to contain the secret sauce that went into the creation of the greatest middle distance runner of his time.

The book—a weighty tome as big as a textbook that runs nearly 300 pages—carries a warning about the need to balance the tension between training and stress. It's healthy advice, then and now. But Coe and Martin also advise against running at your hardest for more than 20 minutes. They suggest a top college 10,000-meter runner will do fine training at a 6:30 pace for 10 miles and topping out at 75 miles per week. The book supports "capacity training"—what in Larsen's world are known as threshold runs—but not for longer than 5 or 6 minutes.

Then there is the so-called Rule of Specific Quantity: do the least amount of the most sensible training to bring about improvement. The idea is to err on the side of undertraining rather than over-training. Sensible, yes, but the list of champions who win without spending any time running on the edge—where the Toads and Shorter and Rodgers and Salazar lived—is a short one.

There is also almost no mention of George Gandy, the nationally recognized athletics coach at Loughborough University, with whom Coe spent the fall and winter following his father's high-intensity workouts. Those carried him through the heart of the competitive season. He spent the fall and winter on long, hard group runs with plenty of other top British runners. With Gandy supervising, they endured 80–100-mile weeks on hilly, challenging terrain. This work likely gave Coe a base of endurance. Without it, the high-intensity training may very well have been fruitless.

While everyone spends the 1980s reading the Coe and Martin tome, and gossiping about what felled Salazar, no one bothers paying too much attention to results. Within the results is an obvious, undeniable truth. Despite record numbers of participants, the line of great American distance runners has run dry.

Fall 1993, Between Los Angeles and San Diego

That thought—the desert that American distance running has become—courses through Bob Larsen's mind as he heads south on the 405, on the way to the home of a seventeen-year-old immigrant from Eritrea whose name he can barely pronounce. In the passenger seat is his assistant coach, Eric Peterson. Peterson's main purpose on this journey is to give Larsen a thumbs-up or a thumbs-down each time he tries to say "Keflezighi" correctly. "Kef-LEZZ-ghi" is what it's supposed to be.

The numbers are depressing. No American high school boy has run the four-minute mile in a quarter century, since Marty Liquori in 1967. A young woman from Maine, Joan Benoit, blazed to the Olympic gold medal in 1984 and set world records in the marathon, but there is no one behind her. The marathon world record has dropped below 2:07. Most elite American men can't break 2:10. They are nearly a mile behind the best of the best. The two-mile times that Larsen's Toads were running in high school in the early 1970s would win championships in the 1990s. Prefontaine still has his name in the American distance record books, nearly twenty years after his death. How could this possibly have happened in such a massive, wealthy country where running had boomed during the past twenty years as no one could have imagined it would?

What happened? Larsen is pretty sure the explanation is pretty simple. Elite distance runners in this country simply aren't training as hard as they used to, as hard as the Toads did back when he was spending most of his waking hours trying to figure out the best way to make people run far fast. There are other problems, too. The money in the stick-and-ball sports has exploded. They are pulling the best athletes in ways they didn't a generation before, when no one who played sports made any real money. There are even a few million kids playing soccer now. The sport was barely a thing in the U.S. a generation ago. It is especially kind to slender kids with freakish endurance, kids who might have turned into terrific distance runners with the right cultivation.

Also, the shoe companies, which have largely replaced the old collection of regional running clubs, haven't helped the situation. Americans dominate the sprints and struggle in the distance races. So the big money and sponsorships from places like Nike and adidas have flowed to the champions, the people who bring home the Olympic medals. Meanwhile, the best American distance runners are having trouble making ends meet. They are scattered across the country. They run alone.

Larsen knows he may be part of the problem, too. He's taken his eye off the ball. While producing all those gold medalists in the speed events at UCLA, he's barely given any thought or money to developing the next generation of distance demons. That isn't a coincidence. He's part of a college system that disincentivizes funding a distance runner. College coaches are paid to win track meets and championships. They have a dozen scholarships to share for the whole team, and they largely go to those versatile speed guys. Even now, on this 150-mile journey to San Diego, Larsen figures maybe he will offer a half scholarship to this kid whose name he can barely pronounce. Anything else would be a form of professional suicide.

As Larsen and Peterson approach the Keflezighi home, Larsen gets that sense of nostalgic comfort he often has when he comes to his old stomping grounds. He is back where it all began. He knows he is different now. He's driving down in a Mercedes, but he knows what happened here in this place—where the farm boy sold newspapers and worked his way through college and got his degrees and became a teacher and coach and a father figure to all these young men—is the essence of who he is.

The Keflezighis live near downtown San Diego, not far from where Bob Larsen grew up. They've been here for five years. He doesn't know all that much about them, just that Meb was born in a country called Eritrea and somehow landed in the U.S. in seventh grade. He's been winning lots of races ever since. Since Larsen first saw him run at Drake Stadium in the spring of his junior year, he's had a whale of a cross country season. He ran a course record 15:04 for 3.1 miles at San Diego's Morley Field to win the section championship, and a 15:02 in Fresno to take the state title. He finished second in the national championships, running a 14:53 on the same Morley Field course where he'd run that 15:04 a few weeks before. Larsen walks into the cramped, spotless Keflezighi home, and he realizes the times and the titles are just a tiny sliver of what the Keflezighis are all about.

First, there are a lot of them. Meb is one of nine children, and there is another on the way. They have been in the U.S. since 1987. Before that, they lived in Italy, the country Meb's father, Russom, had fled to during the thirty-year war between Eritrea and Ethiopia. The story of that escape has become a family legend. In 1981, Russom learned that Ethiopian troops considered him an enemy and wanted to kill him. He trekked 225 miles on foot, dodging Ethiopian soldiers, bandits, and hyenas along the way to safety in Sudan. From there, he caught a boat to Italy, where he lived for four years until he saved up enough money to send for his family. In 1987, the Keflezighis received permission to move to the U.S. They arrived with a few suitcases of clothes and a few hundred dollars. No one spoke much English. In Eritrean, their son Mebrahtom's name means, "Let there be light."

On one of his first days of school, Meb runs a mile in a little more than five minutes. His gym teacher called a local track coach to tell him he had a kid who is going to go to the Olympics one day. Thirteen years later, Meb will prove him right.

The Keflezighi household was hardly a sports haven though. Each day the children came home from school and sat for hours at the kitchen table studying English. A family from Mission Hills, the Van Camps, befriended Meb at a track meet early in high school.

Several days each week, Meb traveled to their house after school for tutoring sessions. The work did not come easily. English is Meb's third language, after all, but his grades and his running times were strong enough to attract interest from Harvard and Princeton and now Bob Larsen from UCLA.

Larsen and Peterson show Meb a video about UCLA. They talk about John Wooden and Kareem Abdul-Jabbar. Meb, as well as his little brother, Merhawi, known as "Hawi," are pretty much hooked. Larsen is, too. He has come here planning to offer Meb a half scholarship. He changes his mind. The Keflezighis represent the country at its best—the land of opportunity coming to life as it can when citizens offer to help, as they often do. After meeting the Keflezighis and hearing their story, he decides to offer Meb a full ride.

As he leaves the Keflezighi home that day, Bob Larsen knows he has done the right thing. He also is beginning to dream, to think about something far bigger than UCLA and NCAA championships. He knows Meb is plenty fast, but there is something about his dedication. There is this intangible fiber that has set Bob Larsen's mind racing. Maybe, he thinks, we can do something truly special with this kid. Who cares if all those foreigners, all those East Africans, have essentially taken over. Maybe, one day, this kid with the funny name, Meb Keflezighi, can make America fast again.

The one woman I have thought about leaving my wife for was an eighty-one-year-old former Minnesota farm girl named Joy Johnson.

Joy, the most aptly named person I have ever met, had sturdy, pointed shoulders, smooth, tan skin that resembled soft leather, and a leggy, slim-waisted figure women fifty years her junior would kill for. She rose with a burst in the darkness of 4 a.m. at her 1950s, four-bedroom ranch house on a quiet street in south San Jose. She read her Bible for an hour, then set out into the eucalyptus- and citrus-tree-scented air on her predawn run, her running mantra from the Book of Isaiah buzzing through her head. "But they who wait for the Lord shall renew their strength. They shall mount up with wings like eagles. They shall run and not be weary, they shall walk and not faint."

How Joy loved to run. And how she loved to race. Never mind that she didn't start to run until she was in her fifties and didn't run her first marathon until she was sixty-one.

In 2007 she won the eighty–eighty-four age group at the New York Marathon, but she finished in seven hours and 15 minutes. That was far too slow she decided. So she cranked up her training. She ran 50 to 55 miles each week instead of 30 to 35. She ran hills and bleachers at the local high school football field, and she worked to build up her core strength at a running camp in Minnesota.

The following October she ran the Twin Cities Marathon in six hours, six minutes, and 48 seconds, more than an hour faster than her time in New York the previous year.

Like any aging runner, Johnson faced enormous obstacles. Aging affects every system the body uses in long distance running. An elderly heart doesn't pump as fast or as hard, so oxygen—the body's gasoline—doesn't circulate as efficiently. An average sixty-year-old pumps 20 percent less oxygenated blood than a twenty-year-old. Like all human tissue, the lungs become stiffer and less expansive. Muscles atrophy at an increasing rate and ligaments and tendons grow brittle making injuries far more likely. Muscle strength generally peaks at thirty. After seventy, it declines 30 percent per decade. Knowing that, Joy never skimped on the strength training at the running camp Dick Beardsley (remember him, second in the Duel in the Sun) put on in Minnesota. He pushed her through a series of stomach crunches, push-ups, and hovers (holding the body in a push-up position) that helped her avoid becoming hunched as her body tired. Into her mid-eighties she ran eleven races each year, including three marathons, the 12-kilometer Bay to Breakers race through San Francisco, and the 13.1-mile Securian Frozen Half Marathon in St. Paul each January. "Cold as the dickens but it's so much fun," she told me one morning when we ran together. "I want to die running," she said.

On November 4, 2013, my girl completed the New York Marathon for the 25th time, even though she tripped at mile 16 and suffered cuts to her face. She was still bleeding when she crossed the finish line in the dark nearly eight hours after she started. She got bandaged up in the medical tent but didn't bother going to a hospital for further examination. She woke the next morning and followed the ritual that had become a part of her New York Marathon routine—she went to stand outside the Today show studios with her medal to say hello to Al Roker. As usual, Roker found her and shared a few words. She felt tired after that venture and went back to her hotel room to lie down. She fell asleep and never woke up. She was eighty-six years old.

I cried in the middle of the Wall Street Journal newsroom when I learned of her death. Then I sat down at my computer and wrote her obituary while wiping tears off my face.

A friend and fellow runner wandered over to console me as I typed. "She lived for eighty-six years, completed a marathon, and went to sleep," he said. "That's about as good a death as anyone could ever get."

Maybe he was right.

Higher

Sydney, Australia, September 2000

Bob Larsen is knocking on doors.

Everyone else has come to the Australian capital to watch or participate in the Olympic Games. He has come to do a little of that, too. His star pupil, Meb Keflezighi, is here to run in the 10,000 meters. Bob and Meb both know he has little chance of winning. That's fine with them. He's just twenty-four years old, a year out of college. His time will come. Bob just needs to figure out how to prepare him the right way. That's why he's knocking on the doors of sponsors and benefactors of the sport he can find here, 7,000 miles across the Pacific. Bob Larsen has an idea. He needs money to make it happen.

The money is not for him. Bob is just fine on that front. He retired from UCLA in the spring as one of the most successful and respected college track and field coaches. With nearly forty years of service to the state of California, he has a healthy pension and plenty of money socked away for retirement. He also got into California real estate at the right time, investing in opportunities throughout the state in addition to owning a home in Brentwood. But now that he no longer has to win championships for UCLA he has a mission. He needs to figure out how to make the U.S. competitive in distance running again, for Meb's benefit, and for his own.

He has been pondering this problem since he convinced Meb to come to UCLA back in 1993 and through those four years when Meb was beginning to develop into a grown-up runner and competing as a Bruin. Finding a solution has become more urgent the past two years, ever since Meb graduated and decided to try to make a go at life as a professional runner. In the professional game, if you don't win you don't eat.

For Larsen, it is both personal and public. He was there at the creation of the distance running boom, then he was part of the glory years in the 1970s. Distance running is like the music of his youth, an essential part of who he is that will never go away. He is going to be named the distance coach for the U.S. team at the 2004 Olympics. That means he is on the clock, and there is a ridiculous amount of work to do between now and then if his team is going to deliver something approaching a respectable performance. Here in Sydney, the U.S. has just one man in the marathon. He qualified into the team's automatic spot. Rod DeHaven, the U.S. qualifier, won the U.S. Trials, but he failed to run faster than 2:12:00. So his spot in the race is essentially charity.

There are plenty of folks, most of the running cognoscenti in fact, who believe Larsen's mission is not possible. There are no U.S. men or women ranked in the top 10 in the 800 meters, the 1,500, the 3,000-meter steeplechase, the 5,000, the 10,000, or the marathon. Even Meb, Larsen's great prodigy, is far off the pace of his top competitors. The night before the 10,000 final, Meb's father tells him that it is God's will for him to win the race. Meb and Bob appreciate the sentiment, but the 10,000-meter champions of the era, Haile Gebrselassie of Ethiopia and Paul Tergat of Kenya, can complete the distance in 26.5 minutes. Meb has just figured out how to break 28 minutes. Whether Meb's father likes it or not, God's will is going to have to wait.

Larsen believes God has enough on his plate at the moment without worrying about the fate of American distance running. Larsen, on the other hand, has been obsessing about this problem nonstop in recent months after years of having it gnaw away near the back of his mind. It's what this kid deserves, he thinks. It's what this country's distance runners deserve—those quirky souls who were once the envy of the world. And who cares what the running aristocracy thinks. There was a time when no one thought much of Monte Vista High, or the Grossmont Griffins, or a bunch of Toads.

Larsen didn't know exactly what to expect of Meb when he arrived at UCLA. He sized Meb up as a very good 5,000 guy with good range, a runner who could drop down to the mile when needed or jump up to the 10,000. There were bumps the first couple years. At

Meb's first NCAA championships, he figured he could compete for the title in the 5,000. He hung with the leaders, thinking he had gained enough speed since high school to compete with the big boys. With two laps to go, he fired his engines and closed in 1:57 for the final half mile. The leaders closed in 1:53. That meant he was a good 30 meters behind the best college runners at that distance.

Part of Meb's problem was figuring out how to manage the all-you-can-eat buffet at the UCLA cafeteria. Growing up poor in a family that would ultimately include his nine brothers and sisters, training every afternoon, he got used to ending meals a shade on the hungry side. At UCLA he packed in pancakes and waffles and a bagel at breakfast, pizza, a sandwich and soup at lunch, pasta and more pizza at dinner, which he finished off with Klondike bars. His 5'5" frame carried 135 pounds. Other runners his size weighed 10 pounds less.

Then sophomore year, he got seriously pissed when he told an academic advisor he wanted to major in communication studies. She told him it was a difficult major that only elite people should pursue. He heard what any student of African descent might hear—thinly veiled racism. At training, he began to get frustrated with the terrain of busy, traffic-clogged Westwood. He had to drive if he wanted to get to the trails in the hills above Malibu. He didn't like carrying the team of distance runners who weren't his equal. He approached the assistant coach, Eric Peterson, with the idea of transferring to Arkansas, the reigning track and field power of the day. Meb believed he would find a better group to train with there. He wasn't wrong.

Peterson absorbed the suggestion and responded with a question. "Who does Haile train with?" he asked. He was talking about Haile Gebrselassie, the king of distance running. The question carried a message. If he reached his potential, he was going to get to the point that every great runner reaches, when there is no one fast enough or strong enough to keep up. He could be that good and be a trailblazer at UCLA, Peterson said. And so Meb stayed.

He ran in the morning before class with a single teammate and in the afternoons with the rest of the squad. He cruised up the grassy island in the middle of San Vicente Boulevard to dodge the traffic in Westwood. He trekked up to Malibu, or to the beach in Santa Monica.

That spring, he won the 5,000 at the conference championship and believed so strongly he had a shot at the national championship that he visualized the race every day for a week before the meet. Then he came out flat and faded to ninth. The disappointment carried a lesson—trust your training, do not overthink a race to the point of exhaustion. "The hay is in the barn" becomes something of a pre-race mantra for him.

A year later he is the most determined, most prepared collegiate runner in the country. Ahead of the NCAAs, he attempts a six-by-800 workout. It includes one minute rest between each half mile. The idea is to start out hard, and to somehow make each successive interval faster than the last one. This is what the watch says—2:04, 2:02, 2:00, 1:58, 1:56, 1:53. In the 10,000 at the championships, he pushes the pace from the moment the gun fires. He wins by nine seconds.

Four days later, just before the 5,000, Larsen spotted him stretching in a downpour. Everyone else was hunting for cover. Meb smiled at his coach. He doesn't even seem to know it's raining, Larsen thinks. In the race, Meb hung with the lead pack until there were three laps left. Then it was time to go. He won by two seconds to become the first NCAA double-champion in the 5,000 and the 10,000 since 1985. For the first time Meb thought, maybe I can make a living doing this.

In the summer, a stress fracture in his foot hobbled him, so he got a late start to the cross country season. He and Larsen crafted a training plan that had him peaking at the national championships in November. Worry about nothing else, Larsen told him. At the Pac-10 championships, he was leading with Bernard Lagat of Washington State, but developed a stitch in his side. He thought of what Larsen had told him. Keep your eyes on the big prize. He let Lagat go, knowing a conference championship was not the goal. Two weeks later, at the cross-country nationals in South Carolina, he led a pack at the front that included five future Olympians through the first two miles in 9:08. At the four-mile mark he told his friendly rival Lagat it was time to go. Lagat couldn't manage it, so Meb went alone and won by seven seconds.

The spring championships didn't go as well. Meb was flat early in the 10,000 and decided against pushing the pace like he usually did. With 600 meters to go, three Stanford runners jumped him and blew him away. Food poisoning felled him ahead of the 5,000. It's fine, Larsen told him. He still had one of the great college running accomplishments on his résumé—he'd been just the third NCAA runner to win the 5,000, 10,000, and cross country championships in the same calendar year. He won the indoor 5,000 national championship that year, too. More importantly, he had embraced the idea of being a trailblazer.

With his four years of college eligibility gone, it was time for Meb to figure out how to be a professional runner. He and Coach Bob decided the path of least resistance was to take advantage of his five-year scholarship and its free room and board so he could stay in Westwood and train with Larsen. Larsen even sold him his first car—a 1973 Ford LTD. It was about as big as a small aircraft, but at $50 the price was right.

He solicited all the shoe companies and got a $30,000 sponsorship deal with Nike that included some nasty reduction clauses. If he didn't perform, the salary dropped. It's the best he can do. Welcome to the cruel and uncoddled world of pro sports. There was also a wakeup call that summer, when he ran the 10,000 at the Goodwill Games in New York. He got lapped. Welcome to the senior circuit, son. Then, with his scholarship complete, he had to find yet another way to fend for himself, so he moved to the United States Olympic Committee's Training Center in Chula Vista, about fifteen miles south of downtown San Diego. It was a spartan life. A shared room and a basic daily routine of eat, train, sleep, repeat. There is good food though and Meb also had a part-time job at the welcome center of the complex to make a little cash.

Larsen, who was finishing his last year at UCLA, drove down a couple times a week to oversee Meb's training. It sort of works.

He bunked with a race walker named Tim Seaman, who taught him the trails through the mountains on the edge of the Mexican border. His friend and college rival, Adam Goucher, invited Meb to move to Boulder to train with him. Meb considered the offer, but then decided that his LTD probably wouldn't make it all the way, so he stayed in California.

He boosted his mileage. Larsen had been upping it 10 percent each year, and it finally surpassed 100 miles a week for the first time.

He took seventh at the national cross country championships, which got him a spot in the worlds, where he finished 26th and was the top American. He did two 5,000-meter tune-ups ahead of the Olympic Trials in Sacramento.

In that race, Meb did what Meb had been doing since high school. He stayed cool for the first chunk of the race, in this case the first six kilometers. Then, with two miles to go, he put down a 63-second quarter to separate himself from the lead pack. Pushing the pace, he stretched his lead to 20 and 30 meters. It nearly disappeared on the final straightaway, as Alan Culpepper, the six-foot Texan, sprinted to try to catch him. Not that it mattered all that much. In the Olympic Trials, third is as good as first. At the finish, Meb raised an arm and leaned to win by three hundredths of a second in 28:03.02.

It was a nice win, and it was Meb's first professional national championship. But he and Larsen both knew how much distance remained between Meb and the world's best distance runners, those vaunted East Africans who had been hogging medals and victories and posting record times no one thought possible just a few years before. There was plenty of chatter about the supposed genetic advantages of the Kenyans and Ethiopians. Some suggested that the unique shape of their long and thin lower legs, and even something as yet undiscovered about the innate efficiency of their hearts and lungs, made the East Africans so much better. The difference between Bob Larsen and nearly everyone else in the U.S. was that he thought all this theorizing about the advantages was way overstated. Now it was a matter of figuring out how to prove it.

For several years now Bob has been studying the science of altitude training. It's not so different from the early 1960s, when he became obsessed with the connection between heart rates and success. Back then it was an understanding of the heart as a muscle like any other. The more it works the stronger it gets. Train the heart to beat quickly for a longer period of time, over all those miles of running on the edge without a break for rest, and you will be able to run farther, faster than you ever have.

From his research, Bob now understands that the East Africans, who are going to take all the distance medals here in Sydney, are doing plenty of threshold training, piling up those 130-mile weeks that America's best runners have grown fearful of, and they are running them in the highlands of the Rift Valley, which lies more than 7,000 feet above sea level. Even better, they are running through the valley, to school, from village to village, from early adolescence. They pack miles into their legs and gain a head start of five or ten years. That amounts to a roughly 18,000-mile training advantage over many of their competitors from the rest of the world.

There's a smattering of elite U.S. runners who train in Boulder, like Shorter did, at 5,000 feet, but most of them do their work at sea level, in or close to America's major cities, instead of in the high air of the Rocky Mountains or the Sierras. They might spend an occasional week or two, or maybe even a month at altitude, but Larsen is certain that is nothing like living above 7,000 feet and training at altitudes as high as 9,000 feet, every day with a collection of like-minded elite runners. They push each other to the edge in a way that is not unlike Terry Cotton and his Toads did back in the 1970s.

The Africans aren't genetic freaks, Larsen thinks. They simply run far and fast in groups, all the time. They are willing to endure discomfort in a way Americans are not, or seemingly haven't been urged to, or haven't been given the opportunity to try. In the U.S., the sprinters are winning all the American running medals, so the money—most of which comes from the shoe companies—follows the medals.

Financial issues aside, the numbers tell the story. Since 1968, more than 90 percent of all the Olympic and world championship medals from 800 meters to the marathon have been won by athletes who trained and lived for long stretches very high above sea level. The human body isn't naturally built for high-elevation living or training. In thinner air, the lungs instinctively breathe harder and the heart beats faster to get the same amount of oxygen. The heavier breathing forces the body to release too much carbon dioxide. That causes the acidity level in the blood to drop, producing the symptoms of altitude sickness, such as dizziness and nausea.

The body is very good at adjusting to the adverse circumstances though. Its solution is to produce more red blood cells. The red blood cells carry oxygen from the lungs to the rest of the body. That includes all the muscles we use when we run. Live at altitude for just three weeks and endurance performance begins to improve. The challenge is to find a balance between training at altitude so bodies get used to the thinner air without overdoing it and overtaxing the athlete. Exertion at elevation is exhausting and far more difficult to recover from, especially in the beginning.

There is a solution, though. Larsen and anyone else interested in the subject have come to know the work of an American cardiologist and former competitive cross country skier named Jim Stray-Gundersen, and two other sports science researchers, Rob Chapman and Ben Levine. Stray-Gundersen has become the world's leading expert on the effects of altitude on sports performance. He works closely with Norway's Nordic athletes, who dominate their sports in ways that no other country dominates another, even though there are only about four million Norwegians. The trio has developed the concept of athletes living at a very high altitude—helping to increase the production of red blood cell and hemoglobin levels—and then moving to lower elevations to train at maximum intensity. Live high, train low, so to speak.

This is the existence Larsen thinks about creating for Meb as he watches the Olympic 10,000 go about how everyone except Meb's dad thought it would. Meb, who has been battling a touch of the flu, is running about 40 seconds behind the leaders, and on the back straight of the final lap, he looks up to watch on the video board as the epic battle between Tergat and Gebrselassie plays out. It's depressing and breathtaking all at once. He's so close to the top of the running world and he is also eons away. It's as though he has a really, really good seat from which to watch the competition. Bob has a plan to change that, a plan to make Meb into something and someone Meb does not yet understand is possible.

The plan to turn Meb Keflezighi into one of the world's fastest distance runners started to take form in the winter of 2000. There were no dramatic pep talks, or an early morning wakeup for an especially taxing run up a mountain. There was merely a moment of concluding thought, after years of consideration, when Bob Larsen finally decided that giving Meb, or any other American runner, a prayer at challenging the Africans was going to take more than just a few extra long runs every month and a few more challenging interval sessions. What Meb needed, what every quasi-talented distance runner in America needed, was nothing less than a 180-degree shift in how runners and coaches at every level, and even the journalists who covered the sport, thought about the life and existence of the long distance runner.

Few who pondered what it might take to create the world's greatest distance runners thought of teams of Toads trying to kill themselves together. Hell, they didn't even think of Oregon's Ducks, even though the Land of the Bills (Bowerman and then Dellinger) had produced Prefontaine and Salazar and a host of other elite runners.

They thought of lonely souls out on roads and woodsy trails at all hours of the day and night, chasing both glory and a kind of ethereal meaning. They gravitated to tales of the so-called runner's high, that alchemist's mix of endorphins and transcendentalism. Distance running was not merely sport but religion. To run long and hard and fast was to pray, to meditate, to search for deeper meaning, a meaning that can only be approached and understood after so many miles, so many hours of rhythmic breathing, after the second wind gives way to the third and a state of levitation. In this state, the feet do contact with the ground, but never actually land on it, and the legs and the heart feel like they can do this all forever, alone. Within the movement lies enlightenment.

Larsen gets all this New Age stuff, but the sport he fell in love with and has dedicated his life to understanding is mostly about competing and achieving in the most elemental way. You head to the start line in little more than a pair of shorts and sneakers, and try to go faster than everyone around you. In a perfect world you go faster than you, or anyone else, has ever gone before. That's Larsen's religion. The meaning comes from winning, or at least running to win, and being as prepared as you can possibly be on race day. You may not always finish first, but you always train and prepare for success.

You don't achieve meaning on some lonely transcendental journey. At least the Africans aren't doing it that way. You do it with a team, training hard together every day, often twice a day. You adhere to a plan that tests and stretches the outer edge of what your body believes it can endure. You make yourself uncomfortable. In the case of the Africans, that means living in modest stone homes, with limited plumbing, eating only the most basic grains and proteins, and existing at altitudes where the comforts of what Americans would consider the basics of everyday civilization don't exist. There isn't anything particularly spiritual about it. It's just the hard life of running—with teammates committed to the same goals you are. It doesn't work if you are alone, and at sea level, with little in the way of coaching or guidance or support. The problem is, that's the way every elite distance runner in the country seems to exist right now.

Larsen doesn't expect the best American runners to move to the wild or live in huts. But he wants them to come together for a cause that is larger than their individual selves, and to learn to live and train so far above sea level that the numbers they see on their watches after training runs won't make any sense to them. At first they will wonder if they are getting slower. Eventually though, they will learn the meaning of living high and, eventually, on some days, running even higher. He also knows there is only one person who can help him teach everyone to do this.

Joe Vigil doesn't look anything like a runner, probably because he isn't one. Built like a mailbox, he never has been a competitive runner, not in any sort of serious competitive way. However, Joe Vigil is one of the country's great running coaches, and he might be the smartest sports physiologist in the world. Bob Larsen is smart enough to know what he doesn't know, and some of what he does not know, or does not have experience with, Joe Vigil does.

Born in 1929, just as the U.S. economy was collapsing, Vigil played football and dabbled in track in high school in Alamosa, Colorado, located just above the New Mexico border. After the Navy, he returned home to Alamosa, to attend Adams State University, where he got a degree in physiology and, eventually, a job coaching football and track at the local high school. He wasn't Knute Rockne or anything, but his mix of tough love, inspiration, and hard work got the most out of his kids and made for some decent teams that punched above their weight.

The first turning point in Vigil's life occurred in 1965, when Adams State scheduled an exhibition track meet against his high school squad. Vigil's crew won. Not surprisingly, a few months later, he got offered the job at Adams State. The following year a second crucial turning point of Vigil's life occurred when he decided to attend a running symposium at the University of New Mexico led by Armond Seidler, director of the sports sciences department at the school and one of the pioneers in the new and growing field. Seidler had taken note that the 1968 Olympics were going to take place in Mexico City, at an altitude of some 7,000 feet. This was going to create a unique challenge for American athletes, most of whom lived and trained at sea level.

Seidler decided to attack the issue as a scientific problem, to figure out what challenges running at an altitude very similar to Albuquerque's might pose. He and a team of scientists had divided the issue into twenty-one different modules. They included altitude's effect on blood volume, respiratory capacity, the enlargement of the left ventricle, and the capacity of the body to produce more enzymes that can help ward off exhaustion. As a physiologist, Vigil felt like the subject matter was right up his alley, and he might learn a few things that could help him coach at Adams State, where the elevation is 7,540 feet above sea level.

By the end of the weekend, Vigil had found his calling. Now he understood the potential he could unlock within the runners at Adams State by having them train the right way. There were inherent advantages to living where they did. By the time he was done coaching at Adams State in 1995, his teams had won nineteen NAIA and Division 2 national cross country titles and ten individual championships. In 1992, his runners scored a perfect 15 at the national championships, taking the top five places.

In the 1980s, Vigil became fascinated with how small countries in Europe, especially Finland, with only about five million inhabitants, could produce so many great distance runners. He concluded their system of educating and licensing coaches was superior to what existed in the U.S. The Finns had something else though, something they referred to as "Sisu." The word does not have a direct translation into English, but it is a combination of commitment, stubbornness, fearlessness, and a willingness to risk and endure pain. If American distance runners were going to reverse their increasingly downward slide, they were going to have to learn Sisu.

While Bob Larsen was tending to all those thoroughbreds at UCLA, Vigil was creating a culture unlike anything else that existed in the U.S. He immersed himself in how to measure exertion rates, constantly taking readings of his runners' heart rates; their "VO2 Max," which is the maximum amount of oxygen an individual can process during peak exercise exertion (essentially, the size and efficiency of a person's motor); and their lactate threshold, which is the moment when the production of lactate in muscles begins to rapidly increase, limiting the flow of oxygen-rich blood. He was essentially writing the science behind the concept of running on the edge—and how to do it many thousands of feet above sea level—that Larsen instinctually came to believe in the 1960s.

He preached five fundamental ingredients of a training regimen.

First, there was work on basic speed and power, which took the form of repetitions of 60–400 meters. Intervals of 60–200 meters were all-out sprints. For intervals between 300 and 400 meters, runners should start with their long distance race pace, say, a 4:45 mile, and get faster with each repetition.

Second, threshold runs, performed at 85–87 percent of the pace at which an individual runner reaches his lactate threshold. These runs lasted anywhere from 20 to 80 minutes, depending on the age and health and speed of the runner.

Third, there were the long endurance runs, lasting from 30 minutes to three hours and run at 70–80 percent of the heart rate measured at the lactate threshold—that moment on the edge of exhaustion—or 75–80 percent of the velocity at the VO2 Max. There was an added instruction for this one—the second half should be faster than the first half. So start at 70–75 percent and end at 80 percent.

Fourth were the mid-range intervals—800s, 1-kilometer and 1-mile, and 2- and 3-kilometer repeats. At sea level there are two minutes of rest between each interval. At altitude, it's three minutes. Blood analysis and other testing reveals that these workouts increase fat metabolism. They also speed up the production of the aerobic enzymes that help the muscles use glucose for energy, plus they produce additional capillaries and mitochondria, those cellular power plants.

Fifth were the recovery runs. Nothing like following up a hard morning workout with a 45–80-minute run at 30 percent of the maximum heart rate. Yes, nice and easy, but running to recover rather than resting.

Vigil's runners, their lungs feeling squeezed in the middle of any hard workout, learn how to survive a 12.4-mile run that begins at 7,500 feet and treks up to 11,000 feet in the San Juan range of the Rocky Mountains. There is the 25-mile Rock Creek Run that winds through the high plain. They do that once a week. They run through the soft dirt of the Great Sand Dunes National Park, and they run over the 400 miles of trails on the Forbes family ranch, where, with the exception of the occasional pickup truck, they are alone with the deer, the occasional moose, and all other forms of wildlife. In other words, Sisu.

By the mid-1990s Vigil has spent so much time spreading the gospel of altitude training, and sharing information with foreign coaches, and winning national championships, that thirteen national track federations are sending runners each year to Alamosa to work with him. First stop is the local hospital, where he gets their blood levels so they can develop a baseline. That way they can see how they have improved after four or six or eight weeks at 7,540 feet. Amazingly, of the thirteen national track federations to send runners, the U.S. track and field federation isn't one of them.

Larsen knows the absurdity of that. He knows what Vigil has put into practice is the scientific justification for everything he pushed for with his Toads a generation ago. He knows that Vigil understands the group dynamic of this sport, that the collective gives the individual strength. Vigil has even put words to the evolution that occurs when an elite runner commits to a team and its ideals. The collective integrity of the pursuit becomes the foundation of the mission. We give back to a team and a sport by giving to ourselves, by pushing our physiology into a new territory, to a place of near-desperation.

It was in the winter of 2000, when Meb was tromping through the hills of the Olympic Training Center in Chula Vista, that Larsen first reached out to Vigil. Vigil was working with a small group of postgraduate runners in Alamosa. Larsen, who was trying to get some company for Meb, told Joe to bring his crew out to San Diego for a stint to escape the worst months of the Colorado winter.

Free room and board, and plenty of high-quality trails in the area. Vigil decided to give it a shot. There, Larsen and Joe discussed the ultimate vision of the kind of team he wanted to create. Six men and six women—even though Larsen has barely coached women—based somewhere very high, maybe in Mammoth Lakes, California, elevation 8,000 feet, but within a thirty-minute drive of 5,000 feet and trails scaling to 9,000 and higher. A five-hour drive south is the Olympic Training Center, where they can live and train for free if the snow gets too relentless in the eastern Sierras in the winter, or if they need a few weeks at sea level.

Larsen had been holding camps for his UCLA runners at Mammoth for years. Maybe the owners of the ski area will help out with lodging? They might like the idea of marketing the area as a running Mecca where the elite of the elite want to be based. It's an American version of what the Africans are doing.

Unbeknownst to Bob and Joe at the time, there's also a collection of owners of road races in the U.S., Running USA they call themselves. They love the idea of creating an elite team and are trying to figure out how to support it. They know distance running and their livelihoods will likely collapse if the U.S. can't produce some champions to inspire the masses. It's been fifteen years since Salazar crashed and burned, and the country stands to lose another generation of potential greats.

Joe Vigil is seventy-one years old. He's supposed to be edging into retirement and moving to Arizona. He's still got a group of penniless and good-but-not-great postgraduate runners in Alamosa, including one woman, an Arkansas graduate named Deena Drossin, who is knocking on the door of elite and needs something like what Bob Larsen is talking about, in the worst way. He knows how depressing the numbers are. In 1980, there were 188 Americans who ran the marathon under 2:20. Now there are about 20 who could achieve that. In Japan, over the same time period, the numbers have grown from 59 to nearly 80. In Kenya, it was one in 1980 and more than 500 now.

If we can get the money, Vigil tells Larsen, I'm in.

With Meb's Olympic race over, Larsen is free to resume his hunt for funding. Some of the smaller shoe companies are flirting with a contribution. Larsen wants the big fish, though. He wants Nike. In the final days of the Olympics, he's got a meeting set with John Capriotti, the company's head of track and field. The Swoosh has to support this, he figures.

He sits down with Capriotti over lunch at Nike's hospitality center on a bright warm day of the Australian spring and lays out his plan. Capriotti rolls his eyes. Really? You actually think you can beat the Africans? Yes, Larsen says, he does.

Capriotti is about as convinced as Geoff Hollister was a quarter century before, when Larsen told him he had a pretty talented group from San Diego called the Toads that he thought just might be good enough to do some damage at the national championships. Nike was a fledgling company then, still existing month-to-month, teetering on the edge of bankruptcy every so often, hand-selling its trend-setting products. Now it is a multibillion-dollar, worldwide enterprise that owns basketball, thanks to Michael Jordan. It even has a golf division, launched to support its new flavor of the month, Tiger Woods. The Swoosh has become one of the world's most powerful brands.

Well, Capriotti explains, if Nike were to get involved, it would expect to get a clean shirt, meaning the runners would wear a singlet with the Swoosh on it and nothing else.

That's not what this is about, Larsen explains. This isn't as simple as a commercial opportunity, a sponsorship to promote shoe sales. This is about reviving U.S. long distance running, the sport that is the reason Phil Knight and Bill Bowerman created Nike in the first place.

Sorry, Capriotti says. The payoff is too unlikely. We're going to pass.

That's fine, Larsen tells himself. This is how it always is.

When he meets up with Meb for a post-Olympics sit-down, the conversation quickly turns away from the lessons of the Olympic track to how much work remains and what's next. Then Coach Bob breaks the news to his star student. We're going to the mountains, he says. Those Africans who take all the medals in these championships, we're going to make you into one of them.

That is exactly what Meb Keflezighi wants to hear.

"Look at me," the doctor says.

I am sitting on the edge of the table in his examination room. The bottom of my legs hang over the side. He wants me to look at him so I don't look down at the eight-inch needle he is about to slide into the soft notch on the side of my right knee. Behind the needle is a glass tube filled with cortisone, the steroid that you really aren't supposed to put inside your body. JFK used to have shots of cortisone every day for his back. They say it was eating away at his body by the end.

There's an MRI that shows I have a torn meniscus. I remember feeling the rupture as I lunged for a soccer ball during an early morning game with a bunch of middle-aged hackers some months before. Then there was five days of skiing with my girls out in Utah. I ate lots of Advil because other than running, skiing is the thing I always want to do. I live to fly through powder and ride the chairlift with my growing girls. A couple of them are teenagers now, women of few words when it comes to talking to their dad, except on chairlifts, where they talk to me all I want. A few days after that trip, I followed through on my plan to run the Central Park Marathon. It's an unfancy neighborhood race that covers five laps around the lower loop of the park. It has about 1 percent of the participants of the New York City Marathon and zero percent of the support, though such races have their own, low-key charms. My knee hasn't stopped aching since. Now I can barely walk. I really don't want to have surgery.

"Don't look at the needle, look at me," the doctor says again. He's a sports medicine physician, a friend and a hard-core runner and triathlete. He wants me back on the roads almost as badly as I do. That's why I go see him.

It slides through skin and tissue and I feel the pressure of the fluid being pushed out of the syringe and into the swelling mass around the meniscus. He tells me the relief will come almost instantly, that within minutes I will *be able to straighten my leg as I have not been able to in weeks. That will allow me to work the muscles around the knee, build some strength back on the bike and in the pool and with some bends and squats. This is what I have to do if I want to keep running as I age. "There's nothing wrong with you other than you're getting older," he says. "It's what we do." He pushes on the top of the syringe one more time to get the last bit of fluid out of the needle. I look down, ignoring his instructions, because I do want to see that thin, long metal buried in my leg.*

"Don't worry," he tells me. "You'll be back."

Up High

*Mammoth Lakes, California, Stanford,
California, Winter–Spring 2001*

This is not the Mammoth Lakes that Meb Keflezighi remembers from his college days. That Mammoth Lakes, the one he enjoyed in the sparkling late summer, was filled with crisp mornings, warm sunshine, and raucous dinners with his teammates.

Meb got his first taste of Mammoth as a freshman at UCLA, when Larsen hauled the cross country team there for a preseason altitude camp. He was running for maybe 20 minutes on the endless trails, the cracking blue sky and the peaks of the eastern Sierras looming above him, when he turned to a teammate and asked him what the chances might be of moving the UCLA campus to Mammoth Lakes. Not so good unfortunately. He and his teammates took turns getting lost on the Inyo Craters trail, which runs off the Mammoth Scenic Loop, and travels through a forest filled with towering, ancient Jeffrey pines. The payoff is a series of volcanic craters, a couple of which are filled with blue-green water and look like small lakes. The views stretch for miles, from the San Joaquin Ridge to the White Mountains. He was a long way from downtown San Diego.

This Mammoth is cold and lonely. The calendar says it's the tail end of the winter, but spring comes late at 8,000 feet. The mornings are more frigid than crisp. The sun isn't all that warm. The company is limited to Bob and Philip Price, a top U.S. distance runner, but hardly a substitute for the entire UCLA distance crew. They are bunking together in a condo each night, then hitting the roads and the trails of the eastern Sierras each morning. It's something of a trial run for Bob, and even for Joe Vigil, who is in close contact with Bob on this little venture. It's a three-week jaunt to altitude at a time when Meb is running as well as he ever has, solidifying his place as perhaps the country's top young distance runner.

The streak started in March, in Jacksonville, Florida, at the Gate River Run, a 15-kilometer race (9.25 miles) across the St. Johns River and through downtown Jacksonville. It's a distance nearly every long distance runner loves—long enough to scare away the speed specialists but short enough to go nearly full tilt on their toes from the start. For the elites, it's the first big race of the spring, a testing ground to show how well-prepared they might or might not be for the more high-profile events of the spring and summer.

When the starter's pistol fired Meb headed to the lead. At the end, a little more than nine miles later, it wasn't even close. Meb averages a 4:39 pace and beats Alan Culpepper by 21 seconds to win in 43:14. Rod DeHaven, the lone American to qualify for the Olympic marathon in Sydney the previous year, is 82 seconds behind, or more than a quarter mile.

Then Meb headed off to Belgium for the World Cross Country Championships, the first international measuring stick of the year. In near-freezing weather, Meb battles his way to 13th place. More importantly, he and Abdi Abdirahman, Nick Rogers, and Bob Kennedy, who at thirty-one is part of a kind of lost generation of U.S. distance runners, manage to take third place in the team competition. There are three Kenyans ahead of Meb, but there are plenty of other East Africans behind him, including Kenyans and Ethiopians. Maybe, Meb thought, I can become one of those Africans who finish at the front. And this was the moment when Bob decided to see just what Meb might be able to accomplish with a month in the mountains. When they returned from Belgium, he delivered the message—it's time to go up high.

Sounds good, Meb said. Then, days later he's sharing a two-bedroom ski condo with Bob and Philip Price, his old rival from Arkansas. There's a sleeping loft that Meb starts out in, since Bob is the coach and he gets one of the bedrooms. Meb has his books, his Bible, even a chilly creek near the condo, with water at roughly 45 degrees, which is perfect for soaking his legs after a run. Still there is little else to do but sleep, eat, train, and do it all over again.

Weather permitting, they can head up to 9,000 feet and run the rugged terrain around Lookout Mountain or Bald Mountain. For intervals, there's a dirt road near the Owens River, where the water is so clear and the sun so bright it looks like the ice-covered, granite faces of the mountains are immersed in it.

If it's snowing too hard up high, they can pile in the cars and drive forty minutes down the mountain to Bishop, where there's even an old gravel track 4,000 feet above sea level. Meb loves that track and the chance he gets to run on the watch and see if this life is actually working. Sometimes it seems like it is, sometimes not. Running at altitude he keeps seeing ugly times when he looks at his wrist, times that wouldn't even qualify them for some of the top competitions.

One afternoon, it's snowy up high and windy and miserable down in Bishop. Running fast is near impossible. The spring season is coming. The social pickings are minimal. He begins to think this might not be working at all. He longs for the warmth and comforts of the Olympic Training Center in Chula Vista, the warm San Diego breezes, a city, even a big town, where the social options might be a little more plentiful. Living like this, so remotely, with such a singular purpose, has never been the American way. "Do we really need to be doing this?" Meb barks at Larsen.

Yes, he says. We do. Trust me.

Meb and Bob stay in Mammoth until the end of April, when Bob decides it's time for a tactical strike. There's an international meet at Stanford the first week in May. The word around the circuit is that Bob Kennedy is eyeing the 10,000 at Stanford for an assault on the U.S. record, set in 1986 by a Minnesotan named Mark Nenow. It's one of those records that annoy the hell out of Larsen when he thinks about the crappy state of long distance running in the U.S. Nenow's mark of 27:20.56 is nearly a minute slower than the world record at the time. The world was already past that American best time in 1984, two years before Nenow set his mark.

How was it possible for the world to have gotten more than a minute faster since then but for Americans to have stagnated? Now, Kennedy, whose U.S. records in the 3,000 and the 5,000 had been set in the mid-1990s, was figuring an American record in the 10,000 would serve as the capstone to a career. As the top U.S. distance runner of the post-Salazar generation, he's got a fancy six-figure Nike deal and a sneaker named for him. The "Zoom," it's called.

Meb is still running under his $30,000 deal from Nike, with penalties in the not-very-fine print if his performance slips. Whenever Meb sees John Capriotti from Nike, he asks him what it's going to take to get a six-figure deal. "Cap," as everyone knows him, always has the same answer. Start with an American record, he says, then we can talk.

All April in Mammoth, Meb was fairly certain that the U.S. record in the 10,000 isn't attainable, not by him, at least. He's never gone faster than 27:53 at that distance. Whether he's doing threshold runs along the rolling roadways, or intervals around an old cinder track, the numbers aren't promising much in the way of success. He is sluggish. His legs feel heavy. His lungs struggle to grasp the air that flowed so easily in and, seemingly, all the way out to his fingers and his toes. Larsen tries to remind him he is high above the sea now, running at 4,000 to 8,000 feet. It's a world away from Jacksonville and Brussels. It's supposed to feel crappy, he says.

This is where the biggest challenge of training at altitude comes into play. Running is all about confidence, especially early in a professional career, when you are still trying to figure out who you are as a runner and a person, if you have the courage and the willingness to endure as much pain as you assume all those other guys on the start line are willing to. A developing runner's memory is also dangerously short. In the mountains, it can be hard for Meb to remember what it feels like to run fast when he is feeling sluggish and running slower, to believe he will be fast again. It's no different from the mental strain of an injury, trying to remember what it once felt like to run free and without pain.

Meb also knows that if Kennedy is aiming at this race to break the U.S. record, the field is going to be stacked. Nike will insert rabbits and pacesetters into the field to help him hit his splits. These runners will set the right pace for Kennedy to follow, then drop back and out long before the finish line. Plus, there will be a handful of other U.S. elites there (Abdirahman, Alan Culpepper, Nick Rogers) in addition to a collection of top African runners who are going to win the actual race.

That's why this is your time, Larsen tells him. Kennedy has the weight of an entire Nike-managed production on his shoulders. All you have to do, he says, is show up and run fast.

The week before the race they head down the mountain and stay at UCLA for some last-minute prep work. This is the first time Meb has been on an all-weather track at sea level in more than a month. He isn't running on an old cinder track, or on dirt or gravel trails, or on the rolling roads, and he certainly isn't a mile and a half above sea level in the crisp thin air of the mountains. He's running on the track of UCLA's Drake Stadium, in the moist spring of Los Angeles, and he's flying. On Tuesday and Thursday before the race he does mile repeats that just a week before he struggled to finish in four and a half minutes. Now his times are closer to 4:15. On the other days he works on his speed, ripping off 300-meter near-sprints in 41 seconds. All of it feels easy. Bob doesn't have to say anything. The numbers say it all. Finally, four weeks after first venturing to Mammoth, Meb gets it. He's as fast as he has ever been.

The night of the race, the field is everything Meb thought it would be. Three of Kenya's best are there—Abraham Chebii, Ben Maiyo, and Luke Kipkosgei. Japan's best distance runner, Toshinari Takaoka, has also made the trip, and the best of America is there, too. In addition to Kennedy, Culpepper, Abdi, and Meb, there are also those pacesetters to keep Kennedy on track for a time below 27:20.

As he walks to the start line, Meb realizes no one is even thinking about him, or how or where he has been spending the past six weeks. He knows this is exactly the way any runner would want it, to be the one they never see coming until it's too late. There is a part of him though that burns with rage. He, after all, was the U.S. 10,000 champion the year before. Shouldn't Nike be setting up something like this for him? Isn't he the one who should have a personal shoe and a six-figure salary?

Watching from the side of the track, Bob knows exactly what is going through Meb's head. Meb has been trying to prove to people he is more than simply a spindly refugee from Eritrea for years. It's part of what makes him so fast, so willing to invite the pain that comes with the journey to the edge. That's why this night is going to be his night. It's why Bob told him to come here in the first place.

For the first half of the race, Meb tucks in behind Kennedy and his coterie of pacesetters. They pass through the halfway mark in 13:35. Meb has never felt better, and he knows it's time to do what he always does in races that go like this—push early. He zips past Kennedy and sets his sights on the Kenyans. He picks up their rhythm. With three kilometers to go, Kennedy quits, and Meb knows the night will belong to him. He stays on the heels of the Africans, and crosses the finish line in 27:13.98, seven seconds faster than the record that has stood for fifteen years. He's also 40 seconds faster than his personal best. He doesn't win the overall race. The Africans are still supreme. But Meb is now faster than any American has ever been at this distance, and he sure as hell is going to get that boost up to six figures from Nike.

Then, a simple and obvious question ripples through America's elite running circles—what in the world went on up there in Mammoth Lakes?

And now it all comes together. Joe Vigil is ready to put his plans to retire on hold. The Running USA group, those race organizers that desperately want an American star to rev up interest in their races, decide to cast their lot with Bob and Joe and their concept of a team that trains together in Mammoth Lakes. Allan Steinfeld, the director of New York Road Runners, the organization that owns the New York City Marathon, says he will kick in one dollar for every American entrant into his race. They have 20,000 runners now, but the race is going to grow. The Houston Marathon organizers agree to contribute, and so do the folks from the Atlanta Track Club, who are connected with the massive Peachtree Road Race, one of the biggest in the country. They will buy the team a van.

Larsen also has gotten a call from his friend at Nike. Capriotti, who was once so skeptical, says he has reconsidered. After all, distance running is at the foundation of the company. It's only right that Nike be a part of this, even if they can't get a clean shirt. Plus, it's not like the folks who are going to end up in the camp are on the cusp of winning anything, so the exposure will be minimal anyway. This is about doing the right thing, he says.

Nike's earnings in 2000 are some $500 million. The company will pay Tiger Woods more than $10 million. Capriotti says Nike is willing to give Team Running USA about $30,000. Absurd, yes, but it's $30,000 Bob Larsen very badly needs.

Mammoth Lakes, California, Fall 2001

Deena Drossin is hungry. She comes by her hunger honestly. It's dinnertime in the southern Sierras, which means Drossin has already run twice today. That will build up anyone's appetite, but as her eyes glance around the ski condo where she has come to eat, her mind somehow drifts away from the pizzas and salads and a stomach that has been growling, if only for a moment. She can't actually believe all these people, with all this potential have come here to run together. This is not how things are usually done in her vast country. But as she looks around this ski condo that her coach, Joe Vigil, has rented here in the mountains five hours from the Los Angeles megalopolis, she sees most of the best runners in the U.S. Larsen, with Vigil's help, has sold the elite on their concept—if we train very hard, very high, together, we will win together. Now it's time for the two of them to put it to work.

On the men's side, among the best ones there are Meb, Deena's fellow Olympian from the previous summer, and Phil Price, who ran for Arkansas' national championship teams. Nick Rogers, an Olympian in the 5,000 in Sydney, has come. There is word that Abdi Abdirahman, the Somali-born American who was also in Sydney, will be joining them in the coming months. As for the women, Deena is here, fresh off her Olympic debut, and so is the U.S. cross country champion Amy Rudolph, as well as Jen Rhines, who won three 5,000-meter championships in college in the mid-1990s and placed second to Drossin in the 10,000 at the Olympic Trials in July. Leigh Daniel has come, too. She is best known for the collegiate 10,000 final in 1999, when her shoe came off in the middle of the race—and she still won.

As the pizzas begin to emerge from the kitchen and are placed buffet style on a dining table, Vigil tells them to fill a plate and then to listen. Bob Larsen is lurking in the background, working the room with his dry Midwestern sense of humor and sarcasm. He's letting Vigil do the talking tonight. This is Vigil's kind of room—a dozen elite runners gathered high above sea level with a singular purpose—so why not let him have center stage. The runners load up their plates and gather round to listen to one of the country's wise men.

"We believe in coming to the best place with the best people," he tells them simply. They are the best America has to offer. The rest of the world may not take them all that seriously, but that is not their fault, and that is going to change. Everything they think they know about their sport is going to change.

For Deena and most of the rest of the crew here, the road to Mammoth has been a meandering one. Born in Boston and transplanted to southern California as a young girl, Deena was the kid who rarely spoke—reserved, shy, or sometimes just plain terrified of verbal human contact. No one really knows why. Maybe it's because she is the Easterner in a world of valley girls, or the Jewish girl in a land where there aren't too many of them, or adopted. Does the reason even matter?

Then at twelve, she begins to run. She is fast, faster than anyone around, faster than all the boys, and this is how she finds her voice. Her father notices something odd. When Deena is stationary she is silent. When she runs, or when she has just finished a race, she never shuts up. At Agoura High School, Deena grows to a sinewy 5'4", and becomes one of the fastest girls in the state. The pattern holds as she wins three consecutive state cross country titles. In class or in the school hallways, she moves in near-silence. On the track, or during practice, running on the streets and hills of the San Fernando Valley, she is a chatterbox. Her talent gives her authority, a kind of power. Everywhere else she is a kid people find easy to overlook. When she is wearing shorts and a pair of running shoes, and has just blazed over a cross country course and broken the tape, other kids and adults, even coaches, shower her with attention and ask her for advice. She dispenses it freely and with joy. The running, her God-given speed, makes her feel significant.

She decides to attend Arkansas for college. It's the best track and field school in the country. Nestled in the Ozark Mountains in the northwest corner of the state, Fayetteville provides near-perfect training terrain. Here though, running becomes more complicated. For the first time she is very good but not great. She wins a handful of conference championships, including two in the indoor 5,000, that mind-numbing 25-lap race around a 200-meter track, but she can never quite break through and become a national champion, which is the thing she was so sure was going to happen after high school. She is as surprised as anyone that there are women who simply seem more talented than she is. When she doesn't win, she doesn't decide she needs to work harder. She decides that the hard work may not come with much of a payoff since she may not have the final gear that the women who are edging her out at the end of the race seem to possess.

She hangs around Fayetteville to train some after graduation. She wonders why she is doing this. The women who beat her in college will still be there, and then there are all those other women from both the U.S. and other countries that probably have more than she does. How can she possibly top them?

One afternoon, she goes to see her coach, Milan Donley, and she tells him she thinks she is done with running. It's time to get on with the rest of her life. That's fine, he says. She's done plenty for him and helped his Razorbacks collect a couple more conference and national championships. He has just one question—have you done everything you possibly could have done to become the best runner you can possibly be?

He knows she hasn't, and he knows she knows this, too. She knows she has never fully committed her body and her mind to being the best. She has never lived the ascetic, all-consuming life of a professional long distance runner, a life that usually happens in a remote area, where the air is thin and a small collection of like-minded souls toil together. She also knows why. That level of commitment carries a certain risk. To do everything possible and to still come up short is to know that you really don't have something that the people finishing in front of you have. As satisfying as it might be to know you have given something every ounce of energy you have, the satisfaction carries the most painful truth for any prodigy when it ends up falling short.

Maybe you don't need this, Donley says, but if there is a part of you that needs to do everything you can possibly do before you give this up, then you need to call a coach in Alamosa, Colorado, named Joe Vigil.

Later that day, back in the solitude of her Fayetteville apartment, Deena taps out the numbers to call Vigil. He answers in his usual deep, gruff voice. What could he do for her? Deena talks about races, ones she hadn't won, ones she had dreamed of winning since she first started running. She doesn't know if she's good enough, she says, it isn't clear she has the innate talent she thinks she needs to compete at the highest level. But maybe, she says, she does have it, and training at altitude is what she needs to get over the hump.

Vigil listens, and then he says something no coach has ever told Deena before. You know, he says, the races don't matter. In this sport, success is all about the principles you live by.

He tells her what life is like in Alamosa, running on southern Colorado's high plains, living workout to workout in a city that no one would describe as cosmopolitan. He talks about his team of runners, how they train together and eat together and push and love one another. He doesn't ever mention winning or talent. Running, he says, is about building great relationships, setting goals for personal development, then trying to reach them, about bringing people into your life and venturing out on a journey with them.

As Deena listens, she begins to think that she knows nothing about the sport and how to pursue it. It is an awakening, the moment she hears a truth she has never heard before. When she hangs up the phone, she looks around her apartment and begins to think how long it will take to pack up everything. Not long, it turns out—by the next afternoon, her Jeep is packed and she is on her way to Colorado.

There she waits tables to pay the bills and she runs, roughly a dozen times a week, usually with the men, because Vigil doesn't have any other women in his stable. Slowly he boosts her mileage, from 70 to 80 and then 90 and 100 miles a week. Every run has a purpose, everything is measured. There are races, too, those things that Vigil says aren't supposed to matter, until they do.

She runs only with men. The men count her as one of them until she starts winning. Then, as the wins pile up, they have one of those weird, jealous athlete moments. They tell her they don't like her much and never did. She's hurt, but fuck them. She's here to stay whether they like it or not—and they get a talking-to from Vigil that gets them back on track. She becomes the national cross country champion in 1997, and sets a personal record of 15:40.83 in the 5,000 in 1998. The next year brings another national cross country championship, and in 2000 she wins the Olympic Trials in the 10,000. At the Sydney Olympics, she battles an Achilles injury and finishes a disappointing 18th.

After recovering over the winter, like Meb, she wins the 15-kilometer Gate River Run in Jacksonville. Deena goes at a 5:18 pace. She wins by 13 seconds at 49:09 over thirty-four-year-old Sylvia Mosqueda, a former national half marathon champion. She wins Frank Shorter's Bolder Boulder 10K in June, and then the moment that changes her life happens to Deena on a summer visit to her parents in the San Fernando Valley.

She decides to set out on a morning run from Sycamore Canyon through the hills northwest of Malibu down to the ocean. It's an astonishingly beautiful nine-mile run, through largely undisturbed park land that feels even more isolating because it is so close to the center of Los Angeles. It is a bright California morning, the kind that reinforces all those native emotions about this being the most spectacular state in all the land. When she gets to the beach, she pauses for a moment to gaze at the ocean. She leans down to pick up a clump of sand, then lets the grains sift through her fingers.

She hasn't actually thought about how she is going to get back to her car, but as she looks back from whence she came, back to those pale green and yellow desert mountains, she knows she wants to run back. She doesn't care that the return, away from the sea, will be basically uphill. If someone asked her at this moment if she felt like running to San Francisco, she would undoubtedly answer "yes, of course." And so she starts the trek, rising, sometimes severely, sometimes gradually, through the hills back toward her car and home.

The whole venture is over in a little more than 100 minutes. She is faster at the end than she is at the beginning. When it's done she's ready to go 100 minutes more. Driving back to her parents' house, she's knows exactly what she is going to do when she gets there. As soon as she is at her childhood home, she puts in a call to Joe Vigil. She tells him about the run to the beach. She tells him she wants to try the marathon. He has never mentioned the distance to her because he wanted her to reach this conclusion on her own. He tells her he has been waiting to hear her say these words for two years, and that they are going to Mammoth Lakes to turn her into one of the best marathoners in the world.

This is not a decision anyone makes lightly. Being a competitive marathoner is a relatively miserable existence. The essence of training the body to run fast after 20 miles is borderline torturous. Seemingly endless miles in high remote locations. Long journeys at the threshold, even a bit of speed work to make sure the legs can come alive in the final mile if the competition requires it. Then, after intense training cycles that last anywhere from ten to sixteen weeks, race day approaches. Because the stress on the body is so intense, there are only two bites at the apple each year for elite marathoners. Come down with the sniffles, or a fever, or a queasy stomach, or tweak your calf muscle in the days leading up to the race and, well, tough darts. As for the race itself, running 26 miles at a pace that ranges from roughly 4:55 to 5:30 per mile, is a very good way to become incomparably nauseated, or worse. Sometimes, marathoners die.

Let's do it, Deena says.

They gather each morning at 8:30 in town at the Looney Bean coffee shop, then head off in different directions in small groups, depending on what the day calls for. Bob has let them in on the routes Meb and Phil Price ran in the spring. Want to press? Head up to 9,000 feet and run the rugged terrain around three lakes. The intervals happen on that two-mile loop around Lake Mary. On one section, Deena figures out a way to cut out a section of the loop just so she can beat Meb occasionally and boost her confidence.

They measure their progress on an 8–10-mile run that will become their standard and a test for anyone who ever goes to train in Mammoth. It begins on Benton Crossing Road, but they eventually call it Green Church Road because there is a little green church there. The road rolls across the terrain of the high valley to a set of rocky peaks known as the Glass Mountains. The phrase "Green Church Road" becomes shorthand for a killer, 6–17-mile test of grit where everyone lays it all on the line. Larsen and Vigil send runners out in stages, depending on their speed, so toward the end of the run they can be racing one another to the finish. They take the drives down the mountain to Bishop, and the old cinder track at 4,000 feet. Deena doesn't like it much. The "Shitbox" she calls it, since it's riddled with holes and ruts and could be a sprained ankle waiting to happen.

Now that she's pursuing the marathon, her regimen shifts. She moves from sets of four one-mile repeats to eight. Her threshold runs stretch beyond 10 and 12 miles. With speed no longer the ultimate necessity, she replaces 400-meter repeats with 5Ks. She goes 135 miles a week, sometimes 25 at a time. There is plenty of pain, but a strange pleasure in the pain, too.

She makes her marathon debut in New York in November. She runs the first half in 1:13:43 and the second half in 1:13:15 to finish in 2:26:58, in seventh place. No American woman has ever run her first marathon faster.

The Road to Athens

Mammoth Lakes, 2003

Running, like most sports, is a copycat endeavor. Whatever the best are doing, that's what nearly everyone else does.

Soon nearly everyone wants to come to the eastern Sierras, or some version of it. After 2001, the best American distance runners stream in and out of Mammoth for stretches long and short to see if the Mammoth magic can rub off on them. Abdi Abdirahman, Ryan Hall, Ryan Shay, Dan Browne, Brian Ball, Elva Dryer, and others all do stints in the mountains seeing what secret wisdom Larsen and Vigil and his protégé, Terrence Mahon, can impart. Some stay, others depart for elite running groups that pop up in the Northwest, where Nike and Salazar launch their Oregon Project. It's a special team for Nike-sponsored athletes. The company pays for coaching and helps with lodging and food—but then they own you, controlling every facet of your health and wellness, including diet and medication, even some that push the boundaries of the world's anti-doping laws.

After getting his promised bump to a six-figure deal with Nike, Meb sticks with Bob, of course. The Hanson brothers, runners and running store owners based in Michigan, launch a similar team in the suburbs of Detroit with the help of Brooks, the shoe company. The idea that distance runners, as individual as their sport might be, are social animals who can thrive within a team structure catches on like wildfire. It turns out no one really knew just how lonely the vast majority of distance runners in the U.S. really were, or how hard it is to get to the edge alone. The Africans in the Rift Valley have been training this way for years. How much did it help? America is about to find out.

Salazar and Nike make their proclamations about setting out to create the best team in the land. They will pursue their goals with the same sense of propriety with which Nike guards all its other research. At the other end of the spectrum are Larsen and Vigil, who are happy to share the information they have gleaned with anyone interested in learning about it.

Want to see Meb's training log? Have a look. A typical week might show a morning with six one-mile repeats, another morning with a 12-mile run on the edge of the threshold, another with three five-kilometer repeats, and still another with a morning at the Shitbox with a series of 400s and 800s that turn his legs into butter. In the afternoons there are shakeout runs for 30 or 60 or 80 minutes.

Larsen and Vigil have no loyalties to anything other than doing all they can to make Americans better at running far fast. But everyone who visits the Sierras learns fairly quickly that the secrets of Mammoth aren't really secrets at all. They are science—sleep high to increase red blood cell production, then wake up and run your tail off with the group—always think about the group. Stack up a combination of long runs, speed workouts, and medium-length jaunts at the precipice of total exhaustion. Don't worry about the time on the watch, focus on effort, intensity, on a total commitment to the task at hand, which is to run, eat, sleep, and then do it all over again.

Larsen's quest is about something else, too, the larger concept of making every mile and every minute count as much as it can, which is something that can help anyone in both running and in life. Because if you do that up high, where it is hardest, then, when you come off the mountain, you feel the power and you begin to imagine doing everything that once felt like a dream.

As the calendar flips to 2002, Meb begins to think hard about the marathon, too. He has made steady progress in the 10,000. He wonders though if he possesses the speed to run with the best of the best at that distance. At Stanford the previous May, when he was breaking the American record in the 10,000, he passed the Kenyan Kipkosgei on the final lap. As he edged past with about 200 meters to go, Kipkosgei glanced over at Meb and said, "Not so fast young man." Then he surged and left Meb to settle for fourth place and his American record. Meb has never officially broken four minutes for a mile.

Meb has shaved 40 seconds from his own personal best and set the U.S. mark, but Haile Gebrselassie's world record is another 50 seconds faster. Meb's fastest 10,000 time is 27:13. Haile's is 26:23. Matching that would mean speeding up his pace by more than eight seconds every mile for 6.2 miles. Championship races, like those at the Olympics and the biennial World Championships, are run at a slower pace, and there is a premium on a runner's closing speed and the final quarter mile. In a tactical 10,000-meter race, Meb can close in about 60 seconds, but to win the race he probably has to close in 55 seconds. That may be more speed than Meb has in his legs. As the old saying goes, sometimes you really can't put in what God left out. He may have to leave the 10,000 to the runners who are just a little bit faster if he ever hopes to make an international podium.

He tells himself there are three iconic distances in track and field—the 100 meters, the mile, and the marathon, especially at the Olympic Games, where the men's 100, raced on the first Saturday night of the meet, and the men's marathon, usually the last event of the Games, serve as bookends to the competition. There are no Olympic Games or World Championships in 2002. Larsen has been nudging him in this direction ever since the American record in the 10,000. With that record he's got his spot in the Nike stable locked up for the foreseeable future. For Larsen, life and running are always about what's next. He tells Meb he can make the jump to the marathon with little change to his regimen other than a weekly long run of more than 20 miles. It's the logical moment to try something new.

In addition to adding new races to their portfolios, Deena and Meb decide to put down roots in Mammoth. Deena and her future husband, the former 1,500-runner Andrew Kastor, who is now her physiotherapist, buy a house, and in April Meb does, too.

He is twenty-seven years old. He has never lived without a room-mate. He has avoided paying rent for much of his adult life. A classic immigrant child, he has banked much of his disposable income and sets his sights on a $492,500 three-bedroom house at 141 Mammoth Knolls Drive in Mammoth Lakes. His older brother, Fitsum, tells him he's nuts. Why in the world would he want to plunk down that kind of money for a house in the woods. Meb says he was born in a village and that is where his heart is. He doesn't need the noise and traffic of the city. Give him books to read, trails to run, a television to watch, and altitude to fill his arteries with red blood cells and he's good. He is comfortable in the quiet. Larsen, who has made himself financially comfortable through real estate investments in San Diego and Brentwood, tells Meb, if you don't buy the house, I will. That's all Meb needs to hear. The mountain creek with the 45-degree water to soak his legs is about a mile from his back door.

With the top male and female American distance runners now turning their focus to the marathon and living within a mile of each other, the focus of Team Running USA falls into a marathoner's rhythm. It is not for the faint of heart or legs. It means 10–140 miles per week, run over twelve sessions. Hence the need for all those baths and massages and muscle rolling and napping and eating right.

It will start with a dozen miles on Monday morning at 8,000 or 9,000 feet, and a weight session in the afternoon focusing on core strength and explosive power from the legs. Tuesday morning is for intervals. The elevation depends on how they are feeling. Wake up ready for a challenge, how about some two-mile repeats at 9,000 feet? If that seems like too much to some, then maybe a group hops in a car and drives down to 5,000 feet for eight one-mile repeats with a couple minutes to recover between each one. There's a three-mile warm-up and a three-mile cool-down before and after each interval session. Tuesday afternoon brings another five to seven miles at a conversational pace and a long weight session at the gym.

Wednesday is a progressive tempo run day, anywhere from 15 to 20 miles with occasional surges built in, followed by a venture to the gym in the afternoon. Those who still have life in their legs head out for a bike ride in the twilight. Thursday is easy day—10 miles in the morning at 7,000–9,000 feet, not a killer pace, maybe 5:45–6:00 minutes per mile for the men, 6:00–6:15 for the women. Then another half-hour run in the afternoon, with more fun to be had at the gym. Friday is hard-core tempo day. Three-mile warm-up, then, depending on how much time remains before the next race, 5–15 miles at marathon pace or faster at roughly 7,000 feet. That has Meb leading the men down to a sub-4:40 pace and Deena taking the women to the neighborhood of five-minute miles. There's a three-mile cool-down to finish things off—for the morning. The afternoon brings another 4–7 miles of easy running.

Saturday means another 10 miles at a relaxed pace in the morning and a 30-minute jaunt in the afternoon. Nothing too heavy because Sunday is the day to go long—somewhere between 20 and 28 miles that may start in the 6:30- or 7:00-pace range but are a minute or more faster than that at the end.

Just as they do on Green Church Road, Bob and Joe figure out how to group the runners in pods of two or three, depending on their speed, staggering the start times so they are finishing in clumps at the end, racing one another to the finish. Bob also loads up his Jeep or the saddlebags on his bike with fluids and food and gets in the right spots so the team can drink and get a snack every three miles just like they would in a race.

At night there are the dinners, a movable feast of carbohydrates and protein, of rice and potatoes, salad and deep-colored vegetables, grilled meat and fish and chicken, whatever can healthfully fill the team with the three and four and five thousand daily calories. Meb especially loves his himbasha, the thick Eritrean bread his mother makes and sends to the mountains or to wherever he is racing. One night the dinner's at Meb's home, where he rents bedrooms to other members of the team. Then it moves to Deena's, then to Joe's place, then on to any of the other ski condos where runners are piled in.

There are jaunts down the mountain for any number of races. Cross country championships, national track meets, and distance races of any and every length, from five kilometers to half marathons. This is not so easy. It means a five-hour drive to Los Angeles or San Diego and then long flights to races across the country.

No matter. Deena has a big moment in Jacksonville in the spring, when she crushes the American record on the 15K by 57 seconds. In the fall of 2002, she takes a shot at the Chicago Marathon in October and Meb signs up for the New York race in November. They do not go all that well. In Chicago, Deena stays with the leaders for the first 10 miles, but by the halfway mark Great Britain's Paula Radcliffe makes it clear that this is her day. She passes 13.1 in 69 minutes and cruises to a best-ever 2:17 finish. Deena trudges to a sixth-place finish in 2:26 on the flat-as-a-pan Chicago course. It's nothing to sneeze at but it puts Deena nearly two miles back of where she eventually needs to be. All part of a process, Joe Vigil thinks. We'll get there.

In New York three weeks later, Meb makes the classic rookie mistake. He surges with the leaders after the 16-mile mark as they come off the Queensboro Bridge and head up First Avenue, through the roaring throngs. Bob told him not to do this. Three miles later he's overheated, the ice water he tosses over his head feels like it freezes his brain. Then he starts going backwards, giving up places and precious seconds. He finishes in 2:12:35. That puts him a mile back of the winner, 35 seconds outside the Olympic qualifying standard, and cuts his appearance fee of $30,000 in half since he doesn't break 2:12. At the finish line, he shakes his head at Larsen. The top-ranked American in the 5,000 and the 10,000 tells his coach he's never doing this again.

Larsen nods and tries to deliver maximum empathy. Inside, he's close to laughter. He knows Meb is full of shit. The kid said the same thing to him when he ran his first college 10,000 at UCLA. He knows how addictive that feeling of flying up First Avenue with the leaders can be. He has no doubt Meb will rest up and recover and be back at this.

Meb spends two months visiting his relatives in Eritrea. When he returns to California in January, he tells Bob he's going to run Boston in April.

There are times in a coach's career when it is just as important to know when to tell someone not to run as it is to tell him how to run. Bob takes his measure of his runner and the calendar and tells Meb this year's version of Boston may not be his moment. During the past twelve months he has racked up national championships at 12K, 10K, 8K, seven miles, and 5K. The New York Marathon is the lone bleak mark on his record. Bob fears that if he sends Meb into a world-class field on a tricky course in Boston, with its deceptively easy first 15 miles and brutal second half, Meb could get so chewed up by the race and the competition that he may wave off the idea of being a marathoner.

Boston is always a crapshoot. A cool day with a wind from the west and it's a course that can produce world-best times. But a warm, early-spring morning, or a storm blowing in from Boston Harbor, and those 26.2 miles from Hopkinton to Kenmore Square can become an absolute bear. Meb might even miss what was then the Olympic cut-off time of 2:12. Also, a rough winter in Mammoth with a race in Boston looming in April could force Meb down to sea level, and at this point he needs every minute in the mountains he can find. Bob tells Meb to aim for Chicago in October, a flat race without the klieg lights of Boston and Heartbreak Hill. It will also give him a solid four months to recover for the 2004 Olympic Trials marathon the following February. Meb has been listening to Bob for a while now. He doesn't stop here.

For Deena though, there is no time like the present. Nearly thirty, she is two years older than Meb, heading toward marriage, and then, before too long, likely motherhood. She has come out of Chicago unscathed. She didn't head to Africa for two months, and with the blessings of her coaches she signs on for the London Marathon in April. Like Chicago, it's another flat, cool course, perfect for someone still learning her way through the distance.

She does not disappoint. It is once again Paula Radcliffe's day. She sets the world record, pacing herself off a handful of elite men and searing London with a time of 2:15:25. No one is close to her. But Deena finishes third and there is so much to like about her performance, so much to prove once again that Joe and Bob are on to something up there in the eastern Sierras. Deena's time of 2:21:05 breaks Joan Benoit's American record, which has stood for seventeen years. It also lowers her own personal best time by five minutes, or about a mile better than she ran just six months before in Chicago.

And yet, it is not just the time but the way she has achieved the time—and a spot on the podium—that has Joe and Bob feeling very good about their little experiment. For the first half of the race, Constantina Dita of Romania and Susan Chepkemei of Kenya fight to keep up with Radcliffe. Deena, meanwhile, pays little attention to the leaders. She has made a plan for the race, and decides to race the plan, clicking off 5:25 miles all morning long. In the final miles, Dita and Chepkemei come back to Deena and Catherine Ndereba, who finishes second, a little more than a minute ahead of Deena. It's the sort of race someone has the smarts and the confidence and the lungs to run after she has a half-dozen marathons under her belt. Deena has just two.

Six months later, when Meb gets his chance to make his coaches look smart on the streets of Chicago, he does. With national championships at 8K, 15K, and 20K already won, his marathon goal is simply to get under 2:12 so he can nearly guarantee a spot at the Olympics if he finishes in the top three at the trials. He resists the temptation to push early and fly with the leaders, and he beats his debut time from New York by two and a half minutes, finishing in 2:10:03, inches away from sub-2:10, the unofficial line between very fast and world-class. When it's over, he cools off by doing something he never could have imagined eleven months before in New York—he goes for a short run.

Southern California, Fall 2003

There are moments when this train ride from Los Angeles to San Diego is as pleasant as modern transportation can be. It's an easy, three-hour glide down the coast. The tracks hug the shoreline for the last hour and a half, from San Clemente down into San Diego. Grab a seat on the west windows of the train and let your mind wander as you gaze at the big blue sea.

This is not one of those moments for Sue Larsen. It's not clear when exactly this train ride shifts from reverie to misery. One moment there is the sea and the sun out the windows as she makes the journey from her home in Brentwood to another one they have purchased on Mission Bay in San Diego. The next, everything goes black. The train is making an emergency stop. Sue Larsen is being rushed to the closest hospital.

It's the second time this fall Sue Larsen has passed out. The first time, doctors quizzed her about her days leading up to it and got the usual rundown of activities—up by 5:30, gardening, tennis, some housework, more gardening, checking in with her grown children. Not much in the way of fluids. Dehydration, she was told. This episode will prompt a new battery of tests. When they are over, the diagnosis she receives will be far less benign. Twelve years ago, when she was forty-eight years old, Sue underwent a mastectomy to treat the aggressive cancer doctors found in her left breast. Now the cancer has returned. It's all through her abdomen, in five organs. Treating it requires some of the most potent chemotherapy modern science has created. Doctors tell Sue Larsen that they might be able to buy her three years.

For thirty-three years, Sue Larsen has been the consummate coach's wife. While Bob worked to recruit and develop athletes virtually every day of the week from early in the morning until into the evening, driving vans to meets and races, providing meals and premium care for other people's children, Sue Larsen took care of theirs—a son, Erik, and a daughter, Michel, feeding and raising and driving them to school and all manner of sports and other activities. When game time arrived, Bob would swoop in at the last moment, just before the tip-off or the kickoff or the sound of the starter's pistol.

Sue was also there for the other kids, too—all the Grossmont Griffins and UCLA Bruins. Her lemonade became famous among dozens of Toads and Griffins and Bruins. Long after Sue began providing the post-race training pancakes and lemonade to those Toads at the old house in the East County near Grossmont, or driving out to the beach to pick them up in the van after a 15-mile hard run, Larsen's Bruins would run three miles to the base of the Brentwood hills. Then they climbed two miles and 1,000 feet up the mountain to the Larsen home. There, they could break for some lemonade, or on a weekend have some pancakes. These were her kids as much as they were Bob's. So every other man or woman who wore UCLA's light blue and yellow. Whether Bob was in town or not, Sue tried not to miss many hoops games at Pauley Pavilion or a football game at the Rose Bowl.

Now she is facing round after round of chemotherapy for the rest of her life. That essentially means an endless case of stomach flu and a slew of other nasty side effects. The timing is awful, though isn't it always? The Olympic Trials marathons are just a few months off. The Athens Games are less than a year away. Bob is scheduled to spend many weeks during the next year at Mammoth, getting Meb and Deena ready for the biggest of stages.

Don't worry, he tells her, I can have Joe handle things in the mountains. I will stay down here and take care of you.

Sue Larsen will hear none of it. You need to be in the mountains, she says.

Bob does end up making certain adjustments. During some weeks of heavy treatment, he will make it up to Mammoth just in time for a key workout. He will rise at 3 a.m., be on the road by 3:30 and make it to the Looney Bean by 8:30 to greet Meb and Deena and the rest of the team. There are some days when they are staying in San Diego when Larsen will rise early, drive three hours to Westwood to make an early morning track workout for a middle distance runner he is working with, then hop back in the car to get to Mammoth in time for a mid-afternoon session.

Once in the mountains, he rarely mentions to the team what is happening in the hospitals and cancer treatment centers 300 miles away, where his wife is fighting her battle. He doesn't have to. They all know what he is going through. They don't pry. He doesn't want them to, and going on about personal struggles isn't his way. What helps is being around the mission, talking about pulling off this attempted resuscitation of distance running that makes him and all his runners feel they are working toward something larger than they are. Whether Sue wants him with her or not, and of course she does in some way, he will be back on the coast soon enough, helping her try to win each day merely by the act of living the only way she has ever lived—fully.

The only real tension arises as the Olympic Games approach. Bob knows how busy he is going to be there as the U.S. distance coach. He is also worried that Sue will feel too ill to be abroad, and there are few things worse than becoming seriously ill in a foreign country, 7,000 miles from your personal physicians. Her coming to the Olympic Games might not be the best idea, he says.

After all the work they have put in, how can she not be there? She has a plan. They have friends, friends who are happy to care for her in Athens while Bob is shuttling back and forth between the capital and the team base camp on Crete where the American runners are staying, and then overseeing the competition once it begins. Very quickly he realizes she is telling him what is going to happen more than discussing the matter with him. She is going to Athens, she says. Bob knows better than to challenge her on this one.

Spring–Summer 2004, California, Crete, Athens

An Olympic marathon is unique in the sport of long distance running. In addition to the weight and history of the race, the competition brings a unique challenge. In all the other major marathons, runners return to the same streets each year. They become familiar with the nuances of each course. In New York, they know about the deceptive hills in those five bridges, and that the real race doesn't begin until Central Park at the 24th mile. They know that Boston is flat and downhill for the better part of 16 miles, mostly uphill for five, then down again to the finish. They know about the damp chill of London, the almost eerie flatness of Chicago. The fast straight boulevards in Berlin. They come to them again and again and run them in their mind as they find similar terrain in training.

In every Summer Games, the event on the Olympic marathon course is the first and likely the last time the race will take place on that exact route. An Olympic marathon course is once-in-a-lifetime. There is no learning curve, no chance to acclimate yourself to its unique falls and rises, its prevailing weather, the sounds of its crowds and the feeling of the pavement beneath your feet, the special approach to the Olympic Stadium.

Bob Larsen first travels to Athens to check out the marathon course in the summer of 2003, following the track and field World Championships. The course has already been laid out. It will follow the historic, 42.5-kilometer journey from Marathon to Athens that gives the race its name and also a good portion of its drama—it is after all the course that killed Pheidippides two and a half millennia ago, after he ran to Athens to announce the Greek victory in the war with the Persians. As Larsen begins his drive in the village of Marathon and heads inland, away from the sea, two things strike him.

The first is he can't believe how hilly it is here. The start is tame enough as the course heads south from Marathon along the western coast of the Athenian peninsula, twisting through the seaside town of Nea Makri for the first five miles. After that, the slow retreat from the coast begins. The route ascends the cliffs through Rafina, then begins curving to the northeast and the Greek capital about

10 miles in. Running away from the sea generally means one thing—climbing. And that's what happens here. The road climbs and climbs and climbs some more. It doesn't start its slow descent to Athens and the ancient Olympic Stadium until past the 18-mile mark. Interesting, Larsen thinks.

The second thing that strikes Larsen is how relentlessly hot it is. It's a humid, punishing heat, the sun hammers down with an unsubtle brutality. It's manageable until suddenly it isn't. He knows hoping for a cloudy day is silly. There hasn't been a cloud in August in Greece in maybe 800 years. The start times for the marathons are 6 p.m., which should provide some relief, but only so much. The Athens region is one of those places where the temperature sometimes rises in the early evening, even as the sun is on its way down.

There is a reason the city of Athens holds a marathon for its general population in November, rather than when the Olympic marathon will take place, in August. Every Olympic marathon brings special challenges. This one will bring very special challenges. It will bring arguably the most challenging conditions ever, because of the climate and because the course will be so difficult. And this is why he thinks, we can make this work.

For months he says almost nothing about the Athens Olympic marathon to Meb or Deena or anyone else he is working with. What's the point? If anyone qualifies for it, then it becomes something to target. If no one does, there is no need ever to think about what it might take to run a mostly uphill marathon in the dead of summer under a sweltering sun. But then, early in 2004, both Meb and Deena get onto the podium in their Olympic Trials marathons and get to join the most elite field in long distance—they get the joy of trying to figure out and obsess over how to race for 26.2 miles in what will likely be miserable conditions.

Even better, Meb and Dan Browne and Alan Culpepper all beat the qualifying standard, saving the U.S. the embarrassment of getting only that single charity slot. Both Meb and Deena are at the top of the rankings in the 10,000 as well, and they will flirt with the idea of running both races through much of the year, even into the U.S. track and field trials in June. But the marathon is the priority. Let the speed demons fight for the 10K. The longer the race, the more that can go wrong for the favorites, especially in the conditions that Athens promises. The combination of hills and heat and the pressure cooker of an Olympic Games can serve as great equalizers. Who will be better on the day?

And so, having researched the course and studied the weather patterns, Bob and Joe get to work on their plan to get Meb and Deena on the world stage. Bob dives into research on how the body reacts under the stress of extreme heat, speaking to every expert he knows in the country. What he finds gives him hope, because heat appears to tax the body in similar ways to altitude. Stress is stress, he determines, and the lessons the body naturally learns about coping with the stress of running at altitude can be transferred to the experience of running in extreme heat, or even the combination of high heat and humidity at sea level.

At altitude, the body learns to cope with air that isn't ideal and the challenges of dehydration, just as it has to in high temperatures. The additional red blood cells help with the oxygen. Also the lack of moisture in thinner air means dehydration occurs more quickly. But there is a benefit to being slightly dehydrated in training. To counteract the dearth of fluids, the body increases the volume of blood plasma. The increased plasma works to bring red blood cells to muscles that are under stress. So not only will the Mammoth crew have more red blood cells, but by training in a state of slight dehydration because of their environment, they are going to have more plasma to deliver those extra red blood cells to where they are most needed.

As naturally beneficial as this all might seem, Bob and Joe decide this isn't enough. Running far in the kind of heat and humidity that the Olympics will bring is going to be a mental test that will be every bit the match of the physical one. They have a solution for this. As the temperatures rise during the spring and early summer in the Sierras, they tell Meb and Deena to begin bringing running tights and leggings to training, even a beanie for their heads, which is how most of the heat escapes from the body.

Discomfort is the name of the game, they explain. You are going to be uncomfortably hot from the first miles of this race. You need to become comfortable with that discomfort, and the only way to prepare for that is to practice being uncomfortable. So when the rest of the Mammoth crew is stripping down to little more than shorts or sports bras for afternoon training runs, Meb and Deena are covered head to toe in clothing, learning what it means to run fast while being overheated and extremely uncomfortable. Finally there are the runs themselves. Having seen nearly every inch of the course, Bob and Joe scour the terrain around Mammoth and find a route that is eerily similar to the journey from Marathon to Athens—a tame first six miles followed by a 12-mile climb, and then an easier final stretch into the finish. One big difference—the route they find is at 7,000 feet rather than sea level. When Meb and Deena run in August, not only will they feel like they have been on this course before, they should feel like it is easier than the one they have trained on.

Bob and Joe also tell them to stay focused on the 10,000 and try to qualify for that event, too. Just because they have already punched their tickets to Athens in the marathon doesn't mean they should let up on the speed work that helps in the final laps of the 10,000 and the final miles of the marathon, when they assure them they will be fighting for a medal. So they keep up with the strides, keep doing the 200 and 400 and 800 and two-mile repeats, sometimes, at least in Meb's case, in the Shitbox, sometimes on the trail around Lake Mary.

And they do everything else, too. Running tights and long-sleeve shirts and extra sweats and hats in the heat. Ascents that last a dozen miles or more. Training runs in the middle of the day, when the sun is the highest and the hottest. They even start in with half-hour sessions in the overheated saunas. Anything that makes intense heat feel normal. Given how far they have come these past years in Mammoth, Meb and Deena at this point would likely run backward wearing leprechaun outfits if Joe and Bob told them it would improve their performance. There is simply nothing that builds confidence in a runner like results. What they are doing in Mammoth produces results.

In May, Meb and Culpepper and Abdirahman are part of a team that beats the Kenyans in the 10K Bolder Boulder race. Then in June, in the heat of Sacramento, both Meb and Deena run the 10,000 in the Olympic Trials as though they are playing with house money, which they are, since they have already qualified. There is no photo finish this time for Meb. He beats the field by 18 seconds. A future Mammoth training partner, Dan Browne, takes the third spot. Deena wins her race by nearly 50 seconds. The success produces the luxury of the ultimate distance runner's dilemma. Which race should they run at the Olympics, or should they run both, like Frank Shorter did in 1972, when he took fifth in the 10,000 and won the marathon? Ultimately, they both decide to run only the marathon. It is the signature distance competition in any Games, especially this one, on the course that created the race. But the idea that both of them get to ponder this choice, it makes them feel like running royalty, and makes those forgettable finals in Sydney feel like they were a very long time ago.

After the trials, the usual routine for Olympic-bound runners is to enjoy the quick paydays that come with appearances at a handful of meets and races in Europe. Joe and Bob strongly advise against this. They tell Meb and Deena to play the long game here, to return to the mountains and keep that red blood cell level as high as possible until the final moment when they need to travel to Greece. They have read the research and done some of the work on their own. They know that red blood cell counts begin to drop within days of a return to sea level. The Olympic marathons won't take place until late August. Seven weeks gallivanting around Europe could wreck everything they have built these past three years in Mammoth. They are both two-time Olympians and American record holders. Their Nike contracts are solid, given their limited stature internationally, in the low-mid six figures. If they reach the podium in Athens the money will be there, and far more than the few $10,000 or $15,000 checks that could be had across the pond. Meb and Deena listen and do what they are told. Of course they do.

They return to the mountains, to long training runs and speed workouts, at 5,000 and 7,000 and 9,000 feet in winter clothing in the middle of the summer, to getting pushed every morning and afternoon by the teammates who have been pushing them for three years. There are long joyous dinners with these people at a time of year when the sun feels like it never sets, people who have grown addicted to being a part of something far larger than themselves. They start playing around with different uniform designs. They tear holes in shirts and cut them off at the midriff. They try loose shorts and skimpy tight ones. They run with a cap and without one, caps with holes in the top, visors, or ones that don't let any sun hit the scalp. The marathon is all about keeping the body cool. Often, the fastest runner is the one who manages to keep his body coolest for the longest time. Overheat and you are cooked, literally, for the rest of the race. This is why the event often favors smaller people. The smaller the person, the less surface there is and the less work the body has to do to keep itself cool.

Then they learn about the ice vests that are being manufactured and that will meet them in Athens. This is, well, different, Meb and Deena think. You're damn right it is, Bob tells them. They will freeze them the night before the race and start wearing them during warm-ups. Nothing will keep the core cooler than wearing a garment packed with frozen fluid, Bob reasons. If this uncommonly hot Olympic marathon is going to turn on body temperature, then they are going to do everything possible to keep their core body temperature as low as possible for as long as possible. If Meb and Deena are cooler at the start than anyone else, then maybe, just maybe, it will take them ever-so-slightly longer to heat up. To Meb and Deena, this idea does seem a bit nutso. But maybe it will be just crazy enough to work.

During the first days of August, they travel to Crete, to a seaside resort with five pools and a few hundred quiet bungalows. It is one of the benefits of being a part of Team USA's Olympic effort, a wealthy operation that spares few expenses for its athletes every four years. The intervening four years don't pay much in the way of stipends, and a bad year will even cost you your health insurance if you drop low enough in the rankings, but the journey to the Olympics is a first-class operation. When the time comes to head to the Games, they won't even bother with the Olympic Village, opting instead for the American College of Greece in Athens. Fewer people, less chance of picking up some unwanted virus.

But first Crete. Nearly every other country's athletes land directly into the tumult of Athens. Noise, pollution, steamy breezeless nights, venues and an Olympic Village where workers are still finishing construction and painting and plumbing around the clock in the final days before the Games.

The Pilot Beach Resort in Georgioupolis is everything Athens is not. The only sound is the sea lapping against the beach. The Lefka Ori, also known as the White Mountains, are in the distance, with caves where the Greek gods were born. The landscape is dotted with small villages. There are also miles of quiet, hilly roads to put in the final miles in the last weeks before the race.

They are no longer at altitude, but that is by design. These last weeks are all about giving the body what it needs, which is rest. With so much work behind them, their bodies continue to work to become stronger, even without the endless miles high above sea level. For Meb and Deena, the time to taper has arrived, time to search for that delicate balance between dialing back and staying sharp, between rest and rust. Deena will run one more 100-mile week before her race on August 22. Meb will put in two before his race on the 29th. A century week may sound like a lot of pounding but it is a far cry from their peak of 145 earlier in the training. They run. They eat. They sleep. They bathe in ice water. They want for nothing.

One afternoon they fly to Athens to study the course. These are the numbers they have to accept. The starting line is 148 feet above sea level. Just before the 20-mile mark the course peaks at 771 feet. During the middle stretch the course gains about 50 feet every mile, which means racing at marathon pace and climbing a nasty hill every five minutes or so.

Deena sees the course and comes away heartened. The hills aren't quite as drastic as they looked in pictures, or how she imagined them, though she knows the heat of the day and the competition will make them feel larger than they look just then. When they get to the ancient Olympic Stadium where the race will end, Bob asks Meb what time he thinks he can run here. I think I can run 2:12, he says. Me, too, Bob says, and if you run that time you're going to medal. Meb doesn't disagree. In fact, Bob thinks Meb can win.

Bob has rarely been so sure that one of his athletes is going to have success. He's known Meb for a decade. He's good going uphill and going down and he's good when it's hot. It doesn't really make sense. Meb has the 39th best time among the marathoners in the field. Paul Tergat of Kenya, the world record holder, has put up a time that is more than five minutes faster than Meb's personal best. He's a good stretch better than anyone else in the field. No matter, Larsen says. This is different. This is the Olympic marathon, in heat and on hills. A crazy fast time on the flat cool roads of Berlin is irrelevant.

Then, ten days before Meb's race, the thing that no one thinks of happens. Greek islands are filled with unattended dogs that wander the countryside in packs without an owner anywhere in sight, if one even exists. There is little rhyme or reason to where they will turn up. It is impossible to know which ones pay little mind to humans and which ones are aggressive.

On an easy run with Culpepper and the former runner and coach Terrence Mahon, a German shepherd appears. This is a problem. Meb Keflezighi, the boy from the African village, who runs in the wooded mountains of the eastern Sierras, is terrified of animals. It is not a small dog, and he may sense this. Meb can't imagine the dog not picking up on his fear. The shepherd goes right for him.

The dog knocks Meb over and goes for his throat. The scuffle lasts only seconds but in Meb's mind it feels like he is wrestling with that shepherd forever. They tussle long enough for Meb to think while he's trying not to get killed that his luck of avoiding injuries and mishaps the past year has just run out. He has no idea how this is going to end. The dog has near full control of the moment.

Then Terrence and Alan grab rocks and begin pelting it as they run at him. Now it's the dog's turn to get scared and he runs off. Alan and Terrence descend on Meb. Meb rolls over in the dirt, his legs and arms bleeding, his back and hip and knee sore and bruised. All that work, all those years and miles in the mountains suddenly seems for naught. After a minute, he rises, brushes off. He finishes the run, but he knows he is in some trouble.

For the next week and a half his knee aches when he is going up and down stairs. Fearing infections on his cut-up arms and legs, doctors tell him to stay out of the sea, and the pools, and no more ice baths either. He takes anti-inflammatory pills, like Ibuprofen, and he rubs a powder from Eritrea called tsebel on his legs. It's a chalky substance that comes from Christian monasteries in his native country. His mother gave it to him. He knows it has no power to heal his injuries, but he rubs it over his skin because it reminds him of God's power. It's what his mother would tell him to do.

On August 21, Deena leaves Crete and heads to Athens. She sleeps well the night before the race and in the middle of the afternoon boards a van to the starting line in Marathon. When she gets there, she puts on a frozen vest. It is very, very cold, because Bob Larsen spent the day before finding the coldest freezer available in the kitchen of the Olympic Village, with the help of the kitchen worker who secures a spot for the vest. The darn vests for all the marathoners didn't arrive until two days before the race, which sent Bob on a scramble looking for that optimal freezer. No matter. Now there may be faster runners than Deena at the start line, but no one will likely have a cooler core.

That is no small thing. When she gets to the starting area, two hours before the start, she calls her husband and tells him it's nearly 100 degrees. He reminds her how good she is at running in the heat. "Just go slow," he tells her. The temperature on the start line at 6 p.m. is 95 degrees. Deena isn't thinking about the heat. She is thinking about her plan for the race, and nothing is going to stop her from racing that plan. She keeps that ice vest on until just before the blast of the starter's pistol to stay as cool as she can. The other runners look at her like she is a bit of a freak. What is that woman wearing? Finally, when it's time for the gun, she discards it.

A little more than 75 minutes after the gun sounds, all hell breaks loose, just like Bob and Joe figured it might. Paula Radcliffe, the world record holder and overwhelming favorite, leads the fastest group through the first 15 miles but she does not look happy about it. These are not friendly conditions for Brits, never have been, in sport or in war, and Radcliffe runs as though heavy metal music is blasting in her ears. At the 16-mile mark Mizuki Noguchi of Japan makes a move and Radcliffe can't cover it. She waits, and then pushes again, but instead of gaining on Noguchi she gets passed by Catherine Ndereba of Kenya and Elfenesh Alemu of Ethiopia. The world's top female marathoner is in fourth and fading fast. With four miles to go, it will all become too much for her. She will stop, then try to start again. Then she crumples to the side of the road in tears, finished for the night.

Deena has no clue about all this drama, but it won't surprise her when she hears about it. Sensing just how deadly hot and heavy the air is, she basically blocks the rest of the field from her mind. She settles on a slow and steady pace and journeys up the endless incline from the sea to the hills above Athens. She is behind so many runners for so long her coaches don't even bother counting. The scoreboard tells them she is in 12th place at the halfway mark.

Bob understands the strategy. She is like a golfer playing the course instead of keeping track of whether the other golfers are making pars or birdies. He is fairly certain she is overdoing it, though. At times she is a half mile and more behind the lead pack. It's a lot of ground to make up, he thinks. And then, as the miles shrink and the night stays hot, that distance between Deena and the podium gets smaller and smaller. She isn't going much faster, but she isn't slowing down either. The group at the front is. One by one she passes them, gaining strength as she swallows each one. Then, finally, there are just three in front of her, though she thinks there must be four, because she knows she has not passed Radcliffe, and Radcliffe must be at the front, she thinks.

With a mile to go she draws in Alemu. As she passes the Ethiopian, she is so locked in on taking each next step she doesn't process the meaning of the rousing cheers from the side of the road. Only when she enters Panathinaiko Stadium, site of the 1896 Games and the birth of the modern Olympics, does she hear the voice from the public address system declare that she is in third place and cruising in for the final medal. When she hears the words she bursts into tears. She cries all the way across the finish line. It's the first U.S. medal in the marathon since Joan Benoit in 1984, and only the second at a distance of greater than 400 meters since the '84 Games.

At a beach resort in Crete, Meb watches the end of the women's race on television. His knee aches. His hip is sore. He has scabs on his legs and arms. But that's not what he's thinking about. He's thinking this is a very, very good sign. He's thinking that what Deena did in Mammoth worked, that when she runs well, he usually does, too.

—

One week later, on the final afternoon of the Games, it's Meb's turn to compete.

He's in uncharted territory here. The only marathons he has run have been in the morning, when you wake up before dawn, have some eggs and some bread, and then head to the van to the starting line. In Athens, at the American College, he sleeps in. Like most distance runners, Meb is very good at sleeping.

At 1 p.m., he wanders down to the cafeteria for a pre-race meal. He eats pasta, bread with honey, and a banana. He has small portions. Just enough to sate his hunger. Then it's time to gather his belongings for the race. At the last minute, he stuffs his official Team USA sweatsuit in his bag. It's what he will have to wear during the medal ceremony if he gets to the podium. He is planning to be on the podium.

He sits with Bob on the bus to the start line. They go through the race strategy one last time. Relatively speaking, it's not that hot. Temperatures are in the low 80s, which in theory is miserable, but under the circumstances and considering what Deena had to go through, it's downright temperate. In this moment, it's tempting to become greedy. When you prepare for 90 degrees and it's close to 80, you think you can run as though it's 50. Bob and Meb know that's not possible, but maybe the others will make a mistake.

Meb's knee also isn't perfect. He even calls his brother Merhawi to tell him about the pain, that he may have to drop out. Merhawi assures him he will not. Then they are in Marathon. They have a last chat about the runners to watch. Bob reminds Meb that Stefano Baldini of Italy has won races in the summer at the World Championships and is comfortable in the heat. Meb is fixated on Tergat, the world record holder and one of his heroes. Bob, not so much. Like Radcliffe, Tergat has made his name on cool flat courses, not on courses that rise 750 feet during the middle eight miles. He also knows the pressure of being the favorite, and the power of being among the overlooked. It worked out pretty well for those Toads all those years ago. Bob thinks this is going to work out very well for Meb.

Then Bob hands Meb the ice vest. He will wear it for the better part of an hour, staying cool as he can be.

—

In the first miles of the race, Meb focuses on staying calm and within himself. Marathons are never won in the first miles, but they can be lost there. He tucks into the middle of the lead pack, next to his teammates Alan Culpepper and Dan Browne. It's a comfortable spot, especially since no one in the field is doing anything stupid. Alan, who is 6'1", helps him scout out the water stations as they approach, which is a big help for a guy who is 5'6", maybe. After every water stop—they come every five kilometers—he tucks right back into the pack. It's exactly what Bob wants him to do. So when he sees Meb at the 10-mile mark, they trade a thumbs-up and he has just one word for him.

For ten years, they have been on this journey to resuscitate the sport that Bob fell in love with forever ago, in the country that turned him from a Minnesota farm boy into an Olympic coach, and helped transform Meb from a near-penniless immigrant boy who couldn't speak English and barely knew running was a sport into an educated adult with a college degree and one of the world's fastest men. They were on this journey before they ever knew they were on it. That scholarship Bob gave to Meb, it wasn't like the ones for Steve Lewis and Ato Boldon, whose talents were so clearly going to take them to this stage. It was something else—an honor for a family that had come and was seemingly going so far. Then the skinny little kid who hoovered Klondike Bars became an All-American, and an NCAA champion, and then the most dedicated, mission-driven professional runner Bob had ever coached. Live with a roommate until age twenty-seven? Fine. Move as a single man to a remote ski village God knows how far from another black man? Sure thing. Tough out mile after painful mile in thin air and trust that a coach knows what he is talking about when the numbers suggest he does not? Absolutely. Try to disprove conventional wisdom that Africans can't be beat and to overcome two decades of futility in American distance running? Yes, of course.

There are still 16 miles to go in the race. There are many runners in front of Meb who have covered this distance faster than he has. But as Meb sees his coach for the first and last time in the race, there is a simple message Bob wants to deliver.

"Perfect," he says. And he doesn't raise his voice. He knows he does not have to.

Slowly, and then very quickly, the lead pack thins. South Africa's Hendrick Ramaala tries to push ahead before the halfway mark, but no one goes with him and soon he sags. Brazil's Vanderlei de Lima goes 10 seconds in front midway through. Meb keeps his eyes on Tergat, who lets de Lima go, even though the Brazilian has proven he can run in the heat. With eight miles left Meb is part of an eight-man chase pack that includes Tergat and Baldini. They get word from coaches and race officials that de Lima's lead is 46 seconds. Time to go to work, they decide, and so together they push.

Three miles later they have nearly cut de Lima's lead in half. They can see he is tiring. His stride doesn't have the same power that it did a few miles back. Then, to everyone's surprise, Tergat drops away. Meb can count to three now. If this holds he's on the medal stand. He thinks he can do better though. From the recesses of his brain, he pulls out some childhood Italian and tells Baldini the two of them can go get first and second. Baldini isn't a teammate, but they have a common purpose—to catch the guy in front of them—and so on the run they seal a pact to help each other get where they want to go. The group is almost always stronger than the individual.

As they start to push harder, a deranged spectator with a history of interrupting sports events rushes from the crowd and tries to shove de Lima off course. He fails, thanks to the assistance of another spectator, but it's a nail in the coffin for the gold medal hopes of the tiring Brazilian. Nearly sprinting for the lead Baldini passes de Lima with about three miles to go. Meb lets Baldini go but passes de Lima about a quarter mile later. With a mile to go Meb makes one last push to get the gold, but Baldini is too far in front. He finishes in 2:10:55, 34 seconds ahead of Meb on a night when times barely matter. This race is all about medals, and Meb has a silver, to go along with Deena's bronze.

When Meb enters the ancient Panathinaiko Stadium in his final mile, Bob is still fighting his way through traffic and security. He doesn't make it to see Meb cross the finish and win that first American men's Olympic distance medal in twenty-eight years. Sue does. She is there. No matter how her treatment goes, and it doesn't look like it's going to go the way she and Bob want it to, in some way, she will be there, always.

For Bob, this is both entirely expected and completely unbelievable.

It feels like just days ago that eyes were rolling and heads shaking over this silly idea he had to prove that Americans could run far fast again. Everyone else thought it was complicated—all that stuff about genetics and long calf muscles and innate East African hunger. Sure, Meb was born in Africa, but he's as American as anyone Bob knows, and Deena has no African blood. Just run like a Toad would, he thought, to the edge, again, and then again.

Now it is a hot night in Athens. The sun has dropped into the Mediterranean, but the air is still thick and hot and heavy. They meet in the tunnel and share a long embrace, and a good long laugh. In a few hours, Larsen will stand among 100,000 people in the Olympic Stadium. He will watch Meb step onto the podium and bow his head for a medal. The American flag will rise, and then, after some music and dancing and speechmaking, the flame of the Summer Games will be extinguished for another four years.

This is what he knows: There are six medals awarded in the world's most prestigious marathon. The little running team from Mammoth Lakes that he and Joe Vigil started, this odd little experiment of theirs, has two of them.

Perfect, he thinks, or nearly so, which is just fine. Because this doesn't feel at all like the end of something. It doesn't feel like he has crossed some kind of finish line. It never does. It feels like the start.

Harvey Cedars, New Jersey, August 2017

"Hey, why don't you run the Dog Day Race with me," I suggest to my fifteen-year-old daughter.

I'm fully expecting her to dismiss me out of hand. You get used to this sort of thing when you have teenage children, even if you say something like, why don't you help me spend this extra thousand dollars I have burning a hole in my pocket.

We are on vacation on the Jersey Shore. The town where we stay has its annual five-mile race to benefit the local fire department the next morning. I don't usually run short races, but this year I'm thinking there might be an easy age-group award for me to grab. There is a pathetic side of my brain that loves collecting these things. So I am in. Meanwhile, my middle daughter has caught the running bug these past months. She's gotten addicted to healthy living lately. She's a vegan, doesn't smoke, rarely drinks, as far as I can tell, and has inherited my compulsion to exercise every day. More often than not, that is a late-afternoon run. I'm early morning, so we don't run together, but one day maybe, especially if I can get this running bug to stick. Running alone is getting kind of old. I'm going to need a running buddy before too long. I've got my eye on one.

Though I don't tell her that's why I'm suggesting she join the race, there is something about the way her head jerks around when I ask the question that makes me think I might have just hooked a fish here. Now I just have to reel her in. Within seconds, she is spewing self-doubt. She can't race. She's too slow. It will be embarrassing. What if she has to stop.

I know these are all absurd thoughts. She's plenty fast, running anywhere between four and six miles a day at a pace between eight and nine minutes. I love how sweaty and red she is when she is done, that look of exhausted accomplishment on her face at a time in her life when this is all so new. She's on tennis and soccer and softball teams and runs a bit in practice but it doesn't feel anything like this.

I explain to her that a race like this isn't really a race, but more like a group run, a celebration. I will run with her if she wants—she does not— and it's all about the free T-shirt anyway, a sweet yellow and blue thing that she'll have for years and get happy every time she puts it on. She says, "Fine," in that tone where this is something she really really wants to do but doesn't want to admit it, because being too enthusiastic about something as lame as running a race with your dad, even though you aren't running with him, would just be the worst thing ever.

Until, of course, it isn't. Until we cut up one of her T-shirts to turn it into a racing singlet. Until she pins a number on her shirt for the first time. Until she heads across the start line at the blast of a fire horn, moving within this little mass of humanity, a part of the human race. There's a turnaround on the course so I pass her about midway through. She's working. It's a hot, heavy, late-summer morning, but there's no way she's going to stop.

I finish about 13 minutes ahead of her, so I'm there at the finish to watch her last steps. She's still trucking along, running strong to the end. A real official race in the books. Later, after a shower, she comes up to the kitchen for a joyous breakfast. She's wearing the shirt. So am I.

Fall and Rise

Distance races and running itself rarely proceed according to plan. Just when the race appears to be won, when it seems like you have unlocked the secret truths, the unexpected happens. Intense heat or cold or miserable rain on the start line. Tweaked ligaments, turned ankles, stress fractures, busted hips. In this way, running, running far, and trying to do it as quickly as possible, may be most similar to life. Optimism may abound, but unexpected danger that rises with the most unsympathetic callousness is always lurking, always looking to knock back anyone who wants to tempt fate and believe too strongly that his running life is heading upward, ever upward.

Turn a corner and there is a car that has drifted to the wrong side of the road. Visit a doctor for dizziness or headaches, and he begins to speak about a grave illness. These aren't inevitabilities, but they are possibilities, rising to whack us whether we expect it or not. We can think we are prepared to deal with them, but we can't be, just like we can't ever truly be prepared for the torn ACL, the incessant stabbing pain of high hamstring tendinitis. This is why running—and life, too, the most important part of it anyway—always has to be about what we do next.

In its most basic form, the running motion is a controlled, forward burst that ends with a fall. Each step is a leap. Gravity brings us back to earth, where our feet catch us and push us back up and forward again. Rise and fall, and rise again. Do this roughly 40,000 times and you will cross the finish line of a marathon. Success comes not by dwelling on the step that has just happened, or the subpar training session, or even the missed workout, or the disappointing race, or the extra miles that led to the busted knee, or the nagging tightness in the oblique muscle that will not relent. Those miles, those training sessions, they are gone. Over. It can all begin again in some form if we want it to, though we have to figure out how to make it so. A new day. A new run. A new opportunity. There will be terrible races and glorious ones. Miserable, injury-riddled years and years of seeming invincibility. After the thrilling ascendance of youth, life and running become a series of episodes, of ups and down, falls and rises. Really, all that matters is what we do next.

What's that you say? *The past is never dead. It's not even past.* Good writer, that William Faulkner. Probably not much of a runner.

Meb, 2004–7, Mammoth Lakes, San Diego, New York City, Boston, London

Everything is going to fall into place after Athens. Meb Keflezighi is set to become the face of American running. There are all these ugly rumors about American sprinting stars. The doping scandals never seem to end—Marion Jones, Justin Gatlin. There has never even been a whisper about Meb, though. He is also the perfect face for an increasingly multicultural America. Now he has all that and an Olympic medal and the belief in his ability to race with the fastest, strongest distance runners on the planet. Triumphs in the big races will surely follow. Until they don't, for every reason a runner and his coach might imagine.

A little more than two months after taking the silver in Athens, Meb is dueling Hendrick Ramaala into Central Park in the New York City Marathon. At the 24-mile mark, near the Metropolitan Museum, Meb grabs his last bottle of fluid and takes a swig for the final push. That's when Ramaala sprints 40 yards ahead, too far for Meb to catch up. So close, yet second again.

A year later, a ruptured quadriceps muscle at the summer World Championships curtails his preparations for the 2005 New York race. The injury compresses his training to eight weeks. He never registers a single 100-mile week in the lead-up to the race. Still he stays with Paul Tergat and Ramaala until the final miles, only to finish third, 26 seconds back.

In 2006, he and Larsen decided it was time to give Boston a shot. It's the grandest stage in the sport, a race and a route that date to 1897. Healthy once again, he made a classic rookie mistake.

He chases the early leader Benjamin Maiyo at a lightning-fast pace through miles 16–18, those first two hills in Newton. By the 20-mile mark, three-time winner Robert Cheruiyot had caught both Maiyo and Meb and cruises through the final 10 kilometers for the win. Meb finishes third that day, running a 2:09:56, two minutes behind the winner. He tries to feel good about being the top American at his Boston debut. Next time, he thinks.

Seven months later he heads back to New York to give the race yet another shot. He loses his luggage, gets food poisoning, and ends up having to make multiple bathroom stops along the way to a 2:22:02 finish and 20th place. There is no way to feel good about that. So much for the inevitable post-Athens run of glory.

Now it's 2007 and time to begin preparing for the marathon trials for the 2008 Olympics. The race is scheduled for November in New York. He begins his road-racing year in Jacksonville's 15-kilometer race, just as he had started in 2004. He wins Jacksonville easily but ends up with a nasty blister on the bottom of his left foot. In the days after the race, it only gets worse, so he goes to the hospital, where doctors cut out the blister, leaving him with a half-inch gash. Recovering from that surgery costs him three weeks of training ahead of the London Marathon in late April. It also throws off his stride. His right Achilles tendon doesn't like the altered mechanics. After 16 miles in London, the knifelike pain at the back of his foot becomes too much to endure. He leaves the course and boards the tube to get back to his hotel.

Bob and Meb know he needs to get healthy and get ready for the Olympic Trials marathon. He can hear the whispers. Maybe Athens was a fluke, or even his peak. He was twenty-eight when he won there, entering what should be prime years for a distance runner. Yet he hasn't won a major marathon since then. In the months after London, he tries to ignore the doubts but also use them as motivation. Bob has long known that Meb runs best when he has a chip on his shoulder, when he is a little angry at the world. Bob's hopes rise when, at the peak of Meb's preparations for this trial, he runs 26 miles at between 7,000 and 8,000 feet in 2:42 over hilly terrain. It's enough to make him believe that this race in New York will be the start of something new rather than the beginning of the end.

Meb comes down with a stomach flu ten days before the race, but he is well recovered by the time the race rolls around. Bob is there, of course, but Sue Larsen is not, because she may be getting near the end. She's basically been nauseated since 2003. She loves coming to New York, though, loves to walk the streets to the brink of exhaustion. By now, she knows where every public bathroom is on the island of Manhattan. But she's just not well enough to make this trip.

Meb rides the bus to the starting line with his old training partner, Ryan Shay. Shay has moved on from Mammoth, but he was there from 2003 to 2005 with that early pre-Athens group. So many miles, so many meals, so many memories.

The route, specially designed for the Olympic Trials, calls for five laps around the lower five-mile loop of Central Park. It's not the most inspiring course, but it's spectator friendly and the Olympic Trials are the pinnacle of utilitarianism. Complete the distance. Get in the top three. Punch a ticket to the Olympics. To that end, Meb leads the way through the first dozen miles. Then his legs start cramping. He slips to second place. After 14 miles he is in third. The pain isn't going away. He tries to push but goes backwards instead of forward. By 21 miles he's in sixth place. He spends 13 minutes limping through the final 2,000 yards. He isn't going to Beijing, not as a marathoner at least. He's getting slower. Worse, not better. How can everything that worked so well three years ago—all that intense mileage so far above sea level—not work anymore?

After the finish, things go from crappy and disappointing to horrible. Meb learns that Ryan Shay collapsed five and a half miles into the race and was soon pronounced dead at Lenox Hill Hospital. An autopsy will later blame the death on an irregular heartbeat related to an enlarged heart and scarring around the muscle. Meb is inconsolable. In addition to dealing with the grief, he will spend the next several days crawling throughout his hotel room. The cramping that produced such disappointment in the race has evolved into chronic pain in his upper legs and hips.

Months of mystery will follow. Is it a sports hernia? Something more serious? Ultimately, a specialist in New York diagnoses a fractured pelvis, the result of altered mechanics and high, hard mileage.

No wonder he went backwards at the trials and was reduced to crawling through his hotel room.

He's thirty-one years old. He has been running on the edge with Bob Larsen for thirteen years. For the better part of the last six, his almost daily journeys to the threshold of exhaustion have taken their toll, as they do on every elite runner.

For the runner, more running is the go-to solution for just about anything, however mistaken that thinking might be. Bob knows this better than anyone. He also knows that no matter who is the coach, elite running has more in common with Alpine skiing than almost any other sport. What makes a downhill skier great is the willingness to tempt disaster, to fly down a two-mile stretch of ice at 80 miles per hour on two long sticks of carbon fiber. Crashes and other bad things will happen. Timing and severity are the only unknowns. Also, what happens after the high-speed tumble into the crash net. Can the skier shake it off, or fight through six or eight months of rehabilitation and make his way back to the starting gate, willing to tempt death again?

Run on the edge as often and for as long as Bob and Joe asked their runners to run, and injury is essentially as inevitable as it is for the downhill skier. When the pain comes, especially on the far side of thirty, the elite runner has to ask the simplest and most complicated question of his life—what am I going to do next?

Mission Beach, California; Eugene, Oregon;
Beijing, China, Spring–Summer 2008

When the words that every husband and every wife dread hearing finally come, Bob knows there is only one thing to do.

Sue has put up a whale of a fight and she does beat cancer in the most meaningful way. The final result of battles like this doesn't get determined with the last breath. Somehow, some way, nature grabs that last breath every time. Nature is undefeated on that count. Cancer, on the other hand, gets whipped every day by everyone stricken with the disease who lives another morning the way it is supposed to be lived, like a damn good run that enthralls and exhausts, that provides the chance for wonder and illumination, and also contemplative meditation, moments that are fast and moments that are slow, hard ones and easy ones, and others filled with all the possibility that comes with devotion and love.

Sue Larsen has kept trying to show up to all those UCLA sports events. She went to Helsinki with Bob in 2005 for the World Championships. She swam and she tended to her gardens. On so many days that followed bad nights, she asked Bob to prop her up on the hill in the backyard of the Brentwood home. From there she could see the Pacific Coast. On a clear day, the view stretched all the way to Catalina.

He gave her a phone and told her she had to call him if things started to go south, if she needed his help. She pulled weeds all day.

Sue Larsen knows what all the best gardeners know about life—success is 90 percent weeding and 10 percent seeding. Sometimes Bob's phone rang with Sue on the other end needing a hand. Mostly it didn't. Tough woman, he would think, but he knew that already. Every so often, the neuropathy or the pain or the nausea got so intense, she needed to head to the hospital, where doctors would tend to the most crucial problem, then wait for another to crop up. The idea was to keep her strong enough to continue handling the treatments that might extend all this another few months.

There were moments when she would drift, or have to battle one infection or another, and it would seem like the end had come. Then, a few days later, she'd be strong again. She would rise out of the hospital bed, and load into the car, and head home to tend to that garden—90 percent weeding, 10 percent seeding.

Then in May, Bob hears those words. There's nothing more we can do for her, the doctors say. It's time to go home. So Bob and Sue and Eric and Michel decide what that means—San Diego, the house overlooking Mission Bay, where Sue can rest on a bed in front of the window and spend her last weeks watching the water and the birds and the beach where so much of the first part of her life got lived. This is where, in the first hours of July 2008, Sue Larsen dies. She is sixty-five years old.

Bob is a private mourner. He is not unprepared for this. He has known for five years this day would come. On the inside he aches like never before. On the outside he holds himself together by confronting the tragedy of losing his companion of more than four decades, his wife of thirty-eight years, with something bordering on steeliness. Friends can't believe how normal and unfazed by it all he seems. They're wrong, of course. He is the furthest thing from normal. Sue's death is the ultimate blow. He just can't talk about it. He decides the only way he's going to survive is to be around people and do what he knows how to do best.

The Olympic Trials have just gotten under way in Oregon. Meb is scheduled to run in the 10,000 meters on the evening of July 4. Given the injuries Meb has been dealing with the past year, Bob knows this is the longest of long shots. Maybe if he's there, giving his quiet, singular words of advice and encouragement trackside during those 25 laps, Meb will find his way into the top three and make his way to Beijing. Get out of bed. Get on a plane. Get to Hayward Field in Eugene. It's all about taking the next step, and the one after that. Somehow, when Meb walks to the start line just after 9 p.m. on the Fourth of July, Bob is there.

Bob has been around Meb a whole lot more than he thought he would be during these past difficult months. Neither of them wanted it that way but Meb had no choice. When he tried to begin running again over the winter nothing felt right. The pain in his carriage returned. The fracture had failed to heal. The only training he could do was in a big pool. In water, there would be no pounding. So he relocated to San Diego, near his doctors, near Bob, and told him he planned to run each day through the water.

Bob had seen runners try to do this before. They start out full of fire, then they fade. Running in water is slow and deadly dull. You can't go fast. Developing any kind of rhythm is impossible. It doesn't actually feel like running at all. So after several days or weeks, the workouts dwindle, and the runner decides that he will run again and return to fitness when the injury heals. Somehow, Meb always steeled himself to deal with the boredom. He ran in that pool for two and three hours a day. He ran in deep water. He didn't even use a flotation vest to increase his buoyancy. He just powered back and forth through the water, lap after lap as the old folks who came for water aerobics floated a few yards away. Bob stopped by when he could, stealing time from his wife's slow fade to check in with the rest of his life, as he and his children took turns watching over Sue.

As he watched Meb plow through the pool, Bob knew the chances of any near-term payoff were extremely low, but the idea that Meb could do this, that he wanted to do this, suggested he wasn't near done. Yes, the disappointments since Athens, the whispers of doubt that had grown into a chorus since the marathon trials about his best races being behind rather than ahead of him, were taking their toll. But he told Meb they were no different than the doubts everyone always had about the kid who lacked the speed of the fastest runners, but possessed something else. These trials might come too soon, but there will be another race.

Meb got back to the track for the final month before the trials. He even rediscovered some of his power ahead of the race.

In Oregon though, the 10,000 goes about how Bob figured it would. Meb finishes 13th, running a 28:39, nearly a minute behind the winner and almost 100 seconds slower than his American record. They meet up in the warm-down area after. The Minnesotan whose genetic disposition has always kept his emotions on an even keel, and the grown-up immigrant kid raised never to show weakness. All that falls away tonight. They hug each other and have a good long cry together. For the first time since either one can remember. What they are going to do next is anyone's guess.

For Meb, it's a far more complicated question than it has ever been. In 2005 he married Yordanos Asgedom, an Eritrean from Tampa he met at an annual soccer tournament that is part cultural celebration/part mating game for the country's immigrants. They took roughly a year to get from courtship to marriage, and the following year, in 2006, they became parents. In 2008, Yordanos gave birth to a second daughter. They don't plan on stopping there. With Meb's body seemingly abandoning him, the question of whether he continues pursuing his chosen profession grows more loaded. It's not merely about him anymore. Father Time is going to win this race. He always does.

Meb knows a running career at this point in life, on the wrong side of thirty, becomes a game of catch me if you can. If he does keep running, like a boxer in a ring with a relentless, bigger, and more powerful opponent, Meb will have to dance. He will bob and weave, use his smarts to avoid a knockout and last until the final bell. Even if he does everything he possibly can, everything he and Bob and the best sports medicine physicians in the world tell him he must, he still might get crushed during years when he might have been setting off on another career to support his family. But then, is there a larger, unknowable, incalculable cost in not trying?

A month later, even Deena reaches the crossroad. Unlike Meb, her success continued after Athens, with wins in the 2005 Chicago Marathon and in London the next year. She has proven Athens was no fluke. Chicago and London, like Berlin, are where the best come to run fast. She has almost nothing left to prove. The rest is going to be gravy.

She makes it back to the Olympics and figures the minor soreness in her right foot was just a routine ache. Unfortunately, it isn't. Two and a half miles into the Olympic marathon in Beijing, she hears what sounds like a popsicle stick snapping. Her third metatarsal cracks. It is one of the bones that stretch nearly the length of the foot. It's a trauma fracture. Running long and hard for years on end, even when smart people like Bob Larsen and Joe Vigil and Terrence Mahon are doing everything they can to keep you healthy, is not for the faint of heart.

Her race is over. Like Meb and Bob though, she doesn't want to believe anything else is, though biology and her desire to become a mother make her choices a little more complicated than anything Meb or any man will ever have to confront. So what will she do next? A little more than a year after the Olympics, she will finish a disappointing sixth at the Chicago Marathon. Then in February of 2011, she gives birth to her first child, Piper. She has done the most important thing next.

Nearly 25 miles and roughly three-and-a-half hours into the New York City Marathon, I finally accepted that this just wasn't my day.

With my legs telling me they didn't want to run anymore on the final hill in Central Park, just past the Boathouse, I knew there was only one way I was going to get across the finish line. For the first time in a mediocre long-distance career that then spanned sixteen marathons, I was going to walk the remainder of what had turned into a pretty miserable day during the past 45 minutes.

Bonking. Hitting the wall. There are any number of names for it. Bottom line, you can't run anymore, and there is almost nothing you can do about it. But strangely, that's where the fun began.

No marathon can rival New York when it comes to support. The crowds heave behind the barricades for many of the 26.2 miles. With about 50,000 runners in the race—the New York Road Runners estimated a total of 51,392 finishers this year, which would be a new record for the largest marathon in history—estimates often range somewhere between one million and two million fans. I have no idea how they come to those figures, but I do know the fans are screaming at you and blasting music and holding out their hands to be slapped everywhere they can from the moment you get off the Verrazzano-Narrows Bridge until the moment you reach Tavern on the Green.

It's a massive blur of the most awesome sound. Start walking, though, and suddenly it gets incredibly personal—so personal that it almost made me think I'd been missing the point of the whole thing by trying to run as fast as I could all these years.

As soon as I started walking, the pats on the shoulder and the words of encouragement began arriving, one after another from my fellow runners as they passed me. "You're looking good, hang in there," or "Almost there, you're not quitting," many of them told me in one form or another. After a quarter mile, I lost count of how many had slowed up momentarily to make sure I got the message.

Meanwhile, over on the other side of the guardrail, fan after fan was reading my name on my shirt and yelling it out. They told me how great I looked, how close I was to the finish. Grown men and women offered me hugs. Not wanting to be rude, I took several of them up on it. It seemed like every other child under fourteen was yelling "You got this!" at me.

I felt a little bad sucking all the attention from the rest of the field, but I felt something else, too.

It had been a pretty miserable few months in the U.S. It felt like two halves of the country had been screaming insults at each other since July.

Yet on that last mile, the only thing I could hear was a chorus of encouragement and concern and support for the guy who looked like he needed the most help. It was a reminder of what we do best on a personal level.

By the time I turned back into Central Park to the strains of a band covering "Jessie's Girl" (another benefit of walking three miles an hour— plenty of time to enjoy the music), I was practically blissful. I probably could have started running again, but I wasn't going to trade that last 500 yards of strolling and goofing off with the crowd for anything.

Back to the Edge

After broken pelvises and screwed-up hips and dog attacks and holes gouged in their feet, thirty-three-year-old distance runners generally call it a career. That's what everyone was pretty sure Meb would do after the misery of 2008. All that running in pools and those massages and the rehab and the therapy looked like a fool's errand. Sometimes, there is simply no way to account for the damage that a bad-luck injury can bring. So who the hell is this guy locked in a two-man race in the final miles of the 2009 New York City Marathon.

Maybe Meb was stubborn? Maybe he wasn't able to let that chip slip off his shoulder? Maybe he couldn't think of anything better to do, or a better way to make money and provide for his growing family? Or maybe he simply thought somewhere between Green Church Road and that house he has near the ski basin, the boy with the funny name who shocked the world in Athens was still lurking, doing that running version of Peter Pan, where running faster somehow allows you to hop off the aging train, at least for a little while. In fact, it's a little bit of all of this, plus the idea that when he is out there, churning away, trying to prove to everyone that he is something more than they believe he is, he becomes the best version of himself, the true son of the man who dodged hyenas and the Ethiopian army during that very long quest for survival.

And so, after more months of rehab, and physical therapy and pool running and then getting back to the Larsen formula of repeats and the thresholds and the long runs through the mountains, Meb pulls off a win in the Houston Half Marathon in January, and then ends up at the top of the heap at the U.S. Cross Country Championships. Then he puts up a PR in London, running 2:09:21, though no one notices because London is a speed race and the time slots him into ninth place. In July he takes the seven-mile national championship in Davenport, Iowa.

Okay, fine, those are nice wins, but sure a World Marathon Major (one of the world's top five marathons—New York, Boston, Chicago, London, Berlin) with an international field must be out of his grasp. And yet there he is in the fall of 2009 by the reservoir in Central Park, with just over two miles to go in the New York Marathon, battling Robert Cheruiyot, the four-time Boston winner.

Cheruiyot is eight inches taller than Meb. He had a running résumé three times as long. He knows how to put a perennial bridesmaid like Meb Keflezighi away at a moment like this with a $100,000 first-place check on the line. Meb sees the final water station. His mind flashes back five years, to that fateful swig that cost him the lead in the 2004 race. It's too early to push, of course, except it isn't—as Cheruiyot indulges in the water station, Meb pushes the pace, refusing to let this go down to the wire. Come with me if you dare. Cheruiyot cannot cover the move. Meb wins going away by 41 seconds.

He's the first American to win this race in twenty-seven years. He's the only living American man with an Olympic medal in the marathon other than Frank Shorter. This little running career he has crafted for himself, it's a long way from over. Only fools would doubt him now.

Right?

Los Angeles, December 2010

For six months, Hawi Keflezighi has been waiting for the good folks at Nike in Beaverton, Oregon, to give him the word on his brother's contract extension. Hawi has spent the past five years serving as his big brother's agent. Like Meb, he attended UCLA. He wasn't a runner, but he has spent enough time around his brother to know the running game as well as any elite competitor.

Hawi and Meb are like Russian nesting dolls. Hawi's skin is slightly darker, and Meb is slightly taller than his younger brother. But around the eyes, where their high cheekbones suddenly cut into deep eye sockets, they are nearly identical. It's always been this way. When they were young children arriving in Europe to reunite with their father for the first time in four years, he mistook one for the other. As teenagers, they run, they work, they strive, and Hawi follows Meb to Westwood. He gets a law degree there, and he gains his brother's ultimate trust.

Since 2005, he has carved out a comfortable living for Meb. Thanks to his win in New York and the bonuses that came with it, the Nike deal reaches into the mid-six figures, though the penalties for poor performances or an off-year remain, just as they do for nearly every other runner, much to Meb's chagrin. Meb also has sponsorships with Sony, the health supplement UCAN, PowerBar, and the New York Road Runners. In good years, when he wins or places in the top two or three at big races, he can clear six figures in prize money, too. As with any runner though, the shoe deal reigns supreme. It's the key part of any runner's equipment, like a golfer's clubs or a tennis player's rackets. With running though it's essentially the only piece of equipment.

Meb has been with Nike since he got out of UCLA, when the company signed him to that $30,000 a year deal. It went into six figures when he set the American record in the 10,000, then went up again when he captured the silver in the Olympics. Running contracts can be cruel though, even for top runners like Meb. They are filled with reduction clauses that lower payments when a runner's performances slip. The reason doesn't matter. Slowing down because of injuries? That's going to cost you. Can't run because of a balky knee or hip? That will cost you, too. Sidelined by pregnancy? Tough luck. Your salary is going down, and Meb's surely did during the struggles of 2007 and 2008.

The win in New York brought in some $350,000 in prize money and sponsor bonuses. It was a much-needed boost for a thirty-three-year-old who, since the Athens Olympics, had gotten married and had two small children, plus another on the way. There was one problem though. Meb's Nike contract ran for another year, through 2010. Had it been up after 2009, when Meb became the toast of New York and American running, he might have gotten a multiyear deal worth more than $1 million. Hawi had broached the subject of an extension with the higher-ups at Nike soon after the race. They smiled politely and said they looked forward to speaking with Meb in the coming months. In other words, let's see what you do next year, then we'll talk. He took them at their word.

In June 2010, Hawi sent a proposal to Nike. All Meb wants is another two years, Hawi told them. He plans to retire after the 2012 Olympics. Carry him through that and he is happy to be a Nike athlete for life, serving as an ambassador for the brand in retirement, when he plans to coach and continue to show up at major races for charity runs and speaking engagements. Hawi had just two significant requests: keep the deal in the low–mid six-figure range it reached in 2010 thanks to his bonus for winning the New York City Marathon, and dump the reduction clauses. Meb is a big boy, he told them, an internally driven runner. He doesn't need a contract to motivate him. Meb also knows he likes to go for the win in races rather than hold back, so he makes some time like 2:12 that he knows won't be good enough to win but will allow him to avoid a reduction in his payments. Give him the leeway to run to win and risk blowing up, Hawi said. Meb merely wants stability for his young family.

We'll get back to you, the Nike folks told him.

Through the summer and fall there have been any number of emails and conference calls with Beaverton. The brain trust is noncommittal, but they continue to tell Hawi they are working on a counterproposal. He will have it soon. They love Meb. They want him to be a Nike athlete for life, too.

Now the calendar has ticked down to the final days of the year, the final days of Meb's current deal. Hawi wasn't supposed to let it come down to this. He wishes he had a do-over here. There are now only twelve days left before the current deal ends and 2011 begins. The Nike folks told him to trust them. They will do right by Meb. Even with those injury-riddled years in 2007 and 2008, he's still the only American distance runner of his generation, of the past couple generations, to win an Olympic medal or a major marathon. That's worth something, even at thirty-four. They get that, they tell Hawi. But they are also businessmen, and they know the longer they string Hawi along, the more leverage they gain. Meb has a young family. He isn't going to want to be without a shoe deal, is he? So they wait, and wait some more, and tell Hawi they are working on the counteroffer.

Then six days before Christmas, as Hawi passes another tense day in his office in the city where he ran as a collegian and got his law degree and cut deals that landed Meb in a Super Bowl commercial, Hawi opens his email, and there it is. He does not like what he sees. Nike's offer is lower, not higher. The performance reductions are there, too. Hawi picks up the phone. He dials up to Beaverton. In so many words he says, "What the fuck?"

It's not personal they tell him. It's just the nature of the business. Nike is trying to trim its roster of athletes. Meb, who is now thirty-four, has been deemed trim-able. It's highly likely his best performances are behind him, not ahead, they say. Yes, it's great that he won a silver medal in the Olympic Games, but that was six years ago. Yes, they know he won New York last year. This year, just last month they remind Hawi, he finished sixth. And this business about him wanting to run in the 2012 Olympics? He didn't make the 2008 team. His spot on the team is hardly guaranteed. The last time they saw him in an Olympic Trials, in Oregon in 2008, he wasn't even close.

On one level, Hawi understands the Nike logic. It's business. He also knows Nike has its heart set on the bright, fair-haired boy of American distance running, Galen Rupp. Rupp, who is twenty-four, is a running machine from Oregon. Alberto Salazar has been training him since he was sixteen years old, a high school kid Salazar convinced to give up soccer for running. He went to Oregon, like the Nike founders Phil Knight and Bill Bowerman, and Salazar himself, and essentially launched Nike's Oregon Project, a running team modeled on Larsen and Vigil's Team Running USA, so Rupp would have an ideal training atmosphere. Meb had no interest in training with Alberto, or Jerry Schumacher, another Nike-sponsored distance specialist. He stayed with Bob Larsen. That didn't help. Hawi gets all these things.

On another level, though, Hawi is burning. How could they string him along like this after a dozen years? How could they jeopardize the livelihood of someone who has been nothing but loyal to them, who worked tirelessly through painful injuries that would have ended the careers of so many other runners. What he knows, what Bob Larsen knows, what he thought Nike knew, is that Meb doesn't run for money. He runs for love, otherwise he would have quit long ago. Like everyone else he wants to make as much money as he can, but with his athletic résumé and his education, he probably could have made more and endured far less pain doing something other than running. Now the company that has known him since UCLA is questioning that love. That is the implicit message of a performance reduction—without the threat of a pay cut, you won't drag your ass out of bed every day and invite the pain of eight 800s at 8,000 feet.

Hawi tells the folks up in Beaverton that they need to talk about this and work something out. They tell him there is nothing to talk about. Meb has two options—yes or no. Take it or leave it.

Hawi knows his brother better than anyone. He knows exactly what he is going to want to do.

For Bob Larsen, Nike's back-and-forth with Hawi and Meb is like that old Yogi Berra aphorism—déjà vu all over again. For Bob, it's his third go-round with the Nike folks on this sort of thing. They blew off him and his Toads in 1976, and then their support for his Mammoth idea was limited at best. Given the size of the company, that $30,000 or so they sent to Mammoth represented barely a rounding error on the balance sheet, a $20 tithe into the bowl at church on Sunday morning to assuage the guilt. It's almost funny in a way. These guys never learn.

He also knows exactly how this one will go. Nothing motivates Meb like being disrespected and doubted. This is how it was in 2001, when he told Meb to go for the American 10,000 record on the night when Nike was flying in rabbits to Palo Alto to make it all about Bob Kennedy. It's what gave Meb that extra gear in Athens, when no one took the guy with the 39th best time in the field seriously except the two people who knew what had been going on in the Sierras for a year. It's what got Meb another slew of national titles and the elusive win in New York in 2009, after two years of injuries and a consensus in the running world that Meb was done, that Athens was a fluke, or one of those things that happens when suboptimal conditions serve as an equalizer and bring the fastest runners in the world back to the ones who are just a click slower.

Of course Bob doesn't see it this way. This sport, this life, is about a rhythm—fall and rise, fall and rise . . . Since Athens, that moment of ultimate validation for his quest, he's been through the ultimate falls and rises, both on his own, and with Meb. He believes in rising.

Mammoth Lakes, New York, Houston, London, 2011–12

Along with great endurance and a killer set of lungs, temperament and faith have long been two of Meb's true gifts. Through disappointment and injury, he knows to channel his anger and he never asks why. He believes there is a reason things go a certain way. His job is to search for it. Within that search, lies enlightenment. Except now.

This time around—after getting the Merry Christmas news from Nike—he's seriously pissed. He does not understand how a group of people he has worked with and for and proven faithful to for more than a decade would stall and lowball him like this. Worse, they seem to not understand the essence of who he is, what drives him. Wasn't it just fourteen months ago, on the streets of New York, that he proved that?

He believed he could still win anywhere on any given day. With a previous two years like this, including the Olympic medal, how could Nike, a company that prided itself on carrying the heart and spirit of distance running in its DNA, not see this? If they don't see it now, they will soon, he promises. Bob Larsen already does.

There are a few raw, come-to-Jesus conversations with Yordanos and Hawi. Do you really want to keep competing and risking your health, they ask? Yes, he says. And once again he finds his way to channeling the anger.

Each morning in the Sierras he rises with his wife and three daughters, all under five years old, with a mission. Sometimes he meets up with the handful of top runners still hanging around Mammoth. Mostly he runs alone, without training partners, without much in the way of real income. He will have to earn that on the roads, with prize money that will hopefully prove to the folks who run the big shoe companies that this part of his life is not over, that he is going to rise. First, though, he falls again. Nike isn't alone in losing faith in him. In early winter, the folks at John Hancock, sponsors of the Boston Marathon, refuse to offer him a spot and the appearance money that comes with it in their elite field. They tell him his fifth-place finish the previous year, nearly four minutes back of the winner, a minute back of Ryan Hall, simply isn't good enough. Their money is better spent on other, younger runners. Meb is certain they are taking their cues from Nike, conspiring to bring his career to an end so the focus shifts to the other American hopes in the stable.

This sort of thing worried Bob back in the 1970s, when he sensed the shoe companies were poised to take over the sport from the running clubs. Their behavior would not always be benevolent. They would be focused on building brands rather than athletes. He wasn't wrong.

With Boston out, Meb and Hawi hit up the folks at the London Marathon, which holds its race the day before Boston this year. They look at Meb's résumé and they are not impressed. You've never broken 2:09, they tell him. You've got no shot at a flat, cool, speed race like the one we put on. When Hawi pushes back, tells them his brother is far from finished, London paints a different picture. They see a thirty-four-year-old runner who has posted a DNF ("did not finish") and a ninth-place 2:09:15 in his two previous appearances in London. London is the land of Roger Bannister and the four-minute mile, of Paula Radcliffe and Sebastian Coe. They are all about greatest-ever performances. You're not up to our standards anymore, they say. Not worth our sterling.

Now Meb's anger turns into a mild rage. He's got people on both U.S. coasts and across the Atlantic who claim ownership of the essence of the sport questioning who he is. Without a contract to guarantee the major source of income for an elite runner, he knows there is only one thing to do. He puts two dates on his calendar— New York in November, and the Olympic marathon trials the following January in Houston. New York will pay him. New York Road Runners, the organization that puts on the race, will always have a place for the only American to win its marathon the past three decades, and Meb loves both the city and the race. He is an adopted favorite son. He knows he can run strong there. Then, at the trials he can prove that he is still at the top of the heap in the United States, and once he is an Olympian, the shoe companies and everyone else will be there for him.

Bob hears Meb out on this. He has always advised his runners not to get greedy and chase appearance fees. Train hard, the right way, and success and the money will be there. Two marathons this close to each other is far from ideal. Actually, it's a terrible plan. The rhythm of this sport follows a spring/fall schedule. Conventional wisdom warns against running more than two marathons a year, or running two races with anything less than several months between them. New York and the Olympic trials are seventy days apart. That is a tough turnaround for anyone. For a thirty-four-year-old with some dings in the armor, it's a flirtation with disaster. On the other hand, it puts Meb on the edge of crazy, which is where good things have often happened to those who run with Bob Larsen.

In reality, Meb has no choice. He has three children and a wife to support. He has to feed them, and there is only one way to do that. He and Bob and Hawi have a meeting of the minds. The only thing left to do is run.

As Meb returns to the trails and roads around Mammoth, Bob Larsen begins to recover from the loss of his wife. It has been a little more than two years since Sue passed away. For more than a year he was barely able to talk about her without breaking down. He largely avoided the topic altogether. The company he sought—his children, his friends, close and otherwise, picked up on this easily. They knew not to pry. But both he and they also knew their companionship formed his life raft. He got out of bed each morning and sought out the people he loved, people he could just be around and lean on emotionally even though he showed no overt signs of leaning.

Then, in the closing months of 2010, the fog begins to lift. Life begins to round itself out again. Also, his greatest student needs help and is smart enough to ask for it.

Things are different in Mammoth now. Joe Vigil is retired. Terrence Mahon is taking care of Deena, who is very pregnant at the moment. A younger crop of runners who also work with Terrence trickles in and out. What Meb wants is different now, too. He's past middle-aged in running terms. Runners of his vintage are already coaching others. He wants more ownership of this mission, to design the program himself. Instead of looking to Bob for the road map, he comes up with the plan, a daily and a weekly and a monthly training schedule that he gives to Bob for approval.

For Bob, this is a beautiful thing, the true sign, even more than Meb's three little kids padding around the house in Mammoth, that the little boy is all grown up. There are tiny tweaks that he suggests. Mile repeats one day instead of one-kilometer intervals, a little more distance on another. A few more easy running days, but mostly Meb has this down. He tells Bob he wants to coach one day when he is done. This idea that Bob has been chasing—this quest for the right way to prepare to run far fast—it's going to endure.

As winter gives way to spring, they head out to the roads, Bob on his bike, staying close to Meb, as they prepare for the one play he can make to prove himself worthy—an elite showing in New York and top three at the Olympic Trials. He watches the small details—where the trail-leg ankle is higher than the knee of the lead leg as it churns through the running motion, how quickly he can get it back on the ground for the next pop.

He has been doing this for so long he can close his eyes and still know Meb's pace by the length of time his shoe spends scratching the pavement on each step. He can pick up the split-second differences and tell whether Meb is running a 5:10 mile or a 4:58. Giving in to age, they dial back the volume slightly. The 135-mile weeks drop down to 120. (They will eventually get down to 110.) To make up for the lost mileage, they add in more cycling and time on elliptical machines. It's cardio work with far less pounding. That makes it even more essential that every mile has its own purpose, even more so than each one used to. This is Bob's way.

The basic regimen is what it always has been—the magic mix of one- and two-mile repeats, extended runs that build discipline and patience and get the body used to being under pressure for two and three hours at a time, and those medium-long ventures to the edge, the place where all great runners now know they must learn to live. Sure, they tinker a bit with the formula. Some afternoon shakeouts become bike rides or ventures on the elliptical bike. A speed workout might get an extra couple intervals in the Shitbox, while the long run gets shaved by a few miles to save the legs from another 15 or 20 minutes of pounding. They become students of every gadget available. They pack his legs in synthetic casts filled with ice, so he can walk around the house with his joints surrounded by the cold. He spends evenings in compression socks and even sleeps in them sometimes. He guards his sleep like it is the family jewel. He and Bob repeat the mantra of the UCLA great John Wooden like the gospel—practice and training is what you do for two or three hours a day. What makes you excel is how you spend the other twenty-one.

As Bob and Meb do their work, Hawi does his. In the fall, he lands Meb a deal with a Los Angeles–based fashion shoe company named Skechers. It's a leap of faith that has plenty of folks in the running world snickering. Skechers has never made a high-performance running shoe, but they want to start getting into fitness and they want to build this new unit of their company around Meb, make him the face of it. It's what Meb always wanted Nike to do. He understands the risk. He can hear the snickers. But he also understands Skechers is risking something on him and doing it for these crucial next two years. He can be in the lab designing his racing flats and training shoes to his exact specifications. He can help make tiny tweaks in the custom shoes—a little more support here, a little less cushioning, or more, to account for age and the increasing potential for injury. He tells them he believes he has personal records left in his legs and that he is going to the Olympic Games in London in 2012. They tell him they think he does, too, that they want nothing more than to get him and their shoes to London.

First he has to get through New York.

November 6, 2011, breaks bright and chilly. It's near-perfect running weather in the Big Apple, a brilliant, cloudless day. Kenya's Geoffrey Mutai is at the top of his game. In Boston earlier in the year, he ran the fastest-ever marathon up to that point, a blazing 2:03:02. Yes, there was a tailwind all the way, but the time was so fast it got people talking seriously about a sub-two-hour marathon. The mark has long been unthinkable, but Mutai has run a half marathon in 58:58. Now, with Mutai seconds from going below 2:03, the sub-2 in the marathon seems doable, roughly 1,300 meters away.

As Bob watches from Manhattan, Meb goes to the starting line on Staten Island praying for the strength to be the runner he knows he can be. He knows this course as well as any. He can see the whole thing passing through his mind as he stands on the south side of the Verrazzano-Narrows Bridge—the rise and descent across New York Harbor, with the Statue of Liberty and the downtown skyline in the distance off to the left, the seven-mile straight up Fourth Avenue in Brooklyn, the slight ups and downs through the neighborhoods of North Brooklyn and southwest Queens. Then comes the Queensboro Bridge, the roars up First Avenue, a mile in the South Bronx, and the final stretch from Harlem to Fifth Avenue and Central Park.

He sees all of it as the cannon sounds. He shoots across the bridge with the lead pack, feeling as though anything is possible. But what is that strange thing in his right shoe?

As he comes off the bridge into Brooklyn, he realizes he has made one of the dumber mistakes of his career. He has been running with a flexible, plastic strip across the bridge of his nose lately. Most people use them when they are sleeping. Meb uses the Breathe Right strip when he is doing the opposite of sleeping. The strip pulls apart his nasal passages, maximizing airflow, making sure every extra bit of oxygen available can find its way into his lungs. Meb feels the bridge of his nose with his finger. Nothing but smooth skin.

Now he remembers that he slipped the plastic strip for his nose into his left shoe on the way to the starting line. That way he wouldn't forget it, or put it down somewhere, or throw it out. None of that transpired, of course. Instead, he has forgotten it, and it's in a terrible place, under the ball of his left foot. If he stops to take it out, and has to untie and re-tie his shoes, he will surely fall several hundred yards behind the leaders. That's too big a gap on a day like today, given the mission he has set for himself—proving his relevance. So he soldiers on, feeling the nasal strip rubbing at his thin sock and the raw skin underneath. It grows more irritating with each mile, and with each mile the idea of taking it out and losing time and place gets more unattractive because with each mile the opportunity to make up ground shrinks.

Meb hangs with the leaders until the second half of the race. Then Meb's stomach goes south on him in Manhattan. It's a basic hazard of trying to run 26 miles at a 4:55 pace. It happens to every marathoner at some point or, rather, at many points. He vomits on the course and falls nearly a mile back. There is no touching Mutai on this near-perfect running day. He runs a 2:05:06 and wins by a quarter of a mile. Meb crosses the line in sixth place. Somehow, even with the vomit and the nasal strip that felt like a rock in his shoe down the stretch, he lowers his personal record in the distance to 2:09:13. That is faster than the time he ran when he won this race. Also, he is the top American finisher. That is no small thing. It comes with a $20,000 prize in a year when he's mostly been running for cash. He has just posted one of the top American times of the year. And he did it with a plastic strip in his racing flat.

As he wobbles around the finish area, the soreness in his foot begins to set in. When he gets a look at it, it's one whale of a blister, with a nasty purple hue where the skin is worn away. The Olympic Trials marathon is in sixty-eight days in Houston. He has a problem.

Back in Mammoth, the blister becomes infected. It gets worse before it gets better. The raw skin aches when he walks on it. He can't even think about running. How much time does he spend staring at it each day? There are few things more frustrating for an athlete than staring at a body part and waiting for it to heal.

Bob knows this as well as anyone. Watching Meb, it's pretty hard for him not to think about those nasty stress fractures that kept him from proper preparation for so many big races a lifetime ago. He knows something else, though. There is no harder worker than Meb Keflezighi, even at thirty-five.

Yet, the window between New York and the Olympic Trials is so delicate. Some people run marathons and don't feel fresh on a 10-mile tempo run two months later. Here, Meb is going to try to run the race of his life less than ten weeks after a PR in track and field's most demanding single event, while battling a nasty blister that has him sidelined. But there is a not insignificant part of Bob's brain that believes the blister may be one of the great gifts the running gods have ever bestowed on Meb. The blister isn't a strained ligament or a fracture in a major bone. It's a deep skin abrasion that will heal in plenty of time for the race. It's also forcing Meb to rest and rejuvenate. Bob knows Meb is going to be back on the roads before too long, and when he gets there, he just might feel life in his legs that he hasn't felt in years.

Yordanos does not disagree. She knows how the past eleven months, the dealings with Nike and Boston and London, have driven Meb into a quiet rage. She knows he always channels his anger onto the roads and the track—an extra mile on the tempo run, a few extra intervals on a speed workout. In this moment of moments, if he had two healthy feet, she has no doubt how these weeks will unfold. She and Bob remind him how primed he was for New York, where he ran the time of his life—so far. A few weeks of rest won't make that fitness disappear. Settle down. Stay off the foot. Get on the floor and play with all these little children, they tell him. Surely there can be no better therapy than that.

By Thanksgiving, he is back at it. The blister and the infection are mostly gone. The Shitbox and Lookout Mountain and Lake Mary and Green Church Road call to him.

It's damn chilly in Houston the morning of January 14, 2012, with the mercury in the high 30s and not expected to rise much more than 10 degrees above that. More than 100 men are on the start line with Meb, many of them, including him, sport gloves and skullcaps and running sleeves that stretch from their wrists to their biceps. Meb has good memories from here. He has twice won national titles in this city in the half marathon. He's here to pick up another one at a somewhat more substantial distance. Yordanos and Bob were right. The post–New York, infection-induced rest has revived him in a way all the massages and ice-infused casts never could have. He's got fifteen marathons under his belt. He's closer to thirty-six than thirty-five now. For a year he's been arguing with the running establishment about whether any of that means anything. There is no more time for talking. Only running. Third may be as good as first in this race, because an Olympic trial is all about getting on the plane to the Games, but make no mistake, Meb is here to win. Bob is fine with that.

He has his eye on his buddy Ryan Hall, a gifted runner six years younger, who lived in Mammoth and trained with Meb until 2010. Then he and his wife, Sara, decided to move to Redding, 100 miles south of the Oregon border. He is so devoted to God that he has shunned all coaches and instead prays to the Lord for enlightenment about his next workout. If God tells him to run 20 miles that's what he does. If He tells him to ease off, he does that, too, believing that his devotion will be rewarded.

The previous April, when Meb was sitting out Boston, the Lord and the running gods allowed Hall to complete the 26.2 miles from Hopkinton to Copley Square in 2:04:58, nearly three minutes slower than Mutai but the fastest marathon time any American has ever posted. Tailwind or not, sub-2:05 is moving. Now Hall believes no one can stay with him. This race is all about establishing a cushion between first place and fourth and keeping it. This is a fast, flat course that will begin with a 2.2-mile circle and then three 8-mile loops around downtown Houston. Hall's strategy is obvious—he will push hard from the beginning and see if anyone dares to stay with him.

Meb dares. So does his old rival and friend and sometime Mammoth-mate, Abdi Abdirahman. And so does Dathan Ritzenhein, the Michigan native who went to Boulder and is seven years younger than Meb. Everyone calls him "Ritz." Meb remembers watching him cruise past in Central Park four years before when everything went to shit. They fire along at a 4:50 clip for the first four miles, then put up a 4:44 in the fifth one. Mohamed Trafeh, a naturalized Moroccan-American who is among the favorites, remains in the hunt, too, before dropping out ahead of the final stage (and later getting busted for performance enhancing drugs).

After eight miles they are a minute ahead of the second group. The race is now a three-seat game of musical chairs with four dancers. At the 18-mile mark, Meb, Abdi, and Hall put a four-second gap between themselves and Ritz. As they turn past the Houston Convention Center and run along Avenida de las Americas to begin the final loop, they dig for a little more juice. By mile 20, Ritz is more than 100 yards and 20 seconds back. It's all going in the wrong direction for him. Then Meb does what any experienced elite runner would do in this situation—form an impromptu team. Meb turns to Hall and Abdi and tells them it's time to work together and make the Olympics. They've done this before in the Sierras. They know what Bob has always told them—the group is stronger and faster than the individual. Nothing against Ritz. With spots at the Olympics on the line, this isn't personal. They stay on each other's shoulders, taking turns bearing the brunt of the wind and keeping their little clique comfortably ahead. With two miles left and Ritz still lurking, Abdi drops off slightly. It's a game of survival for him now. For Meb though, it's almost time to go. In the 25th mile, he feels Hall slow ever so slightly.

Now he knows the moment a year in the making is mere minutes away. With Hall tiring, he pushes. He digs just enough to hold steady. With three quick turns in the final mile, he disappears from Hall's sight, grabs an American flag, and waves it all the way to the finish line. The clock ticks to 2:09:08. It is his second personal best in three months. The $50,000 winner's check is his. Ryan Hall comes across 22 seconds later. Abdi finishes 17 seconds after that, eight seconds ahead of a surging Ritz. Everyone is under 2:10. On Meb's first Olympic team in 2000, just one male marathoner got on the plane to Australia. It was that charity spot, because no one in the country finished under the Olympic standard of 2:12 in the trials.

That embarrassment got Bob Larsen launched on this whole journey to raise the bar of the sport he fell for a half century ago. In a dozen years Americans have traveled from a place where no one could touch 2:12 to a place where a sub-2:10 doesn't guarantee a spot on the team. That is no small thing. Bob would never say mission accomplished. The mission is never accomplished. It only moves to what's next, but it appears to be headed in the right direction.

Meb's father, Russom, now seventy-four years old, grabs hold of his son and somehow hoists him on his shoulders. Meb isn't done, and he isn't going anywhere anytime soon, except London. He is fairly certain the folks in Beaverton, Oregon, and at John Hancock are seeing this.

London, August 2012

London really is going to be the end. That has been the point of these past years. A third Olympic team and another national title to go along with that silver from Athens and the win in New York. There isn't much left to prove. An Olympic marathon and then maybe one last jaunt in New York. Then it's going to be time to grow up, to not live by mileage logs, from workout to workout, week to week, race to race. It's going to be time to leave the mountains, to move the kids down closer to their grandparents and aunts and uncles in San Diego. It's going to be what the life of a thirty-six-year-old runner is supposed to be—charity races, speaking engagements, sponsor appearances, coaching. Bob gets that. He's come to London to enjoy one last Games, because soon it's going to be time for Meb to step back from the edge.

That doesn't mean Bob has to like it. The concept that he has implanted into the ideal vessel, it's still working. He knows the number everyone else is fixated on—36. But the number he can't get out of his head is 2:09:08, that PR Meb ran in Houston on a day when he likely could have gone faster if he really had to fight for the win instead of just the top three.

It's what he thinks about as he cycles alongside Meb in the mountains during those months leading up to London. A gluteus injury in April costs Meb a crucial month of training. It limits his longest pre-London threshold run to 12 miles. But into the summer, as the Games approach, Bob listens for the scratch of Meb's shoes on the pavement. He knows Meb's knees are still churning through the motion, almost as fast as they ever have—fall and rise, fall and rise. Why stop now?

It's what Bob thinks about here in the shadow of Westminster Abbey and Buckingham Palace, as Meb gets handed the wrong bottle at the first fluid station. It's got someone else's mixture rather than Meb's familiar mix of water, carbs, and electrolytes. He gets sick a few miles later. What a terrible way for this journey to end. At the halfway mark he is in 17th place. Somehow, though, during the next 65 minutes Meb climbs all the way back into the race. In the final miles, as Meb passes Bob, Bob holds up five fingers to tell him he's in fifth place. Keep pushing, you're that close to a medal. Meb finishes fourth. He has run on the edge again, just as he always has. Most see this as a cruel loss, one spot from the podium, a bitter fade into retirement.

For Bob, what Meb is doing at thirty-six years old is the ultimate manifestation of his theory. This career Meb has pursued, and is still pursuing, is one long run on the edge. Back in the 1960s, conventional wisdom said intervals are short and distance runs are slow, until Bob pushed those Toads to understand that neither one of those had to be that way, that the truth of a runner's potential could be found in how long he could stay on that precipice, that threshold of exhaustion. How long could he make it last? How long could he make the pursuit of the epic run—that run that is so hard and so natural it feels like it might last forever. Believe you can make it last longer than everyone says you can and you very likely will. It hurts? Try running a little faster, and now try doing it 8,000 feet above sea level. The breakthrough is just up ahead, around that next bend.

Now the world says thirty-six years old has to be the end of the road for the long distance runner. Why? Because there are days when the gun sounds and the journey to the edge carries unexpected pain in the Achilles, or a blister under the foot, or a turning stomach? Why does that mean that the idea, the possibility of truth and glory, are gone? If Terry Cotton and the rest of the Toads could figure out how to get themselves to the edge and stay there for 14 and 18 and 20 miles, can't Meb make this all last, with the right tinkering?

After the race, Bob listens to what Meb says when the writers approach with their pads and tape recorders.

"May Ryan Shay rest in heaven," Meb tells them, remembering his friend and training partner who collapsed at the 2008 trials marathon.

Then he adds, "I told coach, 'If I could have two more weeks, I know I can run 2:07 or faster.'"

And finally, Bob hears the words he has been hoping to hear. "If I'm still running close to my PRs, God willing, I might still stick it out for a couple more years to see what happens."

Perfect, Bob thinks. There's going to be another race. There will be another journey to the edge.

Right on Hereford.
Left on Boylston.

Boston, April 2014

The day before the 118th running of the Boston Marathon, Meb Keflezighi runs into defending champion Lelisa Desisa of Ethiopia in a hotel elevator. Desisa is a rising star. Tall and lanky and twenty-four years old, he ran under 2:05 in his debut marathon in Dubai the previous year. Then he won Boston a few months later, though few remember anything about the actual competition in that race. Meb wishes Desisa luck. Desisa barks that the race is going to be a war and he plans to destroy the field. Then he storms out of the elevator. It's unclear to Meb whether Desisa even knows who he is, or that he is even a member of the elite field.

It's hard to blame him. Meb was not supposed to be here. After London, he decided to give racing one more year. Skechers wanted to keep him on board. New York Road Runners and the folks in Boston promised to pay him to race. Why not see what happens? Then a foot injury kept him off the start line in Hopkinton in 2013. He spent the day hanging around the finish line, doing hits for the television coverage of the race. With his day nearly finished he heard the blast that changed everything about that day. The explosion killed three people, including an eight-year-old boy who was exactly the same age as his oldest daughter. It destroyed the limbs of sixteen others. On the plane back to California, he vowed to come back and run in their honor. He didn't care whether anyone paid him to do it.

Preparing for New York in the fall, a calf injury and a banged-up knee stunted his training. It showed. In the 20th mile, he hit the wall. He walked for a bit. He thought of dropping out. Then he heard a sub-elite runner from Staten Island promise to help him get to the end. They crossed the finish line arm in arm in 2:23. A sweet story, but not the reason Meb had always shown up on starting lines. He even received a trophy for finishing first in his over-thirty-five age group. If this is what it's come to, I'm done, he thought. But he knew he had to get to Boston.

His life is different now. With his kids elementary school age, he and Yordanos decide they should be in a less remote locale than Mammoth Lakes. Meb has to find a way to get his time at altitude in spurts, in four- and six-week stretches in the mountains before the biggest races. He's living in San Diego now, training on the streets of his youth. He runs in the footsteps of Toads once more. On Fiesta Island and the paths of Mission Bay Park, he nods and waves and gives countless thumbs-ups to the everyday runners who are out there for many of the same reasons he is. The father of a friend of his from high school days rides his bike next to Meb to pace him and carry fluids. Bob drops in and out and is often on the other end of the phone, talking through training plans. As Meb stretches one morning, a woman comes up to him to say hello. He asks her what gets her out of bed and lacing up her shoes in the morning. She tells him she had just finished chemotherapy the day before. Now it's time to run again. Yes, it is, he thinks.

He travels to Houston for the half marathon national championships in January. The old man feels good that day. He pushes the pace early, and wins by 15 seconds. He starts to dream. With Boston three months away, he knows he needs to get up high now that he is feeling healthy again. He has sold his house in Mammoth, so he reaches out to some old friends there. His massage therapist offers him an extra room in his house so he can get the altitude training he needs there. Others cook his meals. The old gym welcomes him back. There is a hiccup ten days before the New York half marathon in March. He strains his hamstring. He decides to run the race anyway, even though he knows he has to set aside his hopes for another PR.

Geoffrey Mutai is competing, and Meb manages to stay with him for 10 miles, then lets him go and finishes in 1:02:53, nearly two minutes off the pace. The performance isn't what he wants it to be, especially one month before Boston. He wanted to battle the best runner in the world to the end and plant the memory of that feeling of matching the best at the forefront of his mind ahead of Boston. Now he's going to suffer from the classic short memory that every runner has. He will remember too well the feeling of fading against Mutai at the most important moment.

Bob tells him to think a little harder, to take the long view. He won the Houston Half once before this year—in 2009, the year he went on to win New York in that same year. That's your omen. Get back to the mountains, and get healthy. You're right there, and because of that fade in New York, you're the only one who knows it. That's when good things happen. Ignore everything else.

With those thoughts in his head, Meb's psyche shifts. When he strains his oblique muscle nine days before Boston, it's nothing more than a small bump in the road. He takes a day off from training, gets a little work done with the massage therapist, and decides he is good to go. The rest will serve him well. The hay is in the barn. His work is done. In many ways, so is Bob's.

There is a quality to the kind of coaching that Bob has pursued that is something like parenting. It's that part where you have a vision of what is most important about life and must figure out how to convey those values and the truths you cherish to the people you love. In the best of circumstances, they embrace what you hope they will embrace, and then search for the boundary of what you believe they can become. In so many other professions, the goal is to make money. Coaches set out to make people, people with roots and wings, with unmatched appreciation for where they started and an unrivaled belief in the dream of where they can go. When they go there, in ways both large and small, they take you with them.

In Boston, Meb Keflezighi knows much of the running world considers him the ultimate underdog, if they even consider him at all. Yet, even he can't conceive the level to which, at thirty-eight, his prospects have faded in the minds of the elite. In the official race hotel, he is Warren Beatty in *Heaven Can Wait*, the unseeable and officially dead former quarterback of the Los Angeles Rams, trying unsuccessfully to get people to realize he is there, that he is ready to play football again. Meb will be on the start line feeling as sure as he has ever been that he can be a factor here. Still, the East Africans don't even discuss him in their pre-race strategy sessions, where they decide the pace for the first 13 miles. They focus only on one another. Most of them weren't even born the last time an

American won this race in 1983. They were children when Meb won an Olympic medal. Boston belongs to them.

Meb doesn't know this, of course. He isn't invited to those discussions. He and Bob have their own plan anyway. It's no different from the plans they made twenty years ago. Stay relevant, then dictate before anyone wants to be dictated to. Make everyone else run your race. The forecast is temperate. Push the pace. Force the issue. He sleeps well the night before. Why not. It's his nineteenth marathon. Then himbasha, the magic Eritrean bread. Then it's time to race.

There are so many runners who are faster than Meb in the field, so on the way to the starting line he focuses on the calm, sunny morning. Clear skies, 50 degrees, a little breeze from the southwest. Bob notices how calm the forecast is. He also knows that at thirty-eight, Meb might be a hair too old to cover the surges that the speedy Africans will likely bring. As they walk to the starting line, Bob tells him there won't be a headwind. If the pack starts slow, you can take a lead without worrying about a battle with the elements. He can't be too greedy, though. Even if there is an opportunity to move out front, he has to maintain an even pace on the notorious course with its second-half hills. To win, he has to set a pace so that the race finishes between 2:07 and 2:10. That's how small his window of victory is. One hundred and eighty seconds, roughly 1,000 yards, over 26.2 miles. If the pace is faster, he won't be able to keep up. If it is slower, he will lack the speed to outkick a rested, younger field at the end. It's a tiny needle to thread.

On the start line with some of the best Africa has to offer, he can see where the money that Nike used to pay him has gone—the training centers in Africa that the biggest shoe companies now run for these men. The chip is back firmly in place on his shoulder. Can he send them and everyone else who counts him out one more message? It's where Bob has always wanted Meb's head to be, and it's right there once more.

Meb has been around so long, and he's the last American to win anything major at this distance. But the win in New York in 2009 was a lifetime ago. There are no Meb signs in the crowd. He is a true afterthought. He and everyone else know the window for him to win a major race is going to close, even for Meb, even for someone who believes he can run on the edge forever. Bob and everyone else can see the skin on Meb's face is getting ruddy. There are tiny sprinkles of gray in his scalp. Maybe the runners surrounding Meb will notice that, too. One more reason to underestimate him. Or maybe, he thinks, they won't bother noticing him at all, until it's too late. That's more likely than anything at this point. Even when Bob has talked Meb up among friendly company lately the reaction he has received isn't all that different from all those other times he believed in what no one else did—Toads, Americans beating Africans, Meb getting back to the Olympics. They smile politely. They say nothing.

Standing on the start line in the silence before the cannon, Meb's mind drifts to the year before, the victims of the bombing. He has written their names on his bib. He closes his eyes. He hopes for peace. Then there is a boom. Time to go.

Bob watches him bound off the line and sprint to the front. Sure, he thinks, why not? Then he loads onto a bus bound for Boston, 26 miles away.

During the first few miles, Meb notices the Africans don't want a fast race. They keep going to the front as a group, trying to block anyone who attempts a surge. The pace is relatively slow—a 4:59 opening mile. The first five-kilometer (3.1-mile) split is a little more than 15 minutes. Meb notices that Desisa's mechanics are off. He seems to have no rhythm. He is fighting rather than running. After five miles, Meb decides to make his first surge—just to see the African reaction. There is none. He's still among the invisibles. Only Josphat Boit, a Kenyan-born naturalized American citizen, goes with him. At the eight-mile mark, Meb tells Boit he has no idea what the Africans are doing. The two draft off each other for the next two miles, trading the lead. Then Boit, better known for shorter 5,000- and 10,000-meter races, opens up a lead of nearly 50 meters from miles 10 to 12.

Meb stays calm. Boit hasn't been here before. He doesn't understand he is falling into the trap that Boston's mostly downhill first half sets for the uninitiated. Newton and its hills await. He glances over his shoulder and sees a large group—the Africans—not far behind. He sprints to catch up with Boit.

They pass the halfway mark in 1:04:21. Meb does the quick 2x calculation in his head. The race is right in his sweet spot. He has no idea why the Africans have let this happen.

Gazing at the crowd every so often, Meb can't believe how big it is. In some spots it's six and eight and ten people deep. Every other one of them seems to be wearing one of those blue and yellow "Boston Strong" shirts that have been all over the streets the past few days, and he has never seen so many flags. It's like a July 4th festival on steroids. Boston is a big city but on this bright blue day it feels like a small, tight-knit village, united behind the purpose of showing the world what it means to be fearless. That energy becomes a tangible thing, a kind of force that he knows he alone is going to feel when it truly counts.

At 14 miles, Boit accidentally clips Meb's foot. It's what happens when a runner tires and begins to lose the rhythm of someone he is working with. Meb is feeling as good as he has ever felt in this race—a race that didn't even want him a few years back. Now he decides to make a move. It's early yes, but there is an opening. Dictate. He starts to push in the 15th mile and runs mile 16 in 4:39. That puts him all alone at the beginning of the brutal Newton hills.

But he is not alone at all. As he pounds up the hills, he can see wonder in the eyes of all these New Englanders lining the streets. There is an American in the lead late for the first time in forever. A kind of mania spreads through a crowd here to celebrate a region's resilience, its relentless need to rise beyond the bombs and the death of the year before. The spontaneous, desperate chants of "USA! USA!" pound in his ears as he turns at the Newton firehouse and heads for the next ascent. This does not feel like a road race, Meb thinks. It's more like a World Cup soccer game. He loves everything about it.

As he climbs, a too-familiar pain returns. Since 2007, when he had that bothersome callus removed from the bottom of his left foot, his foot blisters in every marathon. Sometimes it's a mere annoyance. Sometimes making each step in the final third of the race feels like a nail pounding through his skin. Sure enough it's the pounding nail on this day. But he sees the American flags, he hears the "USA" chants, and he tells himself to ignore the pain. Those cheers carry him through the hills and across the 21-mile mark, where Heartbreak Hill finally crests and descends. And still, he runs alone. Bob Larsen knows there is only one explanation. The Africans behind Meb have no idea who is in front of them.

Just then, a disturbing realization hits Wilson Chebet, the top-ranked marathoner in the field, and the rest of the Africans. The man in the lead is so far ahead he has disappeared. At twenty-eight, Chebet, a Kenyan, is ten years younger than Meb. He has broken two hours, six minutes in multiple races, including two wins in the Amsterdam Marathon. He and his comrades decide that it must be Meb who is up there ahead somewhere. We have a real problem, Chebet thinks. Now or never, he tells himself, and he presses on the gas.

The lead doesn't disintegrate all at once, but after a mile he is roughly 25 yards closer, and after another mile another 25 yards are gone. Meb is now within shouting distance, maybe 50 yards ahead, an actual competitor rather than just a speck in the distance. Then 100 minutes into this 118th running of the grandest of all marathons, after Meb has run alone for better than a half hour, he glances over his shoulder as he approaches the end of the 23rd mile, where Chestnut Hill bleeds into Brookline. He sees an orange blur. He knows immediately it is Chebet, who appears far closer than he was roughly two minutes ago, the last time Keflezighi glanced back over his shoulder. Now Meb must confront an uncomfortable truth—I am being hunted.

The two almost make eye contact when Meb swivels his head a few seconds later to check on how quickly the lead is shrinking. At the 24-mile mark, they zip past Coolidge Corner, feeling the gravity and extra speed that comes with Beacon Street's slight downhill. Fenway Park is not far. Meb swivels his head again. He knows his lead is 25 yards at best, a distance that Chebet might be able to erase with a furious sprint. Then Meb realizes he has another problem. He thinks he is going to throw up.

Meb considers slowing down and letting Chebet catch him. That way he can salvage energy for a sprint to the finish, those last 600 yards on Boylston Street. He quickly decides this is a terrible plan. Eliminating what was once a lead of several hundred yards will undoubtedly inspire Chebet to blaze ahead. "Maintain the gap," Keflezighi tells himself, as he tries to will away the wave of nausea gnawing at him. Meb tries to feel better by reminding himself that if Chebet felt as good as he needs to feel to win the race he would be next to him by now, and he isn't. He is also pretty sure the world thinks Chebet is going to eat him in a matter of minutes, because Meb Keflezighi is nearly thirty-eight years old and trying to win a race that can't be won, not by him anyway.

Bob knows there is another move to make here, that Meb has to do what he always has done when good things happen. He must push before the other guy thinks he is going to push. Go early, not late. But he can see Meb's steps aren't what they were even moments ago. They are more labored, heavier, every one a battle. It's that rare moment in his half-century career where the man who knows everything about this game has no idea what is going to happen, and isn't that the beauty of it all?

In his head, Meb keeps repeating three words—maintain the gap. With a mile to go, the gap has shrunk to six seconds. It's all going the wrong way. They pass Fenway Park. Maintain the gap.

With 1,000 yards to go, just before the slight final rise, Meb thinks of two words—"quick feet." He knows what lies ahead. Two quick turns—the most beautiful six words in distance running. *Right on Hereford. Left on Boylston.* Then he will see the finish. Here, he decides is his chance to put this race away, to rise once more and deliver one final primal scream that he and his country will not be discounted. You're not supposed to push here. It's too early, that last stretch on Boylston can last a lifetime. If you go now there's a better than average chance you are spent with 300 yards left, plenty of time to get chewed up and spit out.

But going early has always been what he has done, and he's way too old to start doing anything differently now. He's going to run those turns so hard he disappears from Chebet's sightline once more. He's going to break that Kenyan the only way he knows how—he runs that turn onto Hereford so hard he pulls even with the police motorcycles leading the race. Turning onto Boylston, he's gone again. Then that deafening roar, an entire city screaming, swallows him whole as he sprints to the end, beating Chebet by 11 seconds. He breaks the tape in 2:08:37. He has never run faster.

For the first time all day, Desisa and Chebet accept the idea that Meb Keflezighi can win the Boston Marathon.

At the finish, Yordanos leaps into the arms of the man who has just blazed 26.2 miles and survived. She then realizes this might not be the best idea. She finally lets go. Then it's Bob's turn. He embraces the champion of the 118th Boston Marathon, and as he holds Meb he is clinging to so many others—all the Terry Cottons and Ed Mendozas and Mike Breens and Tom Luxes who have made him look smart for fifty years. Perfect, once more.

It's a funny thing about these long running races. The start and the route to the finish and the finish line itself are so clear. And yet each one feels like a mysterious journey, each mile bringing another surprise. This quest Bob Larsen has been on for most of a lifetime, it's not so different. At the beginning, there was simply love and fascination with the most elemental activity. That somehow evolved into a drive to make others understand something they could not without him, using methods unlikely ever to be abandoned again. They made a very simple and very complicated attempt to be fast and in doing so become the best version of themselves. Of course it would end up here, in this epic moment, watching an American man win the grandest race with the perfect run to the edge.

This life is one long race. Bob Larsen has won.

Onward

I have run two marathons in torrential rain. This first, in 1997 in New York, was notable for reasons other than the rain.

My wife decided to run her first and, so far, only marathon that year. Her goals were where they should be. She merely wanted to cross the finish line. In training she ran roughly a 10:30 mile pace. We both figured she would finish in about five hours. I would run with her and help her get to Tavern on the Green. Since I was going to run about 90 minutes slower than my usual pace at the time, I didn't train very hard. I never ran more than 12 miles on my long runs.

The gray morning of the race, we passed the hours before the start on Staten Island huddled on garbage bags. When the announcement came that it was time to head for the corrals, my wife delivered some interesting news.

"You go ahead," she said. "I'm going to run alone."

This would have been good information for me to have had a few months before.

"What?" I asked. She repeated her intentions.

I guess she hadn't liked my attempts at inspiration during training. On one run, as we trekked up Harlem Hill, I told her the only hills that exist are the ones we create in our minds.

"Oh, fuck off," she told me. Then she explained that, in fact, we were running up a killer hill. She was right.

Running alone probably was the right move for her, but there I was on Staten Island with only one way to get home. When the cannon boomed I set off over the bridge and figured I would run until I could not run anymore.

I don't remember when the skies opened up. It was early and often. When I slogged past the Boathouse in Central Park about 220 minutes later, I looked down at my shoes and saw water around my ankles. What the hell am I doing here? I thought. I resolved to get to the finish line and never do this again. My wife crossed the finish line in five hours and 40 minutes next to an octogenarian who had run the first New York Marathon in 1970. I've rarely seen her so happy.

I stayed true to my promise for fourteen years. We had three children. I pushed all of them in running strollers, singles and doubles, for miles on end, packing bread and carrots to feed the ducks and horses in Central Park and plenty of chocolate muffins and pacifiers for the small people being pushed along. They were good girls.

Then in 2011, I followed through on a commitment I made long ago to one day run a marathon to raise money for The Hole in the Wall Gang, a camp for kids with cancer and other serious diseases, where I had been a volunteer counselor in 1994. My close friend runs the camp's foundation. He gave me a bib for New York. I raised a bunch of money, and there I was back on the bridge heading from Staten Island to Brooklyn. The drawstring of my shorts broke two miles into that race. A friend I was running with gave me two extra safety pins, which held for the next few hours somehow. I limped across the finish line in 3:44 and figured once again I was done.

At work the next day, a colleague ten years older and significantly faster wandered over to my desk to tell me he had been studying my splits. He told me he thought I could go much faster, and he could help me get there. I told him I always wanted to qualify for Boston. He said that I would.

That was sixteen marathons ago, and fifteen marathons before the other one that took place in a torrential downpour.

God willing, there will never be another Boston like the one that unfolded on April 17, 2018. Or maybe God willing there will be.

I'm sure there have been more epic conditions for this race. They've been doing it for 122 years, after all. But that Monday was as high on the misery index as anyone could remember.

For days, many of the race's roughly 30,000 participants had been staring at weather apps and radars, playing amateur meteorologist and praying that the forecast for temperatures in the 30s and 40s with driving rain and a 20–30-mile-per-hour headwind somehow wouldn't come true. We traded notes all Sunday on what we were going to wear. In the end, I never took off my windbreaker. Neither did the women's winner, Desiree Linden. That never happens.

I rose at 5:54 Monday morning in my cousin's apartment in the South End to the sound of birds chirping. My hopes rose, too.

Then I walked to Boston Common in slanted rain to take the bus to the start in Hopkinton. My shoes were soaked and my toes nearly numb as I took a seat on the bus. I was bundled up like a third-grader ready for a walk to school. In Minnesota. In January. In the next seat was a woman from Utah wearing a racing singlet and running sleeves she planned to discard. It rained here three years ago, she reminded me.

I knew that. I ran that year, too, but in 2015 the rain didn't start until much of the field, including me, was nearly half done. And that year's race felt about 15 degrees warmer than the 37 degrees it was as we journeyed to Hopkinton. Yet there was little question this steely woman from the West was way less terrified of the next few hours than I was.

Any hopes of pre-race comfort in the tents behind the school disappeared when we arrived at the start village behind Hopkinton High School, which had turned into a mud bowl. Smart runners brought a second pair of shoes to change into on the start line. I brought extra socks, but putting a dry sock into a mud-soaked sneaker doesn't work so well.

For the first five miles my feet felt as if they were in ski boots. I couldn't feel my toes as the rain shifted between steady downpour and Noah's Ark–style soaking. I desperately wanted to finish, but I didn't want to lose extremities in the process. I started jogging my memory to recall the hospitals along the route. There are several, thankfully. And then, after about an hour, it all became sort of normal for a bit. I settled into a rhythm.

There were moments during those 3 hours, 24 minutes, and 49 seconds when the rain slowed, though it never stopped, and the wind quieted, and I thought, okay, no big deal. Then, just as quickly, Mother Nature unleashed storm cell after storm cell for a few minutes just to keep us on our frozen toes.

So why not quit? Because long distance runners live for the story. We love you thinking we are just crazy enough to run 26.2 miles in driving rain and freezing temperatures. Could there be anything more rebellious, almost countercultural, just like distance running was in those pre-running-boom days? That spirit lives on. Pre would have loved that Boston race.

Also, while plenty of Bostonians were smart enough to stay inside—this is supposedly the area with the largest concentration of graduate degrees, after all—tens of thousands came out to cheer us on, and did they ever bring it. Bruce Springsteen's "No Surrender" was blasting on the speakers as I passed through Natick. You could hear the Wellesley women screaming in mile 13 a good half mile before we got to them. An old college friend appeared to cheer for me on Heartbreak Hill. Hadn't seen her in twenty-five years. And yeah, of course she lives right off Heartbreak Hill.

Then, finally, it was our turn for the six most beautiful words in distance running. "Right on Hereford. Left on Boylston." I was streaking toward the finish line in Copley Square, airplaning my arms and weaving across the road in delirium. Sure, there was some hypothermia. Another deluge, more gusty winds. Bring it on. In the telling, which is all I have now and all that matters, it's the best Boston—evah.

Unless I meet with some terrible misfortune and die in the middle of a race, there will likely be a time in my life when marathons are something I used to do. People often ask me how many more I will run. I tell them I have no idea, because I'm really so far from being ready to say that I don't run marathons anymore, that I don't get the purest joy from rising early on a weekend morning and heading out on the roads or a trail for a long, long time, or from standing on the same starting line with the fastest people in the world, and 50,000 other like-minded souls all wanting to be a part of something so much larger than ourselves, running to the edge to make some sense of our stupid little lives.

May it ever be thus.

Right on Hereford, April 2018.

A Note on Sourcing

The material for much of this book comes from dozens of first-person interviews with the characters in the book, as well as with people who know a lot more about running than I do and are a lot faster than I am. I did rely on a number of books and articles about running and runners to fill in certain holes and to make myself smarter about this pursuit. They include:

Born to Run: A Hidden Tribe, Superathletes, and the Greatest Race the World Has Never Seen, by Christopher McDougall
The Perfect Mile: Three Athletes, One Goal, and Less Than Four Minutes to Achieve It, by Neal Bascomb
Run to Overcome: The Inspiring Story of an American Champion's Long-Distance Quest to Achieve a Big Dream, by Meb Keflezighi
My Marathon: Reflections on a Gold Medal Life, by Frank Shorter
Two Hours: The Quest to Run the Impossible Marathon, by Ed Caesar
Let Your Mind Run: A Memoir of Thinking My Way to Victory, by Deena Kastor and Michelle Hamilton
Bowerman and the Men of Oregon: The Story of Oregon's Legendary Coach and Nike's Cofounder, by Kenny Moore
Duel in the Sun: Alberto Salazar, Dick Beardsley, and America's Greatest Marathon, by John Brant
14 Minutes: A Running Legend's Life and Death and Life, by Alberto Salazar and John Brant
The Sports Gene: Inside the Science of Extraordinary Athletic Performance, by David Epstein
Shoe Dog: A Memoir by the Creator of Nike, by Phil Knight

In addition to these books, there were many helpful articles I found in the annals of *Sports Illustrated, Runners World,* the *Los Angeles Times,*

The San Diego Union-Tribune, The New York Times, The Associated Press, and *The Wall Street Journal,* some of which I wrote myself and had forgotten I had done so. Also, Dyestat has a remarkable database of nearly every California High School Track and Field Championship going back to 1915, which is pretty remarkable. And Gary Close's scrapbook from his Grossmont days is an amazing thing.

Acknowledgments

First and foremost, this book owes its existence to two incredibly generous and special people.

The first is Bob Larsen, who spent countless hours answering endless questions. He never lost his spirit or good humor, and he never asked for anything in return. I'm not sure they make people like Bob anymore. He has had a remarkably successful life, and yet he has a humility that seems to know no limits. Go ahead and try to find someone who has something really bad to say about Bob Larsen. It's darn near impossible.

The second is Robert Lusitania. Robert made and then released a terrific documentary in 2015 about his old running coach and the Jamul Toads called *City Slickers Can't Stay with Me*. He invited me to a screening the day before the Boston Marathon that year. I went and knew immediately I wanted to write a book on the topic. When I approached Robert with the idea, half expecting him to tell me to go find some other story, he said, essentially, how can I help? He gave me phone numbers and email addresses of old Toads and showed me outtakes from his own interviews with them to provide me with background. He's a gem, and a pretty good filmmaker at that.

With Bob and Robert's entrée, nearly every Toad I reached out to was happy to talk. So thanks to Mike Breen, Ed Mendoza, Tom Lux, Dale Fleet, Thom Hunt, Dave Harper, Kirk Pfeffer, Glenn Best. Gary Close, also a Toad and Grossmont Griffin, has an amazing scrapbook that was ridiculously helpful.

Meb Keflezighi and his brother Hawi are two of the most emotionally generous people on the planet. Meb is pretty fun to run with, too. Deena Kastor shared plenty of terrific stories with me about life and running in Mammoth. She still runs to win, which I love. Joe Vigil is a world-class coach and a world-class storyteller.

I have thanked them before, but I will thank them again and

always, because I had an amazing collection of public elementary schoolteachers who got me going on this writing thing. They include Peggy Richards, Naomi Gams, Kay Kobbe, Barbara Brownell, Allen Falber, Ray Kurek, and Eugene Egan. In high school it was more of the same—Rose Scotch and Mike DiGennaro dedicated their lives to public education and making readers and writers out of countless souls. Thanks for that.

My agent, Suzanne Gluck at WME, stuck with this project even when it seemed like it wasn't going to go anywhere. She didn't have to do that. Thanks, SG. And thanks, Andrea Blatt, for all your help.

Sam Walker told me I was an idiot if I didn't see this project through. He's nuts, but he's a good man and much of my success is because of him. Kevin Whitmer and Chris D'Amico gave me my first shots at sportswriting and changed my life. I wish I could thank Chris while inhaling his second-hand smoke one more time, but sometimes the clock runs out on us.

At *The New York Times*, Jason Stallman, Randy Archibold, Sam Manchester, and Becky Lebowitz have the good graces not to roll their eyes every time I drone on about running. Or at least they don't let me see them doing it, which I appreciate. Talya Minsberg, a fellow marathoner and teammate, also tolerates me and sees to it that everything I write about running finds readers. She's as cool as they come, a really good writer, and damn fast.

There aren't a lot of writers with the good fortune to have a book turn into a childhood reunion. I grew up with Jason Kaufman, and when I heard that he was interested in publishing my book there was no one else I wanted to work with. We share lingering bitterness toward our high school soccer coach and an undying love for Sal's Pizza. Jason is a pretty good word guy, too, and a great friend for forty-four years and counting. Thank you.

Also at Doubleday, thanks to Carolyn Williams, Todd Doughty, Bill Thomas, Mike Collica, Victoria Pearson, and John Fontana.

Barbara Greenberg is a great friend, the perfect godmother to my children, and a master wordsmith.

The good folks at New York Road Runners put on a darn good race each November, thanks in large part to the great George Hirsch, a giant of New York City who has dedicated his life to running and the written word. I'm lucky to have him as a friend and mentor. NYRR's

Chris Weiller always has an answer or a mobile phone number to pass along when I need it most.

Thanks to Dr. Jordan Metzl for keeping me far away from a surgeon's scalpel, and to my hot yoga gurus, Melissa Porricelli and John Salvatore, for keeping me healthy and inspired and believing.

I leaned hard on the great Matt Lewis in writing this book. There are sentences that are lifted directly from his notes. He is a terrific runner who has completed the wild run across Madagascar, and a special friend, who taught me how to point my ski tips down the steep chutes and lean forward, both literally and metaphorically.

My brother Danny is always waiting at mile 7 of the New York City Marathon, and my parents are always there at mile 22 outside Mt. Sinai. My brother David, who lives far from the course, regularly checks up on my training, follows my every 5K on race days remotely, and loves to talk strategy and results. All of this is a gift.

For years, my daughters, Ashley, Tess, and Jolie, endured a lot of mornings being pushed around Central Park in a running stroller, sometimes in pretty bitter weather that could have gotten me reported to child protective services. They made out pretty well in the deal, because I plied them with chocolate muffins, but still . . . God, I miss those days. Now they always show up to yell for me in various races, and they do a damn good job writing "Go Matt" on my hats and shirts. When I come home with a medal or a trophy, they treat me like an Olympian. It does not get better than that.

Finally, my wife, Amy Einhorn, has for years indulged my penchant for disappearing for hours to run or to write. She gets me, and that is pure magic.